MERTON

Merton

An Enneagram Profile

Suzanne Zuercher, O.S.B.

AVE MARIA PRESS Notre Dame, Indiana 46556

Acknowledgments

Excerpts from *Conjectures of a Guilty Bystander* by Thomas Merton, copyright © 1966 by the Abbey of Gethsemani. Used by permission of Doubleday, a division of Bantam Doubleday Dell Publishing Group, Inc.

Excerpts from *Thomas Merton's Dark Path* by William Shannon, copyright © 1982, reprinted by permission of the author.

Excerpts from *The Hidden Ground of Love: The Letters of Thomas Merton on Religious Experience and Social Concerns* edited by William Shannon, copyright © 1985 by the Trustees of the Merton Legacy Trust, reprinted by permission of Farrar, Strauss & Giroux, Inc.

Excerpts from *Thoughts in Solitude* by Thomas Merton, copyright © 1956,1958 by the Abbey of Our Lady of Gethsemani and renewed 1986 by the Trustees of the Merton Legacy Trust, reprinted by permission of Farrar, Strauss & Giroux, Inc.

(Acknowledgements continued on page 215.)

International Standard Book Number: 0-87793-576-9

Cover photo by John Howard Griffin, copyright © 1993 by Elizabeth Griffin-Bonazzi, Executor, The Estate of John Howard Griffin.
Photo on p. 22 courtesy of Thomas Merton Center, Bellarmine College.

Cover and text design by Katherine Robinson Coleman

Printed and bound in the United States of America.

Library of Congress Cataloging-in-Publication Data

Zuercher, Suzanne.
Merton : an enneagram profile / Suzanne Zuercher.
p. cm.
Includes bibliographical references.
ISBN 0-87793-576-9 (pb)
1. Merton, Thomas, 1915-1968—Psychology. 2. Enneagram.
I. Title.

BX4705.M5422Z84 1996 95-52255
CIP

Contents

Continuing the Dialogue

Enneagram descriptive research continues to ask new questions and explore new territories. Just twenty years ago basic descriptions of the nine types or spaces or life stances—however one looks at the various human incarnations—were the primary emphasis in books about the enneagram.[1] Now that a number of writers and researchers have contributed to articulating the worldview of various kinds of people, other topics that assume this basic information are receiving attention.

Those readers who are not familiar with the enneagram need not be turned away from this book. Its theme is the spiritual path of Thomas Merton, a path he saw and walked from the standpoint of one of these nine incarnations of human experience. As we proceed through a discussion of his unique journey, one he nevertheless shared with others in his particular enneagram stance, the themes and dynamics of his space will be outlined and described. It is Thomas Merton you will recognize, I believe, in these descriptions.

The most important thing to keep in mind about the enneagram is that human beings judge what is important for life, what they value, and what they tend to overlook in themselves and the world around them, depending on their native endowment. This obvious reality becomes, primarily because it is instinctive, what they hear others rewarding them for. It involves those areas of life where they experience ease.

To become persons who can survive in the world, we all need to be told—and also tell ourselves—what these instincts are. We are bent on self-creation, and we start to reinforce these instincts until they become compulsions. In the process we develop our characters, our egos.

As life continues and we realize the distortions of our personalities these compulsions have caused, we are appalled. If we are people serious about our lives and our spiritual journeys, we respond initially by trying to wipe out our native endowment. After all, it has led to distortion and self-deception; it has bound us up instead of making us free. Yet, human life is destined to be contemplative, not "athletic." The journey to the Divine, we discover as our life moves along in adulthood, is not one we can control or force or determine. We learn by experience that all of our efforts to remake ourselves perpetuate our slavery. We remain unfree and compulsive, unchanged from the point of view of conversion. If our lives are to turn around, we need to acknowledge and admit what we have done in the name of spiritual development. When we can do so, we learn the most important lesson of human life: We are not God.

In the wonder of our redemption we are not delivered from our native endowment. It is that very distinguishing characteristic that becomes our contribution to creation. Once our instincts, which we had exaggerated into compulsion, are admitted, acknowledged, allowed, they gradually assume a proper proportion in our lives. They become increasingly natural and free responses. Instead of actively trying to cut out the condemned aspects of who we had become, we grow into perspective about ourselves. Finding such perspective allows us to laugh at our efforts to be God. In spiritual terms we call this process growing in contemplation, a straightforward acknowledgment of what is so. As Anthony de Mello's spiritual master has said, we no longer need to be lied to about anything.[2]

Thomas Merton reveals himself to us around these dynamics of human—and therefore spiritual—growth. He does so from his unique enneagram perspective, using the images, vocabulary, and emphases of his particular kind of personality. When he talks about becoming contemplative, he reveals his unique view of life. He shows us through his behaviors and tells us through his words what helps and hinders contemplation. In this book I hope to underline his issues in ways that are new. It is the enneagram that makes this possible. It is the enneagram which lets us into Merton's world with a nuance not found elsewhere. I believe questions about his responses and behaviors will find answers not available before.

It has been valuable over these years of enneagram study to walk around the nine spaces, simply in order to get to know them better. It has also been important to have people who live in those spaces talk about what it is like to inhabit each. The time has been well spent and the information has been nuanced in important and ever more subtle ways. I feel privileged to have been one of the people involved in the process.

This is my third book on the enneagram. It represents, as do the other two, where I am in my personal evolution regarding enneagram study. In *Enneagram Spirituality: From Compulsion to Contemplation* I attempted to place enneagram theory in the context of the spiritual journey of conversion and transformation. Since human life takes place in community, *Enneagram Companions: Relationship and Spiritual Direction* addressed interactions among various kinds of people, emphasizing how we can better companion one another along the way to fullness of life.[3]

There is often no better way to clarify concepts than to see how they are born out in the life of an individual. Erik Erikson has demonstrated his developmental theory by applying it to people's history, notably that of Gandhi.[4] Perhaps nothing is better than such storytelling to put flesh on ideas and theories.

I have applied something of Erikson's approach to the life journey of Thomas Merton from the point of view of the enneagram. My hypothesis is that Merton was a 4 on the enneagram. As I make this assertion I am only too conscious of the difficulties of such an application of this theory. Having read many books on the enneagram in which the same individual has been offered as an example of someone in various spaces, I realize naming a person's stance is fraught with dangers.

There are very few people about whom I would even venture a hypothesis as to gesture in life. I do so regarding Thomas Merton because of the wealth of information available about him. This abundance of written material, as well as all that modern technology provides to supplement it, makes me secure in my conclusions. It is not lightly that I call Thomas Merton a 4. Only a lifetime of reading Merton and years of study of the enneagram give me confidence to do so.

This kind of effort and application of the enneagram is something which I invite others to engage in. I feel it necessary, however, to caution those who would apply the enneagram to an individual's journey to beware of beginning their study with a judgment. Rather, it is necessary to let the data about any considered person shape conclusions.

To say it another way, I hope those who apply enneagram theory to particular individuals will be both scholarly and reflective. If they are, if the person chosen for study can provide sufficient information from which to draw conclusions, new awareness can result. What is now gathered in brief reports from individuals about how they describe their dynamics and respond in situations can be expanded. A more complete picture of the spiritual journey as it is experienced by those in differing life stances can become available. Teresa, John of the Cross, and Ignatius of Loyola are only a few of the spiritual writers about whom we may know enough to initiate such a study. Perhaps future generations will be better able to choose the spiritual path most consonant with their limitation, virtue, and gift because of such careful research. That is my hope.

Like the other books I have written, this one assumes a basic knowledge of enneagram theory and of the nine stances or types or spaces or gestures of the human person. It also assumes that the reader is familiar with my description of the journey from exaggerated compulsion to embracing one's gift, one's unique word. It is this life of deepening contemplation that creates the ever more self-aware, self-accepting, and humble human being.

If you do not have such background, I suggest you seek out some introduction to the enneagram that is faithful to the oral tradition. The only way to experience the energy of each space is through individual association or responsibly conducted workshops. It is vital to see and hear and interact with people in the nine spaces. Only in this embodied way can descriptions of the nine kinds of human energy be understood. It is only after some time spent experiencing various energies around the enneagram circle that reading becomes helpful.

I regret much of the superficiality of so-called enneagram study. It has given rise to some of the criticism of the enneagram prevalent today, criticism that is often not lacking in foundation. It is important not to trivialize the enneagram. Rather, it is necessary to value it as a genuine help to contemplation and not merely as a means to label people. I hope this book remains respectful of what the enneagram has to offer our understanding of spirituality. I hope, too, that my efforts to contribute responsibly move this worthwhile study ahead at least one small step.

Finally, it is with much joy and enthusiasm that I join here two life interests: the enneagram and Thomas Merton. I first heard of Merton as a high-school student. His presence in my life has been palpable at times; he has provided invaluable help along my own spiritual path. If the reader comes to appreciate this man at least a little more, perhaps a bit differently from before, I will be content. I count it a privilege to write about this significant person in my life, a man whose unique word has enriched my own.

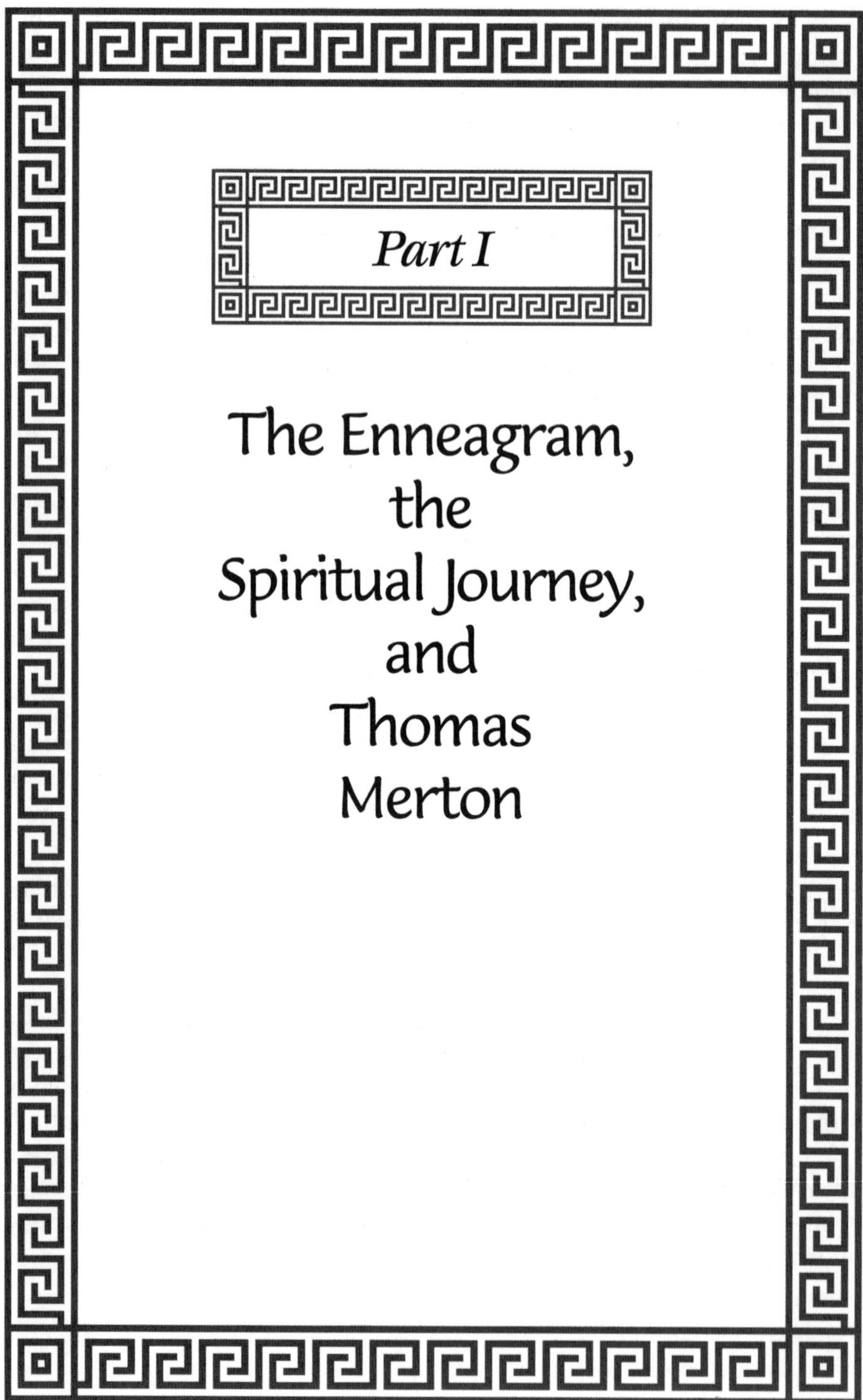

Part I

The Enneagram, the Spiritual Journey, and Thomas Merton

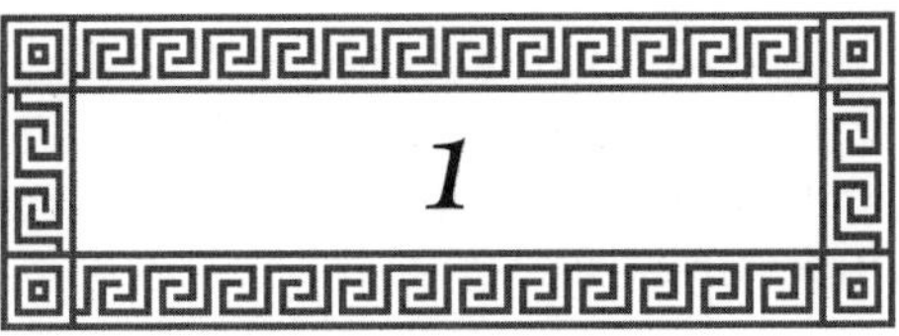

The 4: Ego-Romantic, Ego-Melancholic, Over-Dramatizer

Few people would still maintain that Moslem mystics, or Sufis, originated the enneagram or can be either congratulated or blamed for its development as a theory. Enneagram origins are lost in history, and history itself is laced with sometimes contradictory claims. Surely, I have neither the training nor interest to pursue paths which might or might not lead to the historical origin of enneagram theory.[1] But I do, however, have energy to explore the basis of enneagram study: human nature. My own background in psychology has drawn me to look at applications of this theory to the human person. Enneagram philosophy maintains that everything that exists is some partial manifestation of the All who prisms out the way white light does into varying hues. There are nine such variations in all aspects of creation, according to this philosophy. It is application of this more general theory of creation to nine different human personality types that attracts my interest and bears out my study and observations of people. Such an overview provides a framework for describing the life path that is universal, that all persons are meant to follow. It also accounts for the differing and sometimes contradictory wisdom about the process of transformation as we hear it articulated by various spiritual masters and mistresses.

If we are quite different types of people, if we look out at life and assess it and make response to it from one of nine stances, then it becomes important to find out from which of those worldviews a spiritual leader is speaking or writing. The compulsions that individuals have formed out of their basic instincts lead to certain kinds of problems and issues. The illusions and delusions necessarily built up around creating a self one can live with will be concerned with unique themes. The functions people exaggerate, whether perceptual or affective or behavioral, suggest spiritual approaches that may well contradict one another. Correspondingly, the need for skillful development of the perceptual, behavioral, or affective function these same persons incline to bury will be different.

In many ways the journey is the same for all. In other ways it is quite different, depending on one's unique word, the incarnate person one is. Enneagram theory, which maintains that each person's uniqueness falls into one of nine groupings, does not mean, of course, that every person in that grouping will have identical responses. It does mean that all people in one of the nine stances will recognize patterns and dynamics common to them all.

Spiritual mentors come, of course, from all nine of these gestures in life. This being so, it can prove helpful along the way of conversion and more contemplative living for us to find guides who emphasize what is relevant for our own worldview or life stance. In some ways we all do just that through trial and error. What enneagram study can facilitate is a more informed search. If it accomplishes this, then people who want to live their life more fully in the Divine will be saved from getting lost, if only for a time. They will avoid the cul-de-sacs that contradict their personalities and slow down spiritual transformation. As St. Benedict put it in his Rule for Monasteries, people are looking for the freedom to and energy to "run the path of God's commandments."[2] The enneagram can help focus individuals on how best to live their lives, embodied, as everyone necessarily is, in only one of the nine stances.

A Man Who Told Us Much

Having said this, I turn now to Thomas Merton. I assume he needs no introduction. William Shannon reminds us that Merton viewed life through a wide-angle lens.[3] As a result of his doing so, many of us have gathered around areas of interest we shared with him. These areas are distinct and even disparate, and his fascination with varied aspects of life has brought many of us together. I would like to walk with you through some of what captivated me in this man, both in himself and as he related to others and his environment. At the same time I will develop a description of his spiritual path in enneagram terms.

I present the hypothesis that Merton was a 4 on the enneagram. I do so from a body of information about this nearly contemporary man, someone who not only wrote extensively about his ideas, opinions, and values, but who revealed his issues and dynamics in poetry, fiction, and most especially, in numerous journals.

Merton's journals are of various kinds. They were written in a parallel fashion, covering the same period of his life simultaneously at different levels of personal disclosure. Some are largely notes from his reading with reflections to which these readings led him. Others are more or less descriptive of events from day to day: changes in the liturgical seasons and the seasons of nature, life in the monastery, people he encountered. Still other journals are very private and revelatory; some of the information in these is becoming available only now. Most of Merton's journals are combinations of these approaches.

Besides journal writing Merton carried on an extensive correspondence throughout his lifetime. Indeed, it has been said he contributed much to the literary genre of letter writing. Some of his letters present views on topics such as social justice, politics, the church, and the spiritual life. Others are of a more personal nature and reveal feelings and responses to life situations and relationships with his correspondents. His most significant letters have been gathered into a series of four volumes.

Merton also has many books on the spiritual life, prayer, and relationship to the Divine. If we can assume that authors present their personal problems and traps along the way to God, these writings, too, should yield much information about Merton. If we can also assume that authors write about what has been helpful for them in dealing with these traps, we have an expanded picture of Merton's unique spiritual path. Indeed, such is the assumption underlying my reading of Merton as he talks from his experiential wisdom about illusions and delusions along the way to God. From this assumption I have been led to my primary hypothesis, that Thomas Merton was a 4.

Another primary source for information on Merton exists in his numerous articles on peace, justice, and the spiritual life. Other topics for his periodical writing included reflections on religious life in general and monasticism in particular, the formation of new members in monastic community, and the changing church. Literary criticism, current events, psychology, and theology were frequent topics for him as well. This list is probably not exhaustive, but it does suggest something of the broad interests Merton had. It attests as well to his willingness to present personal opinions even in areas where he had little training.

For some of this daring he has been criticized as superficial; for our purposes here we can be grateful he spoke out on so many issues.[4]

Still another source of information on Merton is that of people who knew him personally and have shared aspects of their relationship with him both in writing and interview. It is not only who we say we are that provides data for assessment, but also how others perceive us. With regard to the enneagram it is maintained that we are qualified to name our own life stance. I believe this to be true, but I also believe that information from others—how they perceive and respond to us—needs to be included in our self-assessment. We do not have a broad body of information on what response Merton had to peoples' impressions and appraisals of him. There do exist, however, a few significant comments by Merton in this regard, notably those in response to Gregory Zilboorg, the psychiatrist, and to monastic superiors and fellow monks.[5]

Besides remarks Merton has followed up with his own evaluation, there are many others on which he made no comment. These indirectly show how the 4 personality affects and is affected by persons in its own and other enneagram spaces.[6]

Besides these time-worn avenues of learning about spiritual leaders we can add others made available by modern technology. Not many writers of spiritual classics are contemporary enough to have been filmed or tape recorded.[7]

Information about Merton from these sources is of special value to our purposes here. The fact that Merton utilized the technology of communication provides a wealth of data to observe what kind of energy he embodied and how he actually lived his life in one of the nine stances. With Merton we not only have the printed words of what he thought and felt and did, we have information about the quality of his energy in his voice, posture, and mannerisms. It is this additional avenue of information that gives me not only courage but confidence in exploring Merton's enneagram space. Without it, the essential element of the oral approach—learning from the particular energies of concrete individuals—would have been missing.

Thomas Merton is, then, a spiritual master who lends himself to enneagram study. With him we have the benefit of knowing both interior dynamics and how these are played out bodily in nonverbal expressions and in life decisions and actions. Inner and outer aspects are vital in assessing anyone's life stance. This is so because people may do many of the same things for differing reasons and in distinctive ways. It is the inner and outer together that contribute to establishing peoples' enneagram stances. Largely because he is a man of modern, technological times, Merton provides data in both areas.

A Look at the Descriptive 4 Labels[8]

Having said all this, I would like to look briefly at what descriptions of the 4 say about the dynamics of this space. To put it another way: a personality formed around the descriptive 4 words melancholy and romantic will have a certain flavor. In the first part of life, the period of ego-development when people form themselves both consciously and unconsciously, 4s make distinctive choices. In the service of self-creation or character development 4s determine, as everyone does, who they are to be. It is from a base of melancholy and romanticism that 4s form both their persona or image and their shadow, the denied and buried aspects of themselves that would contradict that image. The important issues that recur over a lifetime for 4s carry the flavor of this process.

We look, then, at what the word *melancholy* means. Its origin refers to a physiological condition: excessive secretion of black bile. This condition was once thought to be the cause of a disordered mental state called melancholia. Ego-melancholic persons, then, will have reactions similar to people with melancholia. However, the enneagram descriptions are about instincts rather than psychosis. That means that ego-melancholics manifest varying degrees of mental health depending on their response to their inclinations.

It is true that 4s experience a tendency to mood swings from depression to its denial, an affective, high-spirited excitement known as mania. John Eudes Bamberger alludes to this dynamic in Merton, as do many who lived daily life with him over a period of time. He says:

> If you knew him, Merton had a great deal of spontaneous joy and humor but, like so many people who are inclined that way at times, when he was down it was heavy. He seemed to me to be unfair at those times in critical remarks he might make.[9]

We also find in the dictionary other words to describe aspects of melancholy. These include *gloominess*, "a somber, dejected quality and a mournful, whining manner." Terms like these indicate some of the darkness which permeates this stance. They also tell us how 4s meet the kind of world they perceive. Extreme self-consciousness narrows the perceptual world of melancholics. They become absorbed in their limitations. Mary Luke Tobin describes this dynamic in Merton:

> He was a man who examined himself continually. He blamed himself for being too sensitive to the opinions of others, and he often talked about that as his "allergy." I think he lived with this, as all of us must, but in a person of his depth and sensitivity it must have been particularly painful.[10]

There are two other aspects noted in the definition of melancholy. One of these portrays that thoughtful, reflective stance which is often described as pensive and quietly meditative. John Barber, who attended school with Merton at Oakham, distinguishes this quality:

> I suppose you might say that he had a moody side, but I wouldn't say it was moody as much as it was a way of withdrawing into his own thoughts. He thought deeply, you could sense that, much more deeply than most of us who came from a less international background . . . and I would say, even with his bright, sprightly nature, he had a contemplative side. He appreciated being on his own a good bit. That was the strange contrast in him.[11]

The other aspect of melancholy refers to a certain sullen quality that is irascible and ill-natured. This latter response may be manifested in some people as a subtle touchiness. In others it is a more straightforward aggression. W. H. (Ping) Ferry notes Merton's awareness of this quality in himself:

> After carrying on for a long while about, let us say, the then Catholic view of the development of weapons, he would say, "I'm getting strident; I'm beginning to sound just like the opposition."[12]

Such an angry aspect can also be masked as gracious friendliness, a cooperative spirit, but one which may suddenly give way to hostility. When 4s overextend and tire themselves out in social relationship, this aggression rises up as a prelude to withdrawal. Merton describes the dynamic this way:

> The rush and pressure of modern life are a form, perhaps the most common form, of its innate violence. To allow oneself to be carried away by a multitude of conflicting concerns, to surrender to too many demands, to commit oneself to too many projects, to want to help everyone in everything is to succumb to violence. . . . It destroys the fruitfulness of a person's work because it kills the root of inner wisdom which makes work fruitful.[13]

Another description associated with the ego development of 4 people is caught in the word *romantic*. What is an ego-romantic? By definition, romantic refers to something remote in time or place. That kind of distance invites exaggeration, even distortion, of events, feelings and actions. A cloak of mystery, even the invention of details, falsifies reality. It does so by enlarging it to heroic and adventurous proportions, to fantasy and fiction. An ego-romantic, then, is someone who colors life, even to the point of deceiving self and others about what is real. The way 4s tend to be out of the present moment is by withdrawing to an existence with such fictional dimensions. As ego-romantics they escape from the ordinary and everyday either to "good old days" or "bad old days," however they need to see things in the drama of their lives. They do so because they fear mundane reality; they are frightened by the ordinary.

It is this tendency to exaggerate rather than to live their lives that leads to 4s being called "over-dramatizers." Early in life they build up many compulsions in this area as well as the romantic and melancholy areas. In fact, the view that the world is a stage and we but players permeates the 4 energy and interweaves with these other two characteristics. John Eudes Bamberger says that Merton was a very dramatic type of person whose profound insights were more real to him than the stones in a wall.[13] This dramatic quality characterized his dynamism. It is this energy Flavian Burns describes as "lively, hectic, and nervous."[14] Merton compensated for it by discipline, says Abbot Flavian, as do many 4s. This conscious control of the impulse to exaggerate and distort is one cause of the aloofness often attributed to 4s. It showed up in Merton's writing, as Abbot John Eudes tells us:

> Almost anything he (Merton) took a liking to he became enthusiastic about, very quickly, as I learned as the years went on. But that wasn't the impression his books gave. His books

> gave the impression of a person who was on top of things, and who had a very involved but balanced vision.
>
> There was a great openness about him and yet a concealed reserve, too.[15]

Drama involves intense focus on a slice of life. As such it demands an audience which observes and is drawn into the scene. However, 4s do not see themselves "on stage" primarily as the focus of everyone's attention, but rather of their own. As they sit in their own audience and critique their thoughts, feelings, and actions, 4s compare themselves to others as well as to their own criteria of what is fitting and appropriate. Some of the 4 intensity comes from this view of life as a play made up of series of events in which various forces come together.

In the art form known as drama, actors portray not only the events dramatized in the play, but something far beyond them. The little world of the stage focuses in its events and relationships the broader world of its characters, its audience, and human existence in general. The play becomes a microcosm of the issues and dynamics of life, which are intensified for the audience to observe and respond to. For 4s, who are over-dramatizers, life's moments one by one hold something of this flavor of great significance. The life of Thomas Merton contained enough drama even without additional emphasis. The loss of both parents at an early age and a childhood of loneliness caused by frequent moving around would be enough to affect any boy. For Merton, its significance was especially highlighted with a poignancy characteristic of his enneagram space. His autobiography, *The Seven Storey Mountain*, is full of this energy of intense significance attributed to the events of his life. His later journals show how this instinct later relaxed from a compulsive quality to a simple poetic one, which indeed honored his experience without exaggerating it.

As this book proceeds I will underline how these descriptions of the 4 gesture in life weave in and out of the life story, the compulsions, the problems and issues, and the giftedness of Thomas Merton. Those readers familiar with Merton are probably already making applications on their own. The dynamics I have just laid out are the stuff of his personal spiritual journey, the causes of his conflicts and pains and of the distortions and delusions that constitute what he would call the false self. The romantic illusions he found necessary for survival and self-protection forced him at times to deny the concrete reality of his daily life. Frequently he amplified his experience with an intensity hard to endure. The swing from a frustrated hopelessness to enthusiastic excitement followed him all of his days. His unrealistic demands, his angry responses, and the exaggerated significance he placed on everyday disappointments and annoyances colored his monastic experience.

We must never forget, however, the other side of the coin of this 4 instinct. How Merton discovered his compulsions, made peace with them, and let them lead him down the path of humility is of even greater importance. He might have been just another compulsed 4, but he was not. His grappling with, giving up on, eventually turning over to God the instincts of the ego-melancholic, ego-romantic, over-dramatizer are the reasons we remember him today. These dynamics are why he brings us comfort and speaks to our own pain.

Merton made himself into his own creation, as we make ourselves into the creation we are from the raw material of our instinctive incarnation, whether as a 4 or one of the other enneagram numbers. Merton became appalled by who he saw he had become, as we do at some point in our lives when we are able to own what we have done to ourselves. He agonized, perhaps even despaired at times, over this reality, as we must in the "dark night." In desperation he threw himself onto a God he hoped could and would be more accepting of him than he was of himself. If we come to transformation, we do the same. As they did to Jesus in the desert,[16] angels of God in the guise of circumstances and persons came to minister to him, and such moments of darkness and depression passed. Angels of one or another kind come to us, too, in the form of people, events, or simply relief from seemingly impossible situations.

There is good news, also, to be found in the instincts we are born with, the word that is our innate endowment. None of the nine personality types is a mistake on the part of the Creator. The mistake lies in our belief that we must remake who we find ourselves to be. Life teaches reconciliation with our reality and acceptance of ourselves as worthy of love. We discover as we make peace with ourselves that God has always been at peace with, accepting of, who we are. Gradually we free our energy to contribute its unique gift, our unique gift, to creation. James Connor quotes Merton in this regard:

> Do not attach too much importance to any individual happening or reaction, and do not look for very special significances. They are all part of a purification process with which you must be patient. You have an ego which you can obviously not get rid of by ego-willing. The more you try the more you will be in a bind. You cannot scheme, you cannot figure,

> you cannot worm your way out of it. Only God can unlock the whole business from the inside, and when he does, everything will be simple and plain. Obviously, the human element complicates everything, but what else are we? That's all. Identify with the ground, and don't worry too much about the weeds. The ground doesn't. . . . Just don't go on cultivating weeds on purpose with the idea that they are something special, either specially good or specially bad.[17]

In these words we see both the Merton who tended to dramatic intensity and the Merton who eventually relaxed with his reality. It is this latter Merton who came to accept not only his creaturely limitation, but also his goodness. And this Merton has a wealth of words to help us do the same. Because Thomas Merton stayed committed to life, he eventually became this person who freely dispensed his immense richness for us to share.

We are not all 4s; we do not all have to wrestle with the same kinds of demons in the form of compulsions that Merton did. But we all have to follow a parallel path to conversion. The gift of Thomas Merton is that he shared his journey with us in so many ways. Let us now continue our reflections on his story, noting that it is also our own, at least in broad outline. We will be able to recognize the terrain if we ourselves are on our own journeys. The signs along the road, the flavor of the stops along the way, even at times the roadways we choose to traverse the valleys and mountains may not be Merton's. If we are 4s, we will recognize and find helpful even the details of his life journey. If we are not, we can draw help and hope by analogy to Merton's story. It is that of a man who had the courage to look at and accept himself and the wisdom to know he was not God. It is this wisdom that led him to turn in humility as creature to the Creator.

Ultimately, Thomas Merton accepted the word God intended him to be. This ego-melancholic, ego-romantic, over-dramatizer became what he often referred to as his true self. His friend Bob Lax put it this way:

> I think he was just looking for a direction in life. I think if a tree is looking for a direction in life it's just hoping to become a tree. And I think that what Merton was hoping to become was completely a human being, or completely Thomas Merton. . . . What he was after was to become himself.[18]

The Fundamental Sin: A Figure on His Own

One of the most graphic ways to trace the early stages of a person's life journey is to look at childhood photos. In them we find portrayed the early movement to self-creation and beyond it in later life to wholeness. Such photos often reveal not only when and how but often why a person embarks on the path to becoming an individual.

For most of us, it is not difficult to find pictures that capture the wide-eyed openness of infancy. An infant's open, trusting gaze, so arresting to the observer of such a photograph, speaks of security, even immersion in, the protection of an all-provider, usually mother. Actually, this initial life experience becomes equated with the experience of God the all-provider. We live with a human person who is God for us in a paradise of contentment. If such is not the case, if we are deprived of this essential care and basic concern, we will not survive.

Thomas Merton, a human being like the rest of us, certainly knew this time in his own life. Ruth Merton was very much this all-provider in what was something of a paradise, the south of France, where Tom was born and spent his early years. He was the center of her attention, as she was of his. She kept a detailed diary of everything her firstborn did. He sang the songs she taught him and carried on long conversations with her, making use of his extensive vocabulary. One proud entry in "Tom's Book" states that he knew five hundred words by the age of two. Whether she was using hyperbole or had carefully tallied a list, the remark shows how absorbed Ruth must have been with Tom's development.

As it does for all of us, this paradise ended for Tom. We hear him describe his parents in terms of their limitations. His father, Owen, was an artist who would become engrossed in his work to the detriment of the rest of his life. He seems nearly to have forgotten at times some significant persons, including his children. Tom describes his mother in terms of coldness and emotional distance. Whatever the cause, Ruth's relationship with her son shifted from one of an all-provider to one that was harsh and critical. Michael Mott, Merton's official biographer, speaks of her sharp discipline and her aloofness. For example, at the time of her death, rather than saying a personal good-bye to her six-year-old son, she wrote him a letter of farewell and asked her husband, Owen, to deliver it. In the fall of 1921 Ruth Jenkins Merton died, but it seems Ruth Merton had left her child long before.

The accompanying photograph reflects this change in Tom's perception. Mott finds the family snapshot significant enough to single out for comment. For him it portrays Merton's relationship to his family as well as his life gesture. I would say it portrays Merton's enneagram stance.

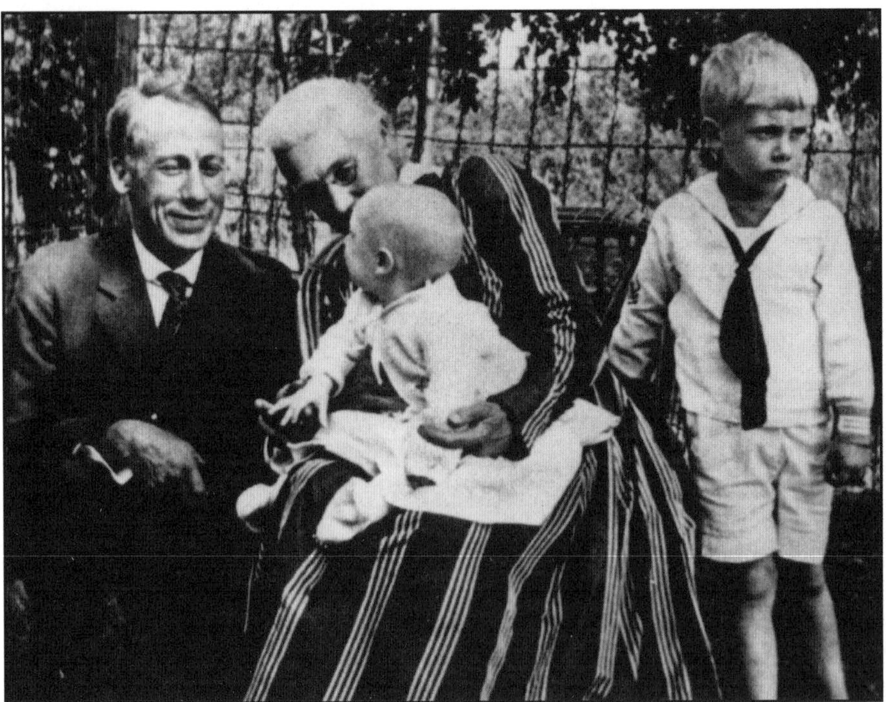

Young Thomas Merton (far right) is pictured with his father Owen, his grandmother Gertrude Merton, and his younger brother John Paul.

> Nothing is easier than to read the wrong things into old photographs, but one of these is certainly arresting. Gertrude sits in the middle holding John Paul and looking down at him. Owen, in a formal suit, squats beside his mother. He is looking at John Paul. All three are smiling at one another. Tom, one hand in the folds of his grandmother's full dress, as if he has been clutching them, and perhaps tugging on them for attention, has turned his back on the group. He stands in a white sailor's suit, scowling out of the picture and far away to his left. All children scowl—certainly small boys of four do—and it usually means nothing. Perhaps Tom is bothered by strong sunlight, though none of the others is bothered by the sun. They are too absorbed in one another. At that moment, only the person taking the photograph could have observed and recorded that Tom was a figure on his own.[1]

For Mott, this photo portrays Merton's relationship to his family as well as his life gesture. I will extend Mott's reflections in an effort to describe Merton, first, as an individual and, second, as an individual who was a 4.

Concrete circumstances in all of our lives make the choice to become a separate individual more desirable than remaining in secure and safe dependence. Nevertheless, we remain ambivalent about losing our paradise. Certainly through adolescence we go back and forth between independence and a childish longing for protection. On the one hand, we yearn for the safe and secure arms of our provider; on the other, we reach for freedom. All who develop normally eventually come down more times than not on the side of independence. Throughout Tom's life we see this ambivalence both in his search for women to provide comfort and his fear of being overwhelmed by them. Already in this photo, which Mott sees as so significant for understanding Tom's choice to become himself, we find this ambivalence portrayed. It is graphically presented in his tentative stance, which expresses hanging on even as he pulls away.

An excuse to go out on our own often demands that we fictionalize our situation, at least somewhat. Perhaps the limitations of Ruth Merton were not as extreme as Tom reported. Perhaps it was a very common and simple life occurrence that caused Tom to feel abandoned; like many of us, Tom was forced at the age of three to share the family spotlight with another child, John Paul Merton. Immediately John Paul seems to have taken over nearly all of Ruth Merton's attention and emotional energy. Rightly or wrongly, we know that Tom experienced the presence of this intruder and his mother's change in attitude toward Tom as rejection. This is the word he used from the vantage point of adulthood to describe how he felt toward his mother. However it occurred, Tom judged that his mother had put him aside.

It is a short journey from feeling unloved to judging that we are unlovable. We see hints of that judgment in the four-year-old Tom's expression and posture. We know from many of the things he said later on in life that he, like the rest of us, rejected himself.

There is in every weak, lost, and isolated member of the human race an agony of hatred born of his or her own helplessness and isolation. Hatred is the sign and the expression of loneliness, of unworthiness, of insufficiency. In so far as we are lonely, unworthy, we hate ourselves.[2]

Part of human development is to look for and find cause to feel unloved. We condemn our very being, a being we see as unacceptable. This judgment of our unlovableness constitutes our original or fundamental sin. Our sense of unlovableness, however, substantiates our decision to separate, to become individuals. At the same time, it forces us to be on our own. Out of this sin come the divisions we create between what we incorporate as part of ourselves and what we determine we must deny and get rid of.

Tom was faced with the task which we all face: the decision to become an individual. Eventually, this choice looks more attractive than being cared for, and we choose life on our own, moving beyond an existence of love and acceptance. We opt for the challenge of independence and the freedom of personal decision. Like every healthy, developing child, Tom used the circumstance of his life to initiate this first of life's tasks.

Although we are all very young when we begin to create our false self, there is an element of choice involved; hence, it can truly be called a "sin," something for which we bear responsibility. As life continues our falsity grows into habit; we wear it as Adam and Eve wore animal skins to hide their reality. That Merton saw human experience this way is evident in this passage:

> We are at liberty to be real, or to be unreal. We may be true or false, the choice is ours. We may wear now one mask and now another, and never, if we so desire, appear with our own true face. But we cannot make these choices with impunity. Causes have effects, and if we lie to ourselves and to

> others, then we cannot expect to find truth and reality whenever we happen to want them. If we have chosen the way of falsity we must not be surprised that truth eludes us when we finally come to need it![3]

Parker Palmer has this to say about original sin:

> I treasure that early Christian theologian who railed against the notion that the fall of Adam and Eve was pure and simple sin. Instead, he called it *felix culpa*, the happy sin, since without it we would still be living in the boredom of dreaming innocence and the great adventure of human history would never have gotten underway. The fall gave us the "gifts" of doubt, ambiguity, alienation. These do not feel like gifts when we first experience them. To know them as the gifts they are, we must enter into the struggles they pose for us. Once inside, we have a chance to find the self that remains hidden when we feel confident and secure, the seeking self that draws us into the human adventure.[4]

Besides the inner division between the acceptable and the unacceptable, we make choices as to what of ourselves we will make known and available to other people and what we will hide away. Such choices come from what we discover in ourselves as more acceptable, more instinctive, and therefore more facile and easy to portray. Who we are, our stance in life, our view of reality, our enneagram space, will shape what we show to others as well as what we deny and bury.

Fundamental sin, then, is a necessary evil; it puts us on the path of that ego-development which is necessary for healthy human life. It is a choice to live, therefore, and its consequence is our taking hold of and creating ourselves. While it is a happy fault, it also holds seeds of destruction and evil. It involves denial of our goodness, of the worth of our being. Not even the God who creates us can possibly find us lovable. This view takes us to the limits of isolation, from God and from others.

> Too often the conventional conception of "God's will" as a sphinx-like and arbitrary force bearing down upon us with implacable hostility, leads men to lose faith in a God they cannot find it possible to love. Such a view of the divine will drives human weakness to despair and one wonders if it is

> not, itself, often the expression of a despair too intolerable to be admitted to conscious consideration.[5]

Merton notes how this view of God is really a projection of our self-image: "Our idea of God tells us more about ourselves than about him."[6]

Such self-rejection also creates distrust of, and hostility toward, others. We find evidence of this self-rejection when we decide that people are hateful and non-accepting. Such a decision is a projection of our own attitude toward ourselves and enables us to survive, to carry on when we find ourselves disgusting. We try to be acceptable; it is others who do not credit us with efforts to re-create and improve ourselves. We are, after all, doing what we can.

How does this conviction of being unlovable show itself in the child Tom? We have his parents' descriptions of the initial, spontaneous, instinctive responses all children have when they are living in the child's version of paradise, the security of the all-provider. We also have photos with the open and trusting gaze of early childhood. As Tom grew older and found that his every desire was not fulfilled, like every child he became frustrated. He expressed this frustration in tantrums for which he inevitably encountered disapproval. It is around this disapproval for his temper displays that the child Tom's split between inner and outer became evident, a split we all learn to make to win acceptance.

Tom became a private person. No longer the apple of his mother's eye, he grew silent about his real concerns and feelings, a habit he was to keep for his entire life. Only once in his adulthood, Mott says, did he display his frustration, anger, and fear in a response similar to his childhood outbursts. This was in reaction to the encounter with Gregory Zilboorg, a meeting which radically attacked the illusions and delusions he had hidden behind for a lifetime. Zilboorg accused Merton of wanting the image of a hermit rather than wanting the life itself. Merton knew there was some truth in the accusation. As a result the exterior warmth and friendliness that disguised more negative feelings fell away for a moment and the frustrated child was visible. The frightened child of that early photo revealed himself in the crisis of the situation. Merton has described this fear as

> Not so much the fear men have of one another as the fear they have of everything. It is not merely that they do not trust one another; they do not even trust themselves. If they

> are not sure when someone else may turn around and kill them, they are still less sure when they may turn around and kill themselves.[7]

It is Merton's letters, journals, and writings in spirituality that best reveal his attitude toward himself. He remembered his mother as the initial source of confusion about his goodness. Mott says, on the one hand she filled him with a sense of his importance; on the other she showed him how inadequate he was. In later life Merton called himself his own mistake. Out of his awareness of who he had created himself to be in order to win acceptance, we have his descriptions of the false self and true self. These articulations of his own dynamics help us his readers see how, in our own circumstances, we have done what he did, indeed, what every person does on the path of life.

Anthony de Mello says, through his spiritual master, that life is not so much about something we do but about something we drop. We need to drop our barriers, those boundaries that separate us from ourselves and from others. We need to stop holding ourselves off from those parts of our reality we early on determined we must deny for survival. We need to refrain from blocking the flow of our lives, placing boulders in the path of our physical, emotional, and perceptual responses. We need to reverse our sinfulness, which told us we must shape how we look and see, how we feel, how we act. Out of this world of barriers we developed our interaction with other people, an interaction laced with distrust and hostility. We, each of us, committed this fundamental sin that resulted in the evil of blocking our life's flow. None of us is the person we might have been had we accepted the value of our being. Yet this is a necessary sin and a happy fault. It is the source of our separate, individual personality.

Fundamental Sin and the 4 Response

This interpretation of the fall from paradise and fundamental sin is the story of every person, whatever that person's enneagram stance. However, each enneagram space with its unique internalization of and gesture toward life responds differently. Early in life each child is immersed in the unconscious as in a sea. With a growing delineation and focus, the ego with its increasingly responsible choice emerges. The child swimmer learns patterns, characteristic strokes, if you will, in response to his or her instinctive enneagram stance through the situation of concrete living. That is why we are all unique at the same time as we share concrete dynamics and issues with others similar to ourselves.

Now we will consider how those in the 4 space, including Merton, deal with experiences of rejection and respond to them.

Some children become openly belligerent and others withdraw to safety in a private interior world. Still others, 4s among them, spend their energy connecting with and adapting to others. For 4s, however, this need to establish some link with other people includes an interior pulling away and insulating themselves from disappointment in, and expectation of, relationship. It is characteristic of children to see themselves as the center of a universe they must control. The way 4s do this is to shape and hone their world and their own response to their surroundings into a pleasant, rhythmic flow.

It is only a very young 4 who expresses willfulness in temper tantrums. In this space children learn early that anger alienates and disturbs. Because of this awareness they give up obvious efforts to force what they want onto others. They move above and away from occasions where they might incur accusation and hostility. It is as though 4s look down from some place above the stream of life. They continue to interact with people, but they do so remotely, saving themselves emotional onslaught and the conflicts of genuine human encounter.

Actual life looks like death to the 4, laced as it is with limitation, crisis, and conflict. Fear of death and slavery to that fear are what motivate the 4's romantic defense, which is manifested in this kind of interior withdrawal. Merton the adult describes such remoteness:

> If you seek escape for its own sake and run away from the world only because it is (as it must be) intensely unpleasant, you will not find peace and you will not find solitude. If you seek solitude merely because it is what you prefer, you will never escape from the world and its selfishness; you will never have the interior freedom that will keep you really alone.[8]

Despite this inner distancing, 4s are instinctively social and come from the social triad on the enneagram. They keep getting caught in nets of friendship and personal attachment in spite of themselves. Actually, 4s want to relate deeply and personally, and they hope their conviction that all relationship is doomed to failure will be proven wrong someday, somehow. In order to maintain harmony and rhythmic flow in life they need to protect themselves from the genuine passion of human relationship: fear, anger, pain, hurt, love, loss. To this end they remind themselves that no relationship can be counted on to endure. Even when the end is due to external circumstances, they usually they see it caused by their own insufficiency as people worth relating to. It is their own feeling of inadequacy that ultimately destroys all of their encounters with others. They examine themselves obsessively, question all of their motivations, and come up wanting every time.

Merton has described what happens to 4s as a result of this ruthless self-examination. Its end is despair; it can only be countered with humility. Merton's summary of the situation is a simple one: "If there were no humility in the world, everybody would long ago have committed suicide."[9]

As we have said, such self-rejection creates distrust of others and hostility toward them.

> It is the rankling, tormenting sense of unworthiness that lies at the root of all hate. The man who is able to hate strongly and with a quiet conscience is one who is complacently blind to all unworthiness in himself and serenely capable of seeing all his own wrongs in someone else.[10]

The luxury of this easy projection, however, is usually denied to 4 personalities. They find it difficult to escape a harshly critical assessment on themselves. Merton goes on to speak of this in the same passage:

> But the man who is aware of his own unworthiness and the unworthiness of his brother is tempted with a subtler and more tormenting kind of hate: the general, searing, nauseating hate of everything and everyone, because everything is tainted with unworthiness, everything is unclean, everything is foul with sin.
>
> . . . Perhaps he cannot feel love because he thinks he is unworthy of love, and because of that he also thinks no one else is worthy.[11]

We see here some of what constitutes the melancholic despair of the 4, and indeed of Merton. We find, too, that dramatic emphasis that intensifies the 4's desperation. Often, as in this passage, such drama assumes a poetic quality, with each word packed with meaning and feeling.

Merton understands that only humility can save those who are 4s from the twists and turns of excessive egoism and self-preoccupation. Only humility can deliver the melancholic from despair and the propensity to suicide, an ultimate escape 4s seem prone to. Having wasted time obsessing on his or her own and others' limitations, the bottom falls out of the activity and helplessness takes over. Only God can deliver the melancholic from such a situation; only God is God.

> In the true Christian vision of God's love, the idea of worthiness loses its significance. Revelation of the mercy of God makes the whole problem of worthiness something almost laughable: the discovery that worthiness is of no special consequence (since no one could ever, by himself, be strictly worthy to be loved with such a love) is a true liberation of the spirit.[12]

This description of the unique way 4s internalize being rejected and abandoned as children carries with it the unique "unlovableness" they experience. Theirs is a sense of not measuring up, of being incompetent. Life becomes a series of efforts to make themselves worthy to belong to the human community, though they believe deep down such efforts are futile. Such attempts cover over the appalling experience, as Merton has put it, of "a general sense of failure, of guilt."[13]

"Guilt over what?" we may ask. Perhaps guilt over their very existence, flawed and imperfect as 4s see it to be. Their very being disturbs the beauty and harmony of creation, especially of the creation which is human interaction. In suffering the intense, instinctively dramatized passion of this guilt 4s who are faithful to their conversion process learn compassion for others.

> I cannot treat other men as men unless I have compassion for them. I must have at least enough compassion to realize that when they suffer they feel somewhat as I do when I suffer. And if for some reason I do not spontaneously feel this kind of sympathy for others, then it is God's will that I do what I can to learn how. I must learn to share with others their joys, their sufferings, their ideas, their needs, their desires.[14]

Merton never did become someone who chose aggressive hostility to deal with people and situations. Those who knew him, especially those who lived with him in community, however, were aware of a sometimes arrogant scorn. His comments on community customs and situations demonstrate such disdain. So, too, do his appraisals of and behaviors around some post-Vatican liturgical reforms; Merton has been said to have walked out of the English reading of the Passion on

Palm Sunday as a protest to its not being chanted in Latin. However, his characteristic affable and inviting smile seems to say that it is usually better to win others than to make them enemies. His anger and frustration expressed themselves more indirectly in apologetic humor sprinkled with shy barbs or else a carefully thought out argument that defied objections.

While we describe the adult Merton here, we see these dynamics already stirring in the boy Tom. The worldview of both child and man are captured in the photo Mott so sensitively chose for just this purpose. Here we find the physical expression of the 4's life view in Merton's posture and stance assumed shortly after what must have been his fundamental sin, his denial of his value. Probably its consequences were just deepening into life patterns of a 4's response, of Merton's response.

We never know with certainty when this fundamental sin takes place in a 4's childhood development. It does so over a period of time through the accumulated experience each child uses to verify suspicions of being unloved and unlovable. It may be that the birth of John Paul was significant as the initial impetus toward Merton's denial of his word, his goodness. Possibly the death of his mother solidified that self-perception. While we cannot be sure how this original sin occurred, we see evidence of it already in this snapshot of four-year-old Tom. The ambivalent stance of both hanging on and pulling away is demonstrated in this photo as 4s characteristically embody it. Tom's sense of inadequacy, of not measuring up to the engaging presence John Paul has to offer, is written in his posture and facial expression.

We see grandmother Gertrude and Owen Merton engaged with Tom's little brother. That engagement seems to be a happy one. Obviously, from the expressions on the faces of the adults, John Paul delighted them, at least in the moment. Furthermore, John Paul seems to be responding in kind. The scene involving this little trio is clearly mutual enjoyment; they are taken up with one another. Tom stands alone to one side of the group, uninvolved in their shared experience. His only physical contact with them is his hand on his grandmother's skirt, tucked unobtrusively behind her body between her back and the chair in that ambivalent gesture already described. His gaze is averted and focused outside the picture. He is obviously not involved with the photographer, either. He stands apart from everyone.

Tom's expression is one of resignation and loneliness. He reaches out in a shy, tentative, and somewhat futile effort to belong to what is going on, though his face shows no expectation of gaining admission to the group. Yet he cannot refrain from reaching out, from feeble efforts to establish connection. Here we see Tom's stance. Here we observe the 4 dynamic: There is no hope of belonging, but one must continue to try if life is to have any meaning.

Mott describes Tom's expression as a scowl. While his deep-set eyes look out and up in a serious way, they would seem to be more calm and aloof, more detached than a scowl might indicate. The pensive 4 quality, the gravity, especially in contrast to the warmth and acceptance the bodies and faces of the others reveal, seems evident. His expression portrays a sense of resignation rather than the hostility a scowl would imply. Even as Tom reaches out instinctively, something in his body seems to say there is little reason to hope he will become a part of things. Yet he appears protected by a calm and control, a poise and quiet. It seems he will survive alone.

If there is any indication at all of anger in Tom's face, it seems to be around his mouth. His lips already have a pouting appearance, one they retained in repose all his lifetime. The anger seems not to be directed at the others in the photo; he appears unaware of them. It is as though he is looking at his situation in life, the lot he has been given, while he gazes off camera. It would seem he already knows in some wordless way that his destiny will be alone, and it is a destiny that cannot be fought against because he is convinced he deserves it. This despair of the 4 Merton describes well:

> Despair is the absolute extreme of self-love. It is reached when a man deliberately turns his back on all help from anyone else in order to taste the rotten luxury of knowing himself to be lost. In every man there is hidden some root of despair because in every man there is pride that vegetates and springs weeds and rank flowers of self-pity as soon as our own resources fail us. But because our own resources inevitably fail us, we are all more or less subject to discouragement and to despair.[15]

Such awareness leads the 4 to a hopelessness that covers an affable, often cheerful, exterior. Throughout Merton's life we find evidence of both of these dynamics.

It is doubtful whether the child Tom consciously registered the ideas described here. Little children cannot reflect on such things. They do, however, experience, internalize, and feel them, and respond accordingly. Children not only make choices about how they will live their lives, they do so from their characteristic instinct or gesture or stance. Were Tom Merton not a 4, he would have judged reality and behaved other than he did.

In the photo of the four-year-old Tom we see captured on camera one moment when he learned about living. This and similar learnings shaped his articulation of issues in the spiritual journey. The picture itself may have been a significant moment in his memory. Surely, at least, it made concrete the gesture that characterized Merton's future living and writing.

The evil of Thomas Merton's life, like the evil of all of our lives, came from the deceptive way he perceived his existence and that existence in relationship with others and his surroundings. As a 4, Tom defined himself as abandoned, an outsider who desperately wanted to be the center of things. Initially he had been. More significantly, he judged himself worthy of this rejection. John Paul's arrival fed Tom's instinct—the 4's instinct—for comparison. The search to belong, to become accepted again, was underway.

For Tom, as for other 4s, this search appeared fruitless and impossible even though it was one he could not resist engaging in. In the photo we see him reach out in a futile little gesture to his grandmother. He did so in a way that was not obvious, did not draw too much attention to himself and his hunger for inclusion. Though he put out his hand, his facial expression seems to say that it does not matter all that much how things turn out. His erect little body indicates that he can get along no matter what happens. His drooping shoulders seem to expect that things won't change.

The hopelessness of the 4 manifests itself in either depression or mania or both. When 4s grow depressed it is because they romantically allow themselves to expect life's meaning to be revealed in flawless, non-conflictual human relationship. Of course they are disappointed in this expectation and their disappointment extends to profound questions about whether life can have any meaning at all since it involves alienation. Even more discouraging, this destiny of loneliness is one 4s conclude they deserve because, as Merton has put it, they have within themselves only emptiness on the one side and falsity and lying on the other. When 4s are manic, it is as a way to escape that abyss of self-deprecation and despair into which they fear admitting their feelings will plunge them.

The grave little boy who looks out from this photo has already chosen somehow to survive, as do all 4s—indeed, all people who live into adulthood. His deceptions have already begun. His body speaks how unloved and unlovable he sees himself to be. He stands alone. There is no one there who seems to care, and he quietly covers over his true feelings. The luxury of tantrums is not allowed to a child who has to adapt and win a place. His frustrations and anger must be hidden behind this calm, cool, aloof facade that says to others that he really doesn't need them after all. His hand on Gertrude's skirt is the only clue that he will entertain their attention were it to be shown. This serious child says all of this in his body stance and even more so in his face and the expression of his eyes.

The evil which results from our "original sin" manifests itself in the barriers we create separating ourselves from our goodness and the goodness of others, from our reality and the reality of the people in our lives. We and they are limited, and that limitation is part of our and their goodness, not a contradiction to it. Already in this picture Tom was about the task of self-creation, of becoming his own God, his own judge of good and evil in himself. His personality was already being built around decisions to banish parts of himself into darkness and shadow so that other parts could be accentuated. He already manifested in this photo the "appropriate" response that 4s reach for to enable themselves to be endured if not welcomed by others. He stays near and seems to—thinks that he—asks nothing. He wants only to hold on unobtrusively so that he can stand alone.

Thus Tom Merton began to taste evil, and he did so in ways characteristic of a 4. Jolande Jacobi has said that evil is not to mature according to our years.[16] Merton himself says something similar, according to William Shannon:

> When Merton speaks of sin, he has in mind, not primarily a moral lapse whereby I choose what is in conflict with my better instincts, but an ontological lapse whereby I choose what is in conflict with my true being. It is not simply that I make mistakes. I become a mistake. For I become what I am not.[17]

In the words of Merton himself:

> [The sense of sin] is not merely a sense of guilt referred to the authority of God. It is a sense of evil in myself. Not because I have violated a law outside myself, but because I have violated the inmost laws of my own being, which are, at the same time, the laws of God Who dwells within me. The sense of sin is the sense of having been deeply and deliberately false to my inmost reality, my likeness to God.[18]

The texture and feel of our sin is characteristic of our enneagram space and the unique circumstance of our individual lives. Tom Merton would have had the patterns of response he did have no matter who his parents were and whether or not they had died early in his life, plunging him into solitary travels through all of his maturing years. No matter what the situation, he was going to deny his word by feeling abandoned, by becoming aloof, by suppressing his anger in as many ways as he could in order to appear compliant and cooperative.

However it might have happened, he would have doubted that anyone could exist as a permanent companion for his life. To make sure that people's departures would not hurt too much he would have maintained a certain emotional distance even as he attempted to connect with them. The little boy standing aside, yet with his hand in his grandmother's skirt, demonstrates these 4 issues.

Knowledge of his guilt and self-deception, of his need to distort himself in order to win his own and others' acceptance, is something Merton was acutely aware of throughout much of his life. He never considered himself the helpless victim, but rather a sinner whose very real, though happy, fault merited a great Redeemer.

Without this sense of the depth of his evil, of the impossibility of saving himself, we would not be able to call Thomas Merton a spiritual guide today. This man who saw himself as a good self-corrector eventually realized that all of his efforts to re-create himself were fruitless. He came to where he could accept he had made a fundamental choice for self-abandonment. This self-abandonment grew out of his experience of being abandoned by others and led to the evil which he told himself: I deserve to be abandoned.

He also discovered that there was no need and no possibility of remaking himself into someone perfect, flawless, acceptable. He came to know and experience over time that he had always been acceptable to a loving God. He learned to assume God's attitude toward himself. Toward the end of his life he could speak of what he—and all of us—need to accept: that we psychically and spiritually cramp ourselves in efforts at self-creation.

> The ego . . . is a self-constructed illusion that "has" our body and part of our soul at its disposal because it has "taken over" the functions of the inner self, as a result of what we call man's "fall." That is precisely one of the main effects of the fall: that man has become alienated from his inner self which is the image of God. Man has been turned, spiritually,

> inside out, so that his ego plays the part of the "person"—a role which it actually has no right to assume.[19]

Merton's created self had the external appearance of confidence, security and friendliness. The knots that developed in his psychic and spiritual efforts at self-correction occurred because he needed to deny anything contrary to that image. As a 4, Merton's particular brand of evil, the special energy in his attempts at self-creation, includes observing himself in all of his complexities of perception, emotion, and behavior. Knowing all about his limitations, he initially hoped, would enable him to control them. In this way he would become self-acceptable and win his way into the lives of others.

In fact, interior controls cannot but be projected out and become efforts at exterior controls. Merton, subtly as is the case for 4s, tried to manipulate those around him to be and to do what he had determined would assist his own growth and life. The relentless efforts to get his hermitage are a case in point. Those who deal with 4s are well aware of such manipulations. From the point of view of 4s who do the controlling, these manipulations are intended as gentle reminders and suggestions that will increase harmony, not only in their own lives but in the lives of those controlled.

Such efforts to shape people and circumstances seem to 4s to be necessary survival attempts. They help manage a world full of anxieties and conflicts. Such controls form experiences, conversations, decisions, and relationships. They result in quiet and firm pressure on others to think and speak and do what 4s need to have thought, spoken, and done. Not only do 4s shape themselves, but they also try to shape others. Out of his stance of abandonment and isolation, Tom Merton tried to make himself lovable by taking control of his own existence. He became his own god, further alienating himself from himself and others.

> When you are led by God into the darkness where contemplation is found, you are not able to rest in the false sweetness of your own will. The fake interior satisfaction of self-complacency and absolute confidence in your own judgment will never be able to deceive you entirely: it will make you slightly sick and you will be forced by a vague sense of interior nausea to gash yourself open and let the poison out.[20]

In Mott's picture Tom Merton was already on the road to compulsion, the exaggeration of those very qualities which were his gift. He was on the road to redemption as well, that freedom beyond the slavery of compulsions, vices, sins, deceptions. This freedom would only come later in life when he surrendered to a God who saves. Merton puts words on what must happen in conversion when he describes how the walls must crumble between creature and Creator. Eventually, barriers built up by self-judgment fall away until these words of God who is life itself are heard in personal experience:

> God said: I do not laugh at my enemies, because I wish to make it impossible for anyone to be my enemy. Therefore I identify myself with my enemy's own secret self.[21]

Part II

Instinct, Compulsion, and Gift: Vice and Virtue in the Life of Thomas Merton

The Fear That Conflict Will Destroy

Perhaps our most significant awareness about spiritual development is that we do not make it happen. Rather, in the course of our lives we reverse early efforts at control and self-creation, yielding to the truth that we are creatures and not the Creator. Life calls us into its flow and shapes us into the person we are meant to be. Only by having the illusion of our own power wrested from our hands can we find our destiny, our true purpose in the scheme of things. We become who we were meant to be, as Thomas Merton has told us in various ways in many contexts.

We become unique individuals, and that uniqueness is reflected in our particular posture or gesture in life, our enneagram stance. From its perspective we respond in certain instinctive ways. We tend to particular kinds of defenses and denials. We over- and under-use our perceptual or feeling or behavioral function depending on who we are. The lies we tell ourselves in the course of self-protection and ego-creation are characteristic ones. They depend on which of the three enneagram centers we live in and out of. We accentuate certain characteristics because they come easily to us and appear positive to us. Such efforts lead to distortions, those compulsions and addictions that in later life are lessened when we relax into life's flow.

A good deal of what we call midlife crisis comes about by our attempts to eliminate those elements of who we are that have led us to our unique illusions and delusions, our self-distortions and ego-exaggerations. When we begin to realize what we have done early in life to "become ourselves," we make efforts to correct what Merton calls this false self. This attempt, of course, is only more self-creation, but it takes us time to realize this. Only when all of our spiritual athletics lead nowhere do we give up in exhaustion and despair, both essential for humility to take root in our lives.

The development of a contemplative attitude helps us see who we are, what we have done to ourselves and others, and that nothing we can do will change our reality. The struggles of midlife, if we are faithful to them, gradually give way to a humble acknowledgment of our human limitation. Out of this virtue fundamental to the spiritual life grows the mature wisdom of contemplation.

Thomas Merton always writes in the context of this theme. He does so because he himself exaggerated his instincts into characteristic compulsions, those of his 4 stance, to be sure, but shaped by his unique life experiences. In efforts to figure out and correct what he had done, Merton, like all of us, relied on such characteristic efforts to eliminate what he initially thought was his to eliminate. Because he was a 4, he did this in the way 4s do it. Life taught him wisdom, as his later writings especially show. Thomas Merton always remained a 4, always retained the instincts of a 4. They never were erased, nor could they be. Were he or any of us able to wipe out our instincts we would attack, as well, our incarnate selves. Life's journey is about reconciliation with our limitation, not elimination of it. That limitation is tied up inextricably with our enneagram stance.

When peace has been made with our imperfect humanity, the gift whose source is in that very same instinct can be freed. Then God can make of us what God intended, because we have moved out of the way, out of the Creator's role. We accept who we are. This is an essential prelude to becoming all we can be—not the limitless Creator, but the limited creature whose instincts, compulsive exaggerations, and unique contributions are characteristic of this limited self.

We hear Thomas Merton say again and again what I have just described. Part II of this book develops the basic 4 instinct and the themes and issues and dynamics of Merton's—indeed, of any 4's—life. We will consider how, in the process of ego-development, Merton exaggerated his instincts and suppressed and repressed their opposites in characteristic 4 ways. Doing so, he formed his shadow and projected out onto others both the positive and negative aspects he could not include within his own self-perception. In this way his world of adversaries and enemies, heroes and heroines came into being.

One by one we will look at some of the issues 4s, and therefore Thomas Merton, know and live with. We will see how he defined himself early in life around the aspects he found positive, pleasing, or at least allowable. We will note how he denied what was contrary to his image of himself, buried it out of his awareness, and then saw it in others either as their limitation or gift. We will also let him speak for himself about a growing awareness that he had done precisely this. We will look at how he learned to relax with himself and how freedom came to him and liberated his instincts from distortion. Finally, we will note how he celebrated his instincts as his gift and contribution, knowing that finding this liberation was God's doing and not his own.

In other words, we will look at Thomas Merton's vices, his illusions and delusions, his exaggerations and distortions, the byproduct of early life and ego-development. We will observe, too, how humility led him to accept his reality and, therefore, to free his 4 gift. This gift he incarnated in unique and personal ways. He was not only a 4; he was Thomas Merton. I believe that readers who know Merton well will enter his private arena of motivation in new ways, ways which shed light on the sometimes complex and unpredictable man we have come to know. My hope is that considering Merton as a 4 will clarify his dynamics and account for what he has emphasized in his spiritual message to others.

The Hope for a Rhythmic Flowing Whole

For 4s, one of the greatest fears is of anger and disruption in the surrounding environment. Should individuals be in conflict, the harmony and rhythm of life is disturbed, and the smooth flowing artistry of life is challenged. Life from the 4 perspective means that all human relationships blend into an organic, moving unity. All of life relationships are meant to be a design balanced and executed by Life, the great Artist. Anger, misunderstanding, hate, and violence hinder that flow, indeed, cut it off. It is as though an essential lifeline were severed; the existence of people united in a flowing rhythm of relationship, which is what life means to a 4, is no longer possible.

When 4s experience this deprivation, it is as though they and all of creation are suffocated. Survival is called into question, because the artistic work of the Creator is disrupted. In fact, such a situation calls the very existence of the Artist/Creator into question. For 4s, this conflict translates into fear that existence may have no meaning; it is the most terrifying of possibilities.

This need for flow and rhythm in life without boundaries between and among people led Merton to the nonviolent stance found in his writing. The source of Merton's yearning for peace is the fear of the destruction which follows when there is no peace. All is lost when conflict arises; consequently, human beings must make every effort toward harmonious bonding. While this is something never fully realized, it needs to be the center of human endeavors if life is to have any significance, even any possibility.

> Hell is where no one has anything in common with anybody else except the fact that they all hate one another and cannot get away from one another and from themselves. They are all thrown together in their fire and each one tries to thrust the others away from him with a huge, impotent hatred.[1]

Merton, whose contemplative living had brought him to the deep sources of his personal dynamics and outlook, deftly put his finger on what it is that makes for this hell of violence, hatred, and destruction. He did so from a distinctly 4 perspective.

> The reason they want to be free of one another is not so much that they hate what they see in others, as that they know others hate what they see in them; and all recognize in one another what they detest in themselves: selfishness and impotence, agony, terror, and despair.[2]

Merton touches here that self-deprecation so characteristic of the 4 personality. Don Richard Riso reminds us that 4s direct their hostility at themselves because they fear something is fundamentally wrong with them. They are angry because they see themselves as defective, and so they inhibit and punish themselves in many ways.[3]

At their center 4s experience a violence which is self-destructive. This violence is covered over early in life with courageous efforts to think positively about themselves. It is often cloaked in a pretense of appearing "naughty." This semblance leads observers to think 4s flippantly dismiss responsibility and guilt. Those who knew Merton were aware of this dynamic in him. As life goes on, however, the rage against their essentially marred existence cannot be denied by 4s. They let go against themselves in unleashed accusation, reproof, and condemnation with its consequent guilt. This is hostility at its most profound level.

It is not what 4s do or don't do that makes them wanting, that constitutes their negative assessment. It is their very being that cannot be justified. The 4 who grows in awareness—and we recognize Merton as one of these—experiences the destructiveness of violence in a very personal way. In his tongue-in-cheek "Signed Confession of Crimes Against the State" Merton describes how permeating is this guilt simply for existing:

> My very existence is an admission of guilt. Placed before a blank sheet of paper, any blank sheet of paper, I instinctively begin to set down the list of my latest crises. . . . All I have to do is think; and immediately I become guilty. In spite of all my efforts to correct this lamentable tendency to subversiveness and intellectual sabotage, I cannot possibly get rid of it.[4]

No human being can endure such a labyrinth of guilt for any prolonged period of time. In an effort to defend against endless self-accusation, projecting wrongdoing onto others becomes a survival technique or, as we tend to call it, a psychological defense. Merton saw this dynamic in himself. He attributed it to others as well who turn to violence and hostility when internalized anger can no longer be endured. I would venture to say that it was the very intensity of his own 4 dynamic that enabled Merton to articulate so graphically the roots of warfare in the world:

> We make the situation much worse by artificially intensifying our propensity to feel guilt even for those things which are not in themselves wrong. In all these ways we build up such an obsession with evil in ourselves and in others, that we waste all our mental energy trying to account for this evil, to punish it, to exorcise it, or to get rid of it in any way we can. We drive ourselves mad with our preoccupation and in the end there is no outlet left but violence. We have to destroy something or someone.[5]

One is struck with the dramatic quality of this and other passages with similar themes in Merton's writings. If one is to believe Riso, such an expression is not experienced as exaggeration. Rather, it is true to the 4 experience and the source of the depression and tendency to despair which plagued Merton. From this negative self-evaluation, the fruit of compulsive personal introspection, he turned outward toward an understanding and appraisal of world violence. Because Merton handled his dynamic this way, we have both a healthier Merton and an articulation of the causes of violence and the importance of nonviolence for our times. Merton turned to fruitful meditation which could have resulted in personal despair. He did so by letting go of his compulsive self-analysis and struggling to find the significance in this 4 dynamic.

> The sage then accomplishes very much indeed because it is the Tao that acts in him and through him. He does not act of and by himself, still less for himself alone. His action is not a violent manipulation of exterior reality, an "attack" on the outside world bending it to his conquering will; on the contrary, he respects external reality by yielding to it and his yielding is at once an act of worship, a recognition of sacredness and a perfect accomplishment of what is demanded by the precise situation.[6]

This passage offers a glimpse into the meaning for Merton of the wisdom of the East. Himself a doer who expresses his activity primarily in complex self-analysis, in "working on himself," he reached from West to East for redemption from his personal instinct-become-compulsion and found insight into the importance of nonviolence—a world where barriers do not exist, and all is one. He returned to his Western heritage, finding in Christ the compassionate one, the source of that mercy without boundary that was his own salvation. He proclaimed it to be, as well, the salvation of our world.

The beginning of the fight against hatred, the basic Christian answer to hatred, is not the commandment to love, but what must necessarily come before in order to make the commandment bearable and comprehensible. It is a prior commandment to believe. The root of Christian love is not the will to live, but the faith that one is loved . . . the faith that one is loved by God.

> In the true Christian vision of God's love, the idea of worthiness loses its significance. Revelation of the mercy of God makes the whole problem of worthiness something almost laughable: the discovery that worthiness is of no special consequence (since no one could ever, by himself, be strictly worthy to be loved with such a love) is a true liberation of the spirit. And until this discovery is made, until this liberation has been brought about by the divine mercy, man is imprisoned in hate.[7]

It is fear, then, that leads to war, according to Merton. He says many times that the only way beyond this fear is the acceptance of a

Redeemer who speaks a message of life at the core of our selves. Such a Redeemer reaches beyond despair and opens life to endless possibility. No longer need Thomas Merton, no longer need the world, be punished. Human beings can hope for life beyond ruthless self- and other-accusation.

> If Christ has died and risen from the dead and poured out upon us the fire of His Holy Spirit, why do we imagine that our desire for life is a Promethean desire, doomed to punishment? Why do we act as if our longing to "see good days" were something God did not desire, when He Himself told us to seek them? Why do we reproach ourselves for desiring victory? Why do we pride ourselves on our defeats, and glory in despair?[8]

Since all are held in the mercy of God there are no longer boundaries of judgment to separate us from ourselves or other people. Peace becomes the reality of oneness beyond "classification."[9] Categories with their parameters dissolve. Racism and nationalism fade away. All of this hope confronts in Merton a strong instinct to return to hopelessness. While he knows that "to stay in captivity is tragic," he is also aware that "to break away from it is unthinkable—and so more tragic still."[10] Because of his personal struggle, we find Merton going over this territory again and again, always ending up in the same place: the embrace of a merciful God. Hope is a tenuous virtue for Merton, as for other 4s. He writes of the struggle between it and despair in many contexts.

The Garden of Paradise is gone forever. This Merton alternately forgets and reminds both himself and us. The peace movement never did—nor can it, despite the 4 romanticism that would restore Eden—make of our world a rhythmic, flowing whole. As a 4 Merton grappled with limited reality and so became a source of courage and perseverance for many dedicated, as he was, to the cause of nonviolence and peace. In a letter to James Forest, Merton revealed how he answered his own temptation to despair, or at least, discouragement:

> Do not depend on the hope of results. When you are doing the sort of work you have taken on . . . you may have to face the fact that your work will be apparently worthless. . . . As you get used to this idea you start more and more to concentrate not on the results but on the value, the rightness, the truth of the work itself. And there too a great deal has to be gone through, as gradually you struggle less and less for an idea

> and more and more for specific people. . . . In the end . . . it is the reality of personal relationships that saves everything.[11]

Concrete human beings with whom one engages—living and struggling and misunderstanding and raging against and forgiving and trusting—all bring the 4 out of self-analysis. The limitations of life, one's personal life, are reality. They take away the preoccupations with perfection and force one into the daily conflicts that are a reminder of universal human limitation. The tapestry of life is appreciated as it is rather than as it could be were it flawless. Merciful acceptance for self and others fills the heart and is the source of compassionate energy which flows out onto others. There is no enemy within and, therefore, none outside. There is life and hope instead of despair and discouragement. To the degree we are peacemakers, we live in the mercy of Christ.

It is small wonder that Thomas Merton understood his mission in terms of nonviolence. Violence wipes out the love for self and others that only God can give. The merciful Christ is at the center of Merton's deepest self. This Christ is found only by giving up struggling self-analysis, shame at his appalling lack, and the helplessness of his own efforts to re-create someone better, more worthy, less disruptive to the pleasing rhythm of creation. When Merton falls into the dark cavern of despair, he finds both his own being and the Being who surrounds him with loving mercy.

The experience of self-acceptance that led Merton to accept others was wrung from the depths of a personal violence we can only know because he so strikingly describes it. And so it is that self-deprecation led Thomas Merton to his mission of peace.

Merton the Doer

At the heart of the 4 dynamic is the instinct to do. The behavioral function dominates the 2/3/4 enneagram center; the response is activity. Around this instinct, then, compulsions build up, and the 4 exaggerates this behavioral/doing/activity function in the process of ego-development only to have to bring it into balance later on in life. Always, despite eventual maturity, a response of doing remains instinctive; it develops into the gift of this enneagram triad. As such it loses the compulsive exaggeration of earlier life and becomes free and free-flowing. Centered activity is the heart of the gratefulness that David Steindl-Rast speaks of as "still and still moving."[1]

There is no doubt that Thomas Merton accomplished much. Besides the doing itself, there was the writing about the doing. When we reflect on the output of articles, poems, letters, books, and other literature—most of which were written on a manual typewriter—we have to acknowledge what a doer Merton was. When we consider as well that for most of his life he fit his writing into a full monastic schedule lived around demanding community roles, we are in even greater awe. His experience taught Merton to discern between ego-inspired pursuits and more balanced ones. These latter blossomed into the gift of action released from enslavement, action beyond compulsion.

> One of the last barricades of egoism, and one which many saints have refused to give up entirely, is this insistence on doing the work and getting the results and enjoying them ourselves. We are the ones who want to carry off the glory for the work done. And perhaps that was why some saints did

> not get to the highest contemplation: they wanted to do too much for themselves. And God let them get away with it.[2]

There was another kind of activity Merton learned, one which the ego did not control: acting according to the Tao. The Tao "is at once perfect activity and perfect rest."[3] Steindl-Rast's "still and still moving" is expressed in Merton's description of the Tao:

> Its effortlessness is not a matter of inertia but of harmony with the hidden power that drives the planets and the world. The sage respects external reality by yielding to it and his yielding is at once an act of worship, a recognition of sacredness and a perfect accomplishment of what is demanded by the precise situation.[4]

This description of harmony, one which distinguishes the 4 from the 9 attraction to harmony, includes participation in the action of the universe. Such participation involves a person in a sort of liturgy of appropriate rhythm, an entering into the dance of sensitive, open, active involvement in reality from moment to moment. At least this was the ideal of action Merton knew about and sometimes experienced.

There were other times as well. Jonathan Montaldo summarizes those more driven, more compulsed kinds of doing which Merton described and which others observed in his life:

> Never sated with ideas and his reactions, always writing compulsively, his quiet prayer more often than not invaded by his monkey-mind's forging new projects, Merton's continual restlessness was an open-mouthed drooling for the God-meat that alone satisfies. There were, therefore, few ideas or persons Merton would not approach with intimacy, sniffing them out, seeking clues on the trail to the next hunting field.[5]

Merton himself was neither as kind nor as poetic in his own assessment of his drivenness. Where Montaldo likens Merton's reactions to those of a hound in pursuit of the Divine, Merton sees it another way:

> I have fallen into the great indignity I have written against—I am a contemplative who is ready to collapse from overwork. This, I think, is a sin and the punishment of sin but

> now I have got to turn it to good use and be a saint by it, somehow.[6]

He goes on in this same vein, acknowledging the irony and the paradox. He says, "I am worn out with activity—exhausting myself with proclaiming that the thing to do is rest."[7] Merton's compulsive doing is one reality that led him to look toward the hermit life, though he realized even it would not afford an escape from the doing dynamic which followed him every step of his way.[8]

As a 4 Merton would never lose this instinct to respond to life by doing something about it. What experience taught him, however, was to discern between compulsion and the Tao, between the stimulus and reactive response and informed and free choice. A lifetime of contemplative honesty made him humble; it also made him articulate. He knew how much the fear of looking like a failure could interfere with the rhythmic dance of doing that was not compulsive.

> One of the greatest obstacles to your growing is the fear of making a fool of yourself. Any real step forward implies the risk of failure. And the really important steps imply the risk of complete failure. Yet we must make them, trusting in Christ. If I take this step, everything I have done so far might go down the drain. In a situation like that we need a shot of Buddhist mentality. Then we see, down what drain? So what? [9]

Again, we see what the cool shadow of Eastern thought provided for this typically Western man who, despite his yearning for silence and solitude, found himself much of the time in a warm lather of activity. He says much the same thing in many other places, one of which is this passage to Dr. Suzuki:

> If one reaches the point where understanding fails, this is not a tragedy: it is simply a reminder to stop thinking and start looking. Perhaps there is nothing to figure out after all: perhaps we only need to wake up.[10]

Merton is well aware how subtly the doing function can overtake the mind as well as bodily behaviors. Life can be turned into a series of mental hurdles for 4s. Analysis becomes as intense an activity as physical behaviors, one which in its own way ends up in exhaustion. He speaks of an inner sanctuary where analytical reflection relaxes into self-awareness. Presence to this true self confronted him with the abyss of "the unknown yet present—one who is 'more intimate to us than we are to ourselves.'"[11] It is in the intuition which follows such presence that the whole person embraces the moment's experience.

Then [the intellectual] rests in this intuition, letting the truth sink in and become a part of himself. Above all, intuition, setting the intelligence temporarily at rest, should leave the will free to adapt itself to the practical consequences of the truth thus seen and to direct our whole life in accordance with it. [12]

The enslavement of doing, Merton came to see, is not so much reacting with bodily behaviors but with mental ones. Once the 4 mind has learned the experience of letting go of its analytical compulsion, freedom follows. Merton uses the word liberation to describe this experience of breaking free from the oppression which results when we "are not entangled in our own body but entangled in our own mind."[13] When we are tied up this way perceptually, our bodily activity becomes compulsive. For Merton, the final subtlety is when we have seen through excessive doing only to find that we are still doing inside our heads. This awareness, Merton tells us, leads to the ultimate letting go into freedom.

> The point is: Learn to act in such a way that thought does not intervene between you and what you do. Just do the right thing without thinking about it. There is such a thing as being in contact with what the situation demands. You just meet it. But for this, you have to get rid of a lot of useless thinking, reasoning, explaining, and putting labels on things and saying, "It's like this," or "It has to be done like that.'"[14]

Merton develops this idea still further when he identifies such simple contemplative living with prayer. It becomes the *Age quod agis* (do what you are doing) of the early spiritual writers. Simply and fully to do what one is doing is the fullness of contemplation in action.

> Work done properly can't stop your praying. Work done properly is prayer. Properly, that means not having to get a bang out of it, not wanting it to be too perfect, doing it as an instrument of God. A deep mysticism is involved in that.[15]

This attitude constitutes the ripeness, as Merton puts it, of the mature person. It is the gift of the doing personality that much is accomplished, but with less and less strain, as life goes on. He describes in an image of harvest what happens when a 4 addresses this doing instinct, early in life exaggerated into compulsion:

> But the ripe fruit falls out of the tree without even thinking about it. Why? The man who is ripe discovers that there was never anything to be done from the very beginning.[16]

It is not that Merton is urging inactivity, something that would have been impossible for him to practice in any case, but rather an immersion in the flow of response that is beyond even reflecting on it.

While it is important for 4s to process their experience, reflecting and bending back on what has already happened in order to know what it was and how it affected them, eventually even this approach falls away. In the moment, the now experience, someone present to self as to another gives over—lets go—to the direct experience of that moment. Such unself-conscious, flowing action is very different from compulsive reaction. It is not characterized by the inability to stop doing, something automatic and independent of any particular stimulus. Rather, it is that rhythmic dance to the motion of the universe which can only be known when the noise of compulsed activity grows silent. Questions die away in the simple response of—and to—what is. Then work itself becomes, as Merton says, the very karma of existence.[17]

To say all of this another way, the spiritual pathway for the 4 in the early part of life is to develop and utilize—over-develop and over-utilize—the instinctive activity function. The self-image, and consequently the early self-worth, of the 4 grows up around being able to serve or care for or organize or produce in order to belong in the community of persons. Reflection assists the adult 4 to experience on all levels—to have a "felt sense" of—the compulsive exaggeration and lack of freedom in this early time. It is necessary along the spiritual journey for 4s to stop and reflect in order to know about their personal reality. In the moment, they will instinctively begin to act; later, upon reflection, they understand the assessments and feelings of that earlier moment, which is now past.

Gradually 4s learn to reflect more immediately and in the present. Eventually, as they grow into wholeness and maturity, they begin to let go into the experience itself. They put aside even the reflection they learned as a help to self-knowledge. Merton comments on this later chapter in the 4's human growth in this very concrete journal entry:

> Beauty of sunlight falling on a tall vase of red and white carnations and green leaves on the altar of the novitiate chapel. . . . The flower is the same color as blood, but it is in no sense whatever "as red as blood." Not at all! It is as red as a carnation. Only that.
>
> This flower, this light, this moment, this silence: *Dominus est.* Eternity. He passes. He remains. We pass. In and out. He passes. We remain. We are nothing. We are everything. He is in us. He is gone from us. He is not here. We are here in him. All these things can be said, but why say them? The flower is itself. The light is itself. The silence is itself. I am myself. All, perhaps, illusion. But no matter, for illusion is the shadow of reality and reality is the grace and gift that underlies all these lights, these colors, this silence. Underlies? Is that true? They are simply real. They themselves are his gift.[18]

Here is the Merton of the "monkey-mind" Montaldo speaks of. Here, too, is the Merton of the Tao. The instinct to do, physically and analytically, was always there. By the time of these journal entries just quoted, the instinct was known and its compulsions unmasked. Merton himself was wise enough and contemplative enough to be at peace with his own dynamics. Because he could name his instinct, his patterned analysis, and then let it go, he fell into an active yet free appreciation of the "simply real."

Merton's photography and his poetry both capture this appreciation of simple awareness. At their best, both expressions hint of the East. They have a haiku quality, asking nothing and giving only nonjudgmental acknowledgment. I choose one example for illustration:

Evening

Now, in the middle of the limpid evening,
The moon speaks clearly to the hill.
The wheat fields make their simple music,
Praise the quiet sky.
And down the road, the way the stars come home,
The cries of children
Play on the empty air, a mile or more,
And fall on our deserted hearing,
Clear as water.

They say the sky is made of glass,
They say the smiling moon's a bride.
They say they love the orchards and apple trees,
The trees, their innocent sisters, dressed in blossoms,
Still wearing, in the blurring dusk,
White dresses from that morning's first Communion.
And, where blue heaven's fading fire last shines
They name the new come planets
With words that flower
On little voices, light as stems of lilies.
And where blue heaven's fading fire last shines,
Reflected in the poplar's ripple,
One little, wakeful bird
Sings like a shower.[19]

This is Merton taken by his experience. This is Merton, who, upon reflection, shares this experience with others. Even his moments of simple awareness turn into products for others to enjoy with him. In that is his gift. Poems like these are communications from his inner world about a once self-conscious, now redeemed person. Through them he reveals what life has taught him. Not all people need to learn how to deal with this way of being, with this instinct around which compulsions form. Some people instinctively merge with their experience rather than analyze it. Merton did not. Because he did not, he was able to teach others who share his struggle the way to active contemplation.

The Special and the Ordinary

Another dynamic of those who are 4 on the enneagram is a feeling of specialness. What happens to 4s seems to them unique and completely original. There is wonder for 4s around the fact that anything so exceptional as their life circumstances could be happening. The intense drama with which they view their living accounts for some of this sense. Their belief that they cannot communicate themselves adequately to anyone flows from it.

An issue rising out of this 4 dynamic is how to address the ordinary. More than something strange and nearly unknown, the ordinary is frightening. Intensity is the stuff of life for 4s, and so reality seems dead without the flavor of the unprecedented. As a result of this fear, 4s tend to see their experience and that of the people around them in exaggerated terms. Instead of walking the daily flatlands of existence, they construct mountains and valleys to affirm to themselves that they are really living. "Better a miserable day than an ordinary one," as a 4 has put it.

We find this instinctive concern around the ordinary and special in Thomas Merton. Surely, some sense of his specialness would have had to have been present for Merton to undertake writing his autobiography. The fact that it was so lengthy and detailed further indicates the uniqueness with which he viewed his life events. The nuances of his writing reveal someone acutely aware and appreciative of his personal story.

In Mott's biography we find Merton talking about his realization that he was not ordinary in one of his talks with the novices. Speaking about Clare Booth Luce's insight into her uniqueness, Mott remarks that Merton himself may well have had a similar sense of specialness as early as his memories of his mother observing him as a small child.[1]

Mott reminds us that Merton always thought of himself and his fate as extraordinary. While he jokingly said that Gethsemani Abbey had its own extraordinary destiny, there is a sense in which his writings indicate he felt that to be true. Even in this unique monastery, he considered himself unique, "a duck in a chicken coop," as he put it.[2] The story of his unusual life in such a remarkable place would be different from everybody else's. While he noted how many people were writing autobiographies at the same time he was writing his, Merton indicated what would make his own attempt special. His uniqueness would lie in the use of small detail to reveal the inner significance of events and to build up a sense of the specialness of place, another favorite Merton theme, says Mott, and one shared by many 4s. The small and the apparently ordinary would reveal the unique. At the time he said these things he was just thirty-three. One wonders whether, without the self-concept that drove his unique message, Merton would have had the energy to introduce himself to us in a life story that became a prelude to his continuing dialogue with his times.

Even in his approach to interior life, Merton sees himself as different from others of his day. The mystical tradition he claimed for himself was that of the fourteenth century. On the one side, he could say with conviction that he must not be ashamed over not being more fashionable.[3] On the other, he was tempted to be part of "a really groovy worldly in-group." The monks with whom he lived, real but "also, for the most part, idiots," made him feel "in exile, humiliation, desperation."[4] Always, his struggle was to be different from or outstandingly above the common issues and people of his times. It was hard for Merton to reconcile himself with anything less than that which was, in one or another way, special.

Even in the most concrete and physical ways, Merton's experience seemed unique. In an interview with Father Matthew from Gethsemani Abbey, Gloria Lewis quotes Merton's fellow monk as saying, upon hearing of Merton's ulcer diagnosis:

> An ulcer way down. It was bad. It was very deep. When I heard it, I said to myself, "Typical, typical. Leave it to him to

> have a deep, deep problem." It was about as far down as you could get and still stay in the body.[5]

His brothers knew him, it seems. Here was a man who, whether he wanted to or not, would never disappear into the ranks. His writing, his spirituality, his history, even his illnesses, were not of an ordinary kind.

Merton reveals his awareness of this dynamic in himself when he asks his readers two questions:

> Who can escape the secret desire to breathe a different atmosphere from the rest of men? Who can do good things without seeking to taste in them some sweet distinction from the common run of sinners in this world?[6]

Undoubtedly, there exist many people who would not identify with such a desire or effort. Merton's assumption that everyone would have this same issue tells us much about him; he assumed everybody was tempted as he was. It is a typical human dynamic to think that all people look at life the way we do. Despite the error in such assumptions, statements like this offer revealing glimpses into the persons who have them; Merton the 4 shows us how he looked at life.

Along with this thread of specialness and uniqueness in the 4 perception is an equally apparent one of the value of the ordinary. All his life Merton was drawn to the poverty and boredom of plain days and pedestrian experiences. Early in his conversion to Catholicism, Merton wrote of his faith life in response to the creed proclaimed at a parish liturgy in Havana:

> The thing that struck me most of all was that this light was in a certain sense "ordinary"—it was a light (and this most of all was what took my breath away) that was offered to all, to everybody, and there was nothing fancy or strange about it. It was the light of faith deepened and reduced to an extreme and sudden obviousness.[7]

Faith like this was mediated for Merton through Hagia Sophia, the Wisdom which was, he insisted, glorious. Such Wisdom crowns Jesus—and we see here Merton's identification with Jesus—with the only thing that is more glorious than glory, more outstanding than the outstanding, which he names weakness, nothingness, poverty.[8] As the 6 personality cannot but address rules and laws, whether to keep or break them, the 4 cannot but grapple with uniqueness, whether that makes him or her stand out as unusual or as so hidden and ordinary that one is noteworthy for being not noteworthy. To say this in Merton's own words:

> [John of the Cross's] way is so humble that it ends up by being no way at all, for John of the Cross is unfriendly to systems and a bitter enemy of all exaltation. *Omnis qui se exaltat humiliabitur*. His glory is to do without glory for the love of Christ.[9]

Merton goes on to speak of this paradox where the ordinary and special come together for the 4 when he describes how John of the Cross might well be "the patron of those who have a vocation that is thought, by others, to be spectacular, but which, in reality, is lowly, difficult, and obscure."[10] Here we see the Merton who wanted to bury himself in the unmarked poverty of a Trappist life so hidden that its ordinariness was unique among religious community expression.

Again, such a view of monastic life and such a motivation for entering a Trappist community can hardly be said to be universal to the monks who choose this life. Undoubtedly, others in Merton's community would not have shared this sense of their own monastic vocation. That it was Merton's picture of monasticism says more about him than about the objective reality of that life. For Merton, as for Thérèse of Lisieux, the ordinariness of day-to-day contemplative community living took on extraordinary redemptive possibilities for self and others. For Thérèse, probably another 4, the spirituality which she termed the Little Way offered profound ordinariness while addressing and responding to the terror such ordinariness could inspire. Merton's initial attraction to the Trappists probably necessitated this merging of the special with the ordinary. Without it one wonders whether he would have had the courage and ego-strength to enter Gethsemani at all.

Merton learned to discern when his desire for uniqueness was pride and self-interest and when it was a quality that infused choices and actions with freedom and life. It appeared too simplistic to him merely to dismiss inclinations toward the different thing, the special thing. Sometimes such inclinations indicated a call it was important to attend to. In speaking of the vocation of Herakleitos, Merton asks and answers:

> Is pride synonymous with an aristocratic insistence upon excellence? It takes humility to confront the prejudice and

> contempt of all, in order to cling to an unpopular truth. In the popular mind, any failure to "conform," any aspiration to be different, is labeled as pride. But was Herakleitos exalting himself, his own opinions, or the common truth which transcends individuals and opinions?[11]

Merton usually tended to embrace opinions different from most people's. For him the source of these interior positions was the simplicity of the contemplative life, a simplicity beyond "all the complexities and pretenses of these intellectual fads and campaigns."[12] When he knew he was standing in his own true experience, Merton, like many 4s, judged it impossible to adapt and compromise for the group. More than that, he found it a necessity to communicate his experience to others and a matter of conscience to hold onto it. That there was compulsion in this seems evident from the agitation it sometimes created. Nevertheless, his intent was to be radically authentic, to stand faithful to his reality.

The threads of simplicity and poverty are often interwoven with uniqueness and specialness in Merton's spirituality. This is frequently the case in the spiritual life of other 4s as well. Such a radical, stripped spirituality makes contemplatives different from others and shapes their mission for humankind. In Merton's words on the subject of the contemplative vocation we find this paradoxical blend.

> [The contemplative's] mission is to be a complete and whole man, with an instinctive and generous need to further the same wholeness in others, and in all mankind. He arrives at this, however, not by superior gifts and special talents, but by the simplicity and poverty which are essential to his state because they alone keep him traveling in the way that is spiritual, divine, and beyond understanding.[13]

It is this blend of the completely original and utterly hidden that inspired Merton's vocation to monasticism, a contemplative life that buries its members in the heart of the community. In his personal monastic, common life Merton learned the lesson of contemplative simplicity.

> Such "walking with God" is one of the simplest and most secure ways of living a life of prayer, and one of the safest. It never attracts anybody's attention, least of all the attention

> of him who lives it. And he soon learns not to want to see anything special in himself. This is the price of his liberty.[14]

Such is the "ordinariness of the present moment with its obvious task,"[15] which led Merton—ever finding himself in unusual circumstances—to the sense he had that his monastic vocation was right for him. At the heart of monastic life is obedience to one another in community. Merton's sense of the call to articulate a new and emerging monastic renewal was continually evaluated against any desire merely to stand out from the crowd. He warns that

> one must avoid eccentricity, self-will, and vain show. If a person is really guided by the Holy Spirit, grace itself will take care of this, for exterior simplicity and obscurity are signs of grace. So too are meekness and obedience. Wherever there is a real conflict with obedience, he who gives in and obeys will never lose.[16]

That Merton found his joined strands of ordinariness and specialness knotted at times is evident from his reflection at Fourth and Walnut in Louisville. The incident is often cited to exemplify Merton's sense of unity with all humanity. This same reflection carries a revealing articulation of the ordinary-versus-special paradox in his life. Merton reveals here that "for sixteen or seventeen years I have been taking seriously this pure illusion that is implicit in so much of our monastic thinking."[17] He describes that illusion, which he said he and all his Trappist brothers held, as thinking themselves "different, or even better, than others."[18] What he found in that simple moment on the street corner was this realization:

> It is a glorious destiny to be a member of the human race, though it is a race dedicated to many absurdities and one which makes many terrible mistakes; yet, with all that, God Himself gloried in becoming a member of the human race. A member of the human race! To think that such a commonplace realization should suddenly seem like news that one holds the winning ticket in a cosmic sweepstake.[19]

In point-counterpoint Merton goes on to speak of both the "nothingness and absolute poverty of the glory of God in us."[20] At this interior center, *le pointe vierge*, Merton's conflict between the ordinary and the special is resolved. The total simplicity and universality at the center of our self is a truly unique existence and experience. Another paradox here, but Merton never shrank from such.

It was this conviction of Merton's that to bury himself in the ordinary was redemptive, if terrifying, that has comforted others whose life seems pedestrian. He discusses the value of boring work, describing the satisfaction he had just sorting pages into piles. [21]

There is another fruit, however, of Merton's grappling with the ordinary and the special. It is a fruit one often finds in 4s as they relate to other people. In their instinctual search for uniqueness, they look for and find that common being which, at the same time as it is universal, has never been nor ever will be replicated. Each individual, each relationship, is, for 4s, an original creation. The result of his own search is that those who knew Merton felt a freshness and newness in the way he met them. Mott notes that this impression was expressed to him by almost everyone who had met Merton:

> When Merton talked to you he made you feel—at least for the time—that you were his most intimate confidant, that he opened himself to you and you opened yourself to him in a way which made it an exchange like no other, and that this friendship could not be duplicated by either of you with anyone else. If at times this was to lead to complications and difficulties . . . it has to be granted that it was a rare gift.[22]

I would add that this is the gift of a redeemed 4, one free of much compulsion, and possessed by Merton to an unusually high degree. Therese Lentfoehr says that Merton "was a man who had the happy gift of going out to each person in a unique way,"[23] truly giving himself in presence to the other. James Finley names his solitary and poor life as the source of Merton's refinement of this gift:

> He woke before dawn with a mind "not totally reconciled to being out of bed." He ate, worked, walked in the woods and prayed. In the winter he was cold and in the summer he was hot. And that is the true self. It is the self that is nobody, that is ordinary and poor. It is this ordinary self that is extraordinary for it is this ordinary self one with the moment, one with the concrete reality of everyday life, that is the self God creates, the poor self made rich in the poverty of the cross.[24]

Merton himself saw this ordinary gift of his, again paradoxically, as unique for our times. In the devaluing of person that Auschwitz represented he found the paradoxical presence of God.

> Never more than today has [God] made His presence felt by "being absent." In this, then, we are most faithful: that we prefer the darkness, and in the very depths of our being, value this emptiness and apparent absence. We need not struggle vainly to make him present, if such struggles are a mockery. Leave nothingness as it is. In it, he is present.[25]

This monk, who insisted on asking whether life could be found in all of one's situations, found his answer in the simplest and least impressive moments of his own existence. Unique as he could not help being, Merton kept on turning away from fame to hide in the unadorned present time, whatever that might offer in human experience. Salvation was there for him, he recognized. It gave him knowledge out of which he could describe a spiritual life that makes sense for today.

> If we constantly over-emphasize those things to which access is inevitably something quite rare, we overlook the ordinary authentic experiences of everyday life as real things to enjoy, things to be happy about, things to praise God for. But the ordinary realities of everyday life, the faith and love with which we live our normal human lives, provide the foundation on which we build these "higher things." If there is no foundation, then we have nothing at all.[26]

In sharing a poem about the Chinese official, Chao-pien, Merton expresses perhaps more simply and clearly than anywhere else his personal resolution of the problem of ordinary versus special. It is in the self that we see our inconsequential and valuable, universal and unique reality.

> The real "I" is just simply our self and nothing more. Nothing more, nothing less. Our self as we are in the eyes of God, to use Christian terms. Our self in all our uniqueness, dignity, littleness and ineffable greatness: the greatness we have received from God our Father and that we share with Him because He is our Father. . . . The laconic little poem then expresses the full sense of liberation experienced by one who

> recognizes, with immense relief, that he is not his false self after all, and that he has all along been nothing else but his real and "homely" self, and nothing more, without glory, without self-aggrandizement, without self-righteousness, and without self-concern.[27]

When Merton found his real "I," his simple self, nothing more and nothing less, he found that ordinary homeliness that shouted to him of God in himself and in everyone else.

6

Life as an Art Piece

Some descriptions of the 4 gesture in life characterize this space as that of the artist. In fact, genuine artists exist in every enneagram space; no one has a corner on either creativity or the expression of it. Nevertheless, there is some truth in calling the 4 an artist. If an artist takes raw experience and works it through image and symbol into a comment on life, then 4s are, in that respect, artists.

Nothing is just left to be, left without comment, for 4s. Instinctively they look for significance all around them. What lies beneath the simple and obvious is always of concern to 4s and, it almost seems, cries out to be addressed. Relationships give life meaning, and so they must be carefully tended, consciously developed, faithfully cultivated. All of life's daily events demand the best, the most appropriate, the most conscientiously studied response. Someone has said that 4s, more than any other people, keep journals consisting of their reflections on and commentaries about their experiences. Whether or not that is so, at least in their minds 4s make what might be considered ongoing journal entries. They search for the right words or images to tell themselves—and often others as well—what life means. Life for 4s does not go unexamined.

At first, 4s assume—as we all assume, whatever our enneagram stance—that everybody responds this same way. Those 4s who grow past the compulsive studiedness and lack of spontaneity into which their instinct gets exaggerated eventually realize its effect on them. They observe how little relaxation their life holds, how intense it so often is, how complicated the smallest of events becomes. It is often people with whom 4s relate who point out this tendency to them. Frequently, too, it is the bodily tension and psychosomatic complaints of various kinds that force 4s to let go of self-demand and seriousness in a kind of despair that can be wholesome and life-giving.

One way 4s learn to deal with finding spirits of significance lurking in every small detail of their lives is to use artistic expression to capture the intensity resulting from such a worldview. Anne Carr summarizes Merton's tendency toward shaping life into significance in her commentary on Merton's remarks:

> Some may try to make a work of art of their lives simply by following an approved pattern. This encourages them to study themselves in order to shape their lives and remodel themselves, "to tune and re-tune all their inner dispositions" and they end up in "full-time meditation and contemplation of themselves." And so they avoid the risk and dread of the unknown mystery of God.[1]

Ultimately, as Carr alludes to, the compulsive honing of existence Merton and other 4s develop is a product of fear. If God is life, then it is life itself in all of its power that 4s are trying to get hold of and control. Real emotions expressed in spontaneous behavior are what 4s try to tame and manage. That way situations won't get out of hand in all their raw intensity. Writing is one art form that relieves such fear, because it converts what often seems crude and vulgar to 4s into a cool, verbal reflection on reality.

Interestingly, when 4s become more transformed, more whole, more free and redeemed, they sometimes put creating art aside. Merton did not do this, undoubtedly because he was one of the genuine artists in this space. It is notable, however, that his writing, his photography, and his sketching took on a simplicity reflective of his freer later life.

It seems that Merton wanted to get into print from a young age. He warns that imperfection is the penalty for such a desire,[2] and it was a penalty he paid his whole lifetime. To say that Merton was a prolific author is to put it mildly; that he was an imperfect writer is what he often stood accused of, many would assess rightly accused of. Mott tells us that Merton entered Gethsemani with a conviction that his writing days were over. Such was not to be, however; he wrote from his very first days in the community.

Writing only about what was worthy of God became Merton's standard. Initially, he published under obedience to Abbot Frederick

Dunne, a man who was himself sympathetic to having an author in the monastery. It was obedience that resolved Merton's original conflict about publishing; of course, at Abbot Frederick's bidding, he would comply. However, later on Abbot James Fox joined Merton in his dilemma and interior debate about himself as an artist. Was it good for Merton's soul to continue as an author? It seems Abbot James and Merton both asked this question, one which Merton kept trying to answer much of his monastic life.[3] That his writing was good for other souls stems, perhaps, from this consistent search to ferret out any motives of prestige or self-satisfaction to which his publishing might have led him.

Merton tells us how, instead of feeding his ego, his writing was a means to a simple honesty, what we might call humility. We can see here the stance which made what he said so fruitful for those who read it:

> To be as good a monk as I can, and to remain myself, and to write about it: to put myself down on paper, in such a situation, with the most complete simplicity and integrity, masking nothing, confusing no issues: this is very hard, because I am all mixed up in illusions and attachments. These, too, will have to be put down. But without exaggeration, repetition, useless emphasis . . . to be frank without being boring. It is a kind of crucifixion. Not a very dramatic or painful one. But it requires so much honesty that it is beyond my nature. It must come somehow from the Holy Ghost.[4]

The reflection on experience necessitated by Merton's writing made him very aware of his romanticism and dramatizations. Writing was possibly where he stated his compulsions most specifically and concretely. He was also brought face to face with what he saw as every talented person's propensity: inconsistency. In his own writing he, like other artists, sought "an outlet and a solution in creative works"[5] as a resolution to such inconsistency. To say it another way, Merton's writing helped him to distinguish, to discern, the difference between compulsive overanalysis and clarity and purity of thought and expression. It did this by holding up the possibility of both to his awareness until he was able to recognize which was operating.

Writing also provided Merton a way to work out the meanings of daily events in his monastic life. When we listen to a 4 speak about personal experience, we often hear philosophical summaries that sound disembodied and distant. Such summaries in Merton's works are a product of grappling with inconsistencies he sees inseparable from living. These objective conclusions seem to have been arrived at serenely. Never be fooled, however. They, too, are raw reality honed into appropriate expression. For this reason, it is essential to an understanding of Merton to read his journals and letters alongside his spiritual writings. The monk who could be enraged and frustrated at the way the Liturgy of the Hours was being prayed in the chapel is the same monk who could write so poetically about the beauty of psalmody in *Bread in the Wilderness*. The same man who struggled with his celibate commitment, with obedience and stability, is the one who could put words on its redemptive value for self and others in *Contemplation in a World of Action*.

As already indicated, Merton's view of art and the artist's vocation holds something of the pragmatic. Merton the artist remains Merton the doer; he wrote because he wanted people to know more, to hear what he had to say. Art for art's sake would never be Merton's attitude, given his product-oriented personality. He describes the artist's mission—his own mission—as follows:

> The genius of the artist finds its way by the affinity of creative sympathy, or connaturality, into the living law that rules the universe. This law is nothing but the secret gravitation that draws all things to God as to their center. Since all true art lays bare the action of this same law in the depths of our own nature, it makes us alive to the tremendous mystery of being, in which we ourselves, together with all other living and existing things, come forth from the depths of God and return again to Him. An art that does not produce something of this is not worthy of its name.[6]

The balance and centeredness in God Merton speaks of here grew into his habitual experience, partly because of his struggle with his own and life's inconsistencies through writing. Merton's search for harmony led him to find it in the rhythm of all things. His writing gave him the experience of how dynamic rather than static true peace necessarily must be.

> The real order of the cosmos is an apparent disorder, the "conflict" of opposites which is in fact a stable and dynamic harmony. The wisdom of man is the product of willfulness, blindness, and caprice and is only the manifestation of his own insensibility to what is right before his eyes.[7]

We see here where Merton's efforts to make an artistic whole of the raw and apparently unrelated bits of personal experience ultimately led him.

Merton was, always, a man of passion, whether or not that passion was detectable in his more "spiritual" books. He tells us that those who have a broad and more universal view of history and humanity have found an inner harmony that "is not achieved merely by a speculative participation in philosophical insight." To be someone who is whole and wise, says Merton, "demands great moral energy and sacrifice." Not content with seeing the objectivity of the *logos*, such persons must "cling to their vision, and defend their insight with their very lives."[8] We recognize the Merton whom people knew as deeply invested in his world and the people in it. Here is the Merton who so vehemently held onto his ideas at community chapter meetings, in conferences with the novices, in individual encounters. Merton the writer, Merton the graphic artist, shaped this passion into art pieces, forming his struggles into meaning.

Given this fact, it is still true that for Merton art was far more than personal therapy or psychoanalysis. He considered the true artist to be lifted above such struggles by the very images and symbols used to express them.

> The soul that picks and pries at itself in the isolation of its own dull self-analysis arrives at a self-consciousness that is a torment and a disfigurement of our whole personality. But the spirit that finds itself above itself in the intensity and cleanness of its reaction to a work of art is "self-conscious" in a way that is productive as well as sublime. . . . Without a moment of self-analysis he has discovered himself in discovering his capacity to respond to a value that lifts him above his normal level. His very response makes him better and different. He is conscious of a new life and new powers, and it is not strange that he should proceed to develop them.[9]

Merton speaks of the genuine artist as one who somehow ends up with an art piece that communicates the Tao. It is the imagery the artist uses that makes this happen. The artist, unlike the photographer, does not merely reproduce reality, Merton tells us; the artist infuses reality with significance by revealing his or her own response to reality through image.[10] One wonders whether Merton's own later fascination with photography came from his no longer needing to share his personal responses to life. Perhaps the poverty and simplicity of his last years gave him the freedom to let reality tell its own story, leaving him more and more in the background.

Merton always saw his art as demanding great sacrifice. Because it showed him his compulsions to self-consciousness he came to realize that the depths of the contemplative experience might very well be denied him. Standing next to his life, observing it, was essential to his art but detrimental to his contemplation.

> What, then, is the conclusion? That poetry can, indeed, help to bring us rapidly through that early part of the journey to contemplation that is called active: but when we are entering the realm of true contemplation, where eternal happiness is tasted in anticipation, poetic intuition may ruin our rest in God "beyond all images."[11]

This 4 instinct to put oneself between experience and a response to it forced Merton to this very subtle distinction and a consequent humility. The man who could help others to contemplative simplicity, to being in God's presence, was able to do so because he often missed such simplicity in his own prayer. Always next to himself, looking on at moment-to-moment reality and his own personal moment-to-moment response to reality, Merton knows how to tell us what contemplative prayer is like, but also how we can miss it.

When Merton was taken out of himself by beauty in nonanalytical wonder rather than in analytical fascination, he experienced simply what is so. For him, such wonder was hard to come by. "Truth often comes on the wings of beauty," Lewis quotes him as saying.[12] Such pure truth, however, often eluded him. Lewis also remarks on Merton's noting of others who seemed to know the purity of beauty that leads to truth. One wonders whether such appreciation also might have included something of the characteristic 4 envy of others, more simple and direct than he himself was. At any rate, his experience made him able to teach the difference between fabrication and life flow in the spiritual life.

It must be said, to be accurate, that Merton himself touched that pure experience beyond analysis at least sometimes. How else could he have talked knowledgeably about both compulsion and freedom? Beyond grasping, he tells us that he came to "live alone and chaste in the midst of the holy beauty of all created things, knowing that nothing I can see or hear or touch will ever belong to me."[13] Such was his expression of freedom.

Merton's struggle with his own life's inconsistency was made all the more concrete for him in the making of his art. He never was able to sustain that feeling of wholeness and balance that he said was art's purpose. He did find, however, the true Thomas Merton, centered and struggling, simple and complex, unself-conscious and self-concerned. Perhaps this is what he meant when he said that

> art enables us to find ourselves and lose ourselves at the same time. The mind that responds to the intellectual and spiritual values that lie hidden in a poem, a painting, or a piece of music, discovers a spiritual vitality that lifts it above itself, takes it out of itself, and makes it present to itself on a level of being that it did not know it could ever achieve.[14]

While this sounds inspiring and uplifting, could it not also mean that in the very act of making art Merton found truth and life and reality—his own reality with all of its compulsion and limitation? Ultimately, humility is the ground of any spiritual life. That being so, Merton did find the height of contemplation he so much wanted; his writing revealed to him an ever fuller vision of both the gift and compulsion of his personality. Merton's art threw him onto God's mercy as surely as any other of his limited actions. This man, obedient to his native instinct as an artist and to his religious superiors who encouraged that instinct, saw his vocation to artistic expression as "the choice of what God has willed," even though it seemed to him "less perfect, and indeed less 'spiritual.'" He says further:

> But it may equally well happen that an artist who imagines himself to be called to the higher reaches of mystical prayer is not called to them at all. It becomes evident to him, that the simplest and most obvious thing for him is to be an artist, and that he should sacrifice his aspirations for a deep mystical life and be content with the lesser gifts with which he has been endowed by God. . . . If he is called to be an artist, then his art will lead him to sanctity, if he uses it as a Christian should.[15]

Here is another Merton paradox. After all, what is the depth of the mystical life if not humility, an admission of our creaturely limitations? Merton must have known this to be so, since he tells us that

> the Christian poet and artist is one who grows not only by his contemplation but also by his open declaration of the mercy of God. If it is clear that he is called to give this witness to God, then he can say with St. Paul: "Woe is me if I preach not the Gospel."[16]

Merton through his art preached not only the gospel of image and symbol, but that of flesh and blood. He did this by being faithful to both his call as an artist and his vocation to contemplative simplicity. Even as he proclaimed truth and shared his response to it, he revealed the truth of his own imperfect life to himself and to other people. It may well be that the fallible and fragile Merton we see in the journals teaches us more about wholeness than the Merton who so poetically places before us more abstract, contemplative ideals. Perhaps it is most true to say that the full picture of Merton as spiritual master is portrayed in his artist's struggle with his personal inconsistencies.

7

Life as a Drama

We have already mentioned what the dramatic quality of the 4 looks like. Daily existence instinctively has the focus and emotional impact of life lived out on some stage. It has been said that 4s are in life's audience—others' audience as well as their own. They look on and into events, finding succeeding moments, days, and years laden with significance. Nothing is exempt from this intensity; framed as if by a proscenium arch, each succeeding now is a stage where life and death, beginning and end, joy and sorrow, grief and celebration play themselves out.

Since all reality leads either to growth or diminishment, and since 4s are instinctively conscious of that fact, they frequently find their compulsions developing around reality enacted in a narrowing spotlight on life's stage. While such focus highlights what is going on, it also tends to exaggerate it. The result of this exaggeration is overdramatization played out in romance, anguish, crisis, and other densely concentrated experience.

We find an interplay in this dynamic with other ones we have already discussed. Merton as artist could not be a stranger to the dramatic; part of the artistic process is to use the language of images and symbols which stand for something more than themselves. Seeing the uniqueness of people and circumstances is also related to drama; there are not ordinary moments in such a view of life where succeeding situations have significant import. Therefore they are unique, special, and unrepeatable; something to be taken seriously; something demanding the attention of anyone who is aware.

Anthony Padovano has observed this attitude toward life in Thomas Merton. Speaking of Merton's organically developing prose, Padovano remarks that "Merton writes out of a dramatic life, a symbolic and archetypal journey, out of personal experiences."[1] *The Seven Storey Mountain* portrays the drama in Merton's early life. In this autobiography Merton seems for the most part still unaware of the dramatic in himself. Later in life he would observe the dynamic operating almost immediately and in the very process of writing his later journals, letters, and books. Earlier, however, we see more of his unconsciously intense attitude in overly reflective and yet, unconscious presentation; to say it another way, the autobiography has something of a consistent dramatic intensity with less awareness on Merton's part that he was being dramatic.

As a boy in Rome, Merton had an experience which was unusual to begin with: he had a strong sense of his deceased father's spiritual presence in the room. Especially interesting for us, however, is his response to the sense of presence as he makes this assessment of his own life:

> In that flash, instantly, I was overwhelmed with a sudden and profound insight into the misery and corruption of my own soul, and I was pierced deeply with a light that made me realize something of the condition I was in, and I was filled with horror at what I saw, and my whole being rose up in revolt against what was within me, and my soul desired escape and liberation and freedom from all this with an intensity and an urgency unlike anything I have ever known before.[2]

One wonders what interior corruption might have led Merton to be filled with such horror. After all, he was only a university student who, while certainly sowing his share of wild oats, can hardly be seen as dangerously malicious. Nevertheless, he painted his condition as he did because he genuinely saw it that way, as in need of a God who would come "to help me to get free of the thousand terrible things that held my will in their slavery."[3] This was not posturing on Merton's part. It was the way he saw himself.

On this same trip to Rome his first attraction to the Trappists blended the romantic with the dramatic. That Merton assumed other people looked at life like he did—a propensity we all share in our early naiveté—shows up in the rhetorical question he poses at that time:

> Is there any man who has ever gone through a whole lifetime without dressing himself up, in his fancy, in the habit of a monk and enclosing himself in a cell where he sits magnificent in heroic austerity and solitude, while all the young ladies who hitherto were cool to his affection in the world come and beat on the gates of the monastery crying, "Come out, come out!"[4]

Interestingly, this question—one to which many would probably respond "yes"—includes a script with stage directions. Scripting can often be observed when one talks with 4s. This can be a frustrating dynamic for those in relationships with them. People often sense there is a part they must play, some lines in the 4's mind which they are meant to deliver. If they do not do so—and how can they unless they are mind readers?—the 4 often withdraws, leaving the other to wonder what speech he or she failed to make.

At the end of this important European trip Merton returned to England and the university. He comments dramatically on Cambridge and his life there:

> I am even willing to admit that some people might live there for three years, or even a lifetime, so protected that they never sense the sweet stench of corruption that is all around them—the keen, thin scent of decay that pervades everything and accuses with a terrible accusation the superficial youthfulness, the abounding undergraduate noise that fills those ancient buildings. But for me, with my blind appetites, it was impossible that I should not rush in and take a huge bite of this rotten fruit. The bitter taste is still with me after not a few years.[5]

Yet another time we see Merton in his own audience in this comment. The scene is paradise; the character is Merton/Adam; the stage direction is to rush on-stage, taking a huge bite of rotten fruit. It might prove interesting to go through at least his autobiography in search of other indications of his dramatic stance/outlook/view of reality and his place in it. The examples cited here occur in the course of less than ten pages; they are far from exhaustive.

Toward the end of his life we find a Merton who has clearly recognized the dramatic instinct in himself. He has also learned the compulsions it can lead to and the danger it poses to authentic spiritual life. In another image of tasting fruit, mixed one notes, with another metaphor, we hear Merton say:

> The idea that you can choose yourself, approve yourself, and then offer yourself (fully "chosen" and "approved") to God, applies the assertion of yourself over against God. From this root of error comes all the sour leafage and fruitage of a lie of self-examination, interminable problems and unending decisions, always making right choices, walking on the razor edge of an impossibly subtle ethic.[6]

The attitude of self-examination and analysis Merton describes here leads to another scenario where God stamps approval on righteous action. The character who is on-stage in this scene is the suffering, misunderstood martyr. Note, this is the martyr as a part written and played, not the martyr who with genuine self-forgetfulness leaps into life and its inevitable deaths.

> In such a religion the cross becomes meaningless except as the (blasphemous) certification that because you suffer, because you are misunderstood, you are justified twice over—you are a martyr. Martyr means witness. You are then a witness. To what? To your own infallible light and your own justice, which you have chosen.[7]

That Merton recognizes all of this self-concern as compulsive is evident in the way he concludes the discussion: "This is the exact opposite of everything Jesus ever did or taught."[8]

Martyrdom was not the only role Merton put himself into imaginatively. There was also the Merton who yearned for the hermit life. Commenting on the characteristic highs and lows of Merton's prayer life, Chrysogonus Waddell remarks:

> More and more [Merton] had to abandon the self-image he had once had of himself as the dedicated hermit; and in the isolation of his hermitage—an isolation mostly of his own imagining, and one that was more spiritual than physical—his pain increased, both physically and psychologically.[9]

Perhaps no one more pointedly commented on the drama and role-playing in Merton's desire to be a hermit than Gregory Zilboorg. In his encounter with Merton at St. John's University the psychiatrist kept repeating that Merton's hermit idea was pathological: "You want a hermitage in Times Square with a large sign over it saying 'HERMIT.'"[10] After he had allowed this appraisal to penetrate his consciousness, Merton was stunned. At first, it seems, he could not take the statement in; hence, Zilboorg's repetitions. Eventually, Merton admitted that there was something of truth in Zilboorg's remarks, and that in some way his hermit focus was, indeed, unhealthy.

Merton's struggle to internalize Zilboorg's remarks seems due to the fact that they included this accusation of pathology. By this time in his life, as much of his writing testifies, Merton was able to admit his compulsion to over-dramatize. But he still resisted the idea that it had developed into a full blown pathology.. Perhaps it was fear of yet another role, that of someone "mentally sick," that made him initially deaf and resistant to Zilboorg's comments. He seems to have grappled with them for a long time, refusing to admit that the characteristic, albeit neurotic, compulsions of his 4 personality indicated mental illness. At any rate, in a much later comment on the blessing of not having gone to Zilboorg for analysis in 1956, Merton uses a dramatic image:

> I think in great measure [Zilboorg's] judgment was that I could not be fitted into that kind of theater. There was no conceivable part for me to play in his life. . . . He had quite enough intelligence (more than enough, he was no fool at all!) to see that it would be a very poor production for him, for the Abbot (who was most willing) and for me. I am afraid that I was willing at the time, to go, which shows what a fool I was.[11]

Nearly destructive as it seems to have been, Zilboorg's assessment and Merton's struggle to understand it led over time to much self-awareness and humility. It may have been what lay behind Merton's distinction between guilt and what he called sin or evil. Guilt, Merton tells us, comes from outside; it results from the scenario writing into which he so often got caught.

> [Guilt] is an anxiety one feels when he thinks he is going to be called to account for a misdeed. The anxiety of guilt is a sign of moral alienation. It becomes active within us when we interiorize a reproof suggested by the presence of an au-

> thority whose edicts we have violated. The sense of guilt is then a sense of physical almost as much as of moral evil. I am guilty when I think someone else believes me wrong. And the anxiety of my guilt is heightened if I secretly want to disagree with his judgment, but do not dare even to feel the disagreement.[12]

One wonders who the "someone" might have been in Merton's imagination when he wrote this passage. No doubt this drama was played out over and over in Merton's lifetime with parents, teachers, superiors, and experts of all kinds taking the antagonist's part. All of these persons join league with Merton, the dramatic critic of his own life, heaping their self-accusation on top of his own. Beyond this scenario, however, is the more simple and direct experience of reality, out of which comes a deeper sense of genuine wrongdoing. He speaks about it this way:

> The sense of sin is something deeper and more existential. It is not merely a sense of guilt referred to the authority of God. It is a sense of evil in myself. Not because I have violated a law outside myself, but because I have violated the inmost laws of my own being. . . . Indeed, serious sin is the death of the spirit. . . . Spiritual death is the sense of having separated myself from truth by complete inner falsity, from love by selfishness, from reality by trying to assert as real a will to nothingness. The sense of sin is then something ontological and immediate which does not spring from reflection on my actions and a comparison with a moral code. It springs directly from the evil that is present in me: it tells me not merely that I have done wrong, but that I am wrong . . . that I am a false being.[13]

We see more of Merton's intense outlook and dramatic writing here. By means of radical self-assessment he communicates dramatically the 4 sense of sin and evil, which for Merton always held the flavor of the narcissistic self-concern Zilboorg so deftly, if not very sensitively, pointed out to him. This self-concern—being in his own audience was the way it appeared to Merton—is one source of Merton's ability to name the false self and distinguish it from the true.

Merton discovered another dramatist along his spiritual path in the person of Thérèse of Lisieux. Her Little Way, as already noted, made an epiphany of all the daily, ordinary routines that were much of her life. In her example Merton saw the gift beyond the compulsion of his instinct to the dramatic. It was when he could laugh at himself that his intensity could relax into more accurate perceptions, more realistic proportions. Humor became more noticeable and significant in Merton's later writing. Mott gives us an example of this shift to greater objectivity:

> For Thomas Merton everything was important. For Thérèse of Lisieux, everything was luminous with supernatural light. Scrubbing a floor was an act of such glory and grace that she trembled and was almost overcome. Merton was reminded that in his letter to the draft board he had talked about digging latrines in a way which made a small melodrama of it all, explaining that it was far more to the honor of God than killing those made in his image. It was an embarrassing memory.[14]

Thérèse was, as Merton commented, overly dramatic. She was also saintly and simple, eventually allowing God freely to direct her life rather than compulsively dictating a martyr scenario in which she offered herself to burn forever in hell so that others might be saved. Like Thérèse, Merton learned to let go and live out his life without turning to watch or "improve" it. Did Merton have some script of how that later role might look? Did he have an image of himself as free and spontaneous? Probably, since to self-observe always remained his instinct. Because it did, however, others know so much more about what prayer is and is not. Thanks to Merton's dramatic dynamic we have eloquent portrayals of what hinders contemplation. Thanks to his later perspective, with the ability to laugh at himself, we also are sure we know a person who attained contemplation's simpler form.

8

Social and Solitary

One of the animals that has been associated with 4 dynamics is the domestic cat. Something of the energy both to move out and withdraw are caught in this excerpt from "The Prayer of the Cat":

> Lord,
> I am the cat.
> It is not, exactly, that I have something to ask of You!
> No—I ask nothing of anyone—but,
> if you have by some chance, in some celestial barn,
> a little white mouse, or a saucer of milk,
> I know someone who would relish them.[1]

Those who are 4s are never psychically removed from people in their current environment or their history. They do not, however, want to be offensive or invasive. As one 4 has said, "I cling, but only on the inside." Important as people are, 4s fear that were they to let others know of their strong energy toward them, they might not find it returned. This would spell rejection and abandonment to 4s, something they always fear and suspect will be their lot.

The early lesson their worldview taught them was the necessity of going it alone in life, of being strong and solitary. This discipline they see as imposed by both human and Divine authority seems only just to 4s because it teaches them maturity. Such maturity translates to control of what they judge in themselves to be excessive desires and unreasonable demands. Like the cat in the poem, 4s ask nothing of anyone, at least directly. To do so would be childish and self-centered. They do, however, obliquely make known their wishes in hopes that the other—and this includes the Divine Other—will hear and respond without their asking, thus assuring there will be no rebuff.

This oblique expression is their testing ground. It keeps them in communication while it avoids conflict and disappointment. They would like it to be their characteristic response, but anger, excitement, and attraction sometimes catch them off guard and they come out directly. When that happens, others are often surprised at the power of the 4 energy toward engagement in the social arena. Something of this dynamic accounts for the back and forth, outgoing and shy rhythm which 4s and those who deal with them experience.

The other factor that seems to figure into 4s' social and solitary instinct has to do with this total involvement with any person or event crossing their path and the exhaustion that this creates. Having given themselves away and allowed themselves to be consumed mentally and emotionally by work or social life or personal relationships, 4s then flee to where they cannot be touched by others and their concerns. There they replenish themselves, returning nourished for another encounter.

We find both the social and solitary themes in Thomas Merton's personality. He was often gregarious, throwing himself into relationship with zest and enthusiasm. He seemed to pour himself out with no need for return. Yet we know from so much of what he has written that he often felt separate and alone, revelatory yet not really understood. We know, too, that his inability to refuse others his attention or presence often drained him so that he pulled away, sometimes abruptly and without warning, only to move out again after relatively short periods for recuperation.

Merton seems to have chosen to be social and outgoing early in his life. Those who are familiar with the enneagram would say that he developed his 3 wing in his youth, wanting to be considered warm, friendly, and somewhat "naughty," a social image 4s often enjoy. Robert Waldron describes this role Merton assumed as a Columbia student:

> Socially Merton continued to wear the persona of rake, boasting to his friends at Columbia that he fathered a child in England. Thus, he would persist in activities which reinforced his persona of sexual athlete and heavy drinker, to the

> point that his college fraternity, dazzled by Merton's sybaritic lifestyle, often referred to him as "our Merty."[2]

This image, although tempered a good deal by his age and his long history in religious life, came back to Merton in the mid-1960s. Many who visited him during that period found him eager to get away from the monastery grounds, frequently for a stop at either a fast food restaurant or a bar.[3] John Eudes Bamberger judged that when faced with both the social and the solitary, Merton would tend toward the former, possibly because of another's needs he felt drawn to address, possibly because of his own gregarious instinct.

> In spite of his deep unvarying and intense attraction to solitude, Father Louis [Merton's monastic name] was one of the most social of men, who had an absolute need for human society. . . . As intense as his longing for silence and solitude was—and this too was a very real, urgent necessity for him—it had always struck me that in an out-and-out battle, if it ever came to that, his social instinct would easily win the day.[4]

Merton surely seemed to welcome a more social life in his last years. On the other hand, he was ambivalent about parties, finding them seductive and unsatisfying. Mott quotes a journal entry after a Fourth of July celebration indicating this other side of Merton, who says:

> What would have been very simple has been complicated by friends and my own reactions. The people who want to take you out—when you shouldn't go and don't want to. I have been definitely at fault in yielding to them and it has made me miserable.[5]

This echoes a number of journal entries registering complaints at the steady line of guests to his hermitage, even as he acknowledges having taken the initiative in many of those meetings.

No doubt some of the reason for Merton's being pursued—much beyond his desire to pursue others, it seems—was his fame. Here his shyness was perhaps most observable. Merton had, of course, a sense of his importance, and yet he was largely detached from it.[6] Willing, even desirous, of being out of any limelight, Merton seems to have been plagued by the 4 instinct toward self-comparison and contrast.

One way to avoid continuously assessing self against others is to withdraw from any semblance of competition. There is a "dis-ease" in

4s concerning competing. On the one hand, if their capabilities are obvious, they are concerned for others who might either see them as braggarts or feel envious of abilities these others may not possess to such a degree. On the other hand, if 4s see themselves as inferior, they withdraw in embarrassment. This former dynamic is manifested in John Howard Griffin's comment that "Merton reacted uncomfortably to any contact that suggested: 'Edify me. Help me become what I think you are.'"[7] The latter sensitivity to personal failure is seen in an incident in which a student compared Merton's class on the prophet Jonah to another teacher's, seeming to find Merton's presentation somewhat wanting. As a result of this student's remark, Merton closed the book, walked out of the room, and gave up scripture teaching for a year.[8]

Merton was always sensitive to his own failings, no doubt due, once again, to the influence of his 3 wing. That, like all 4s, he carried an imaginary measuring stick around with him, by which he rated himself as better or worse than others, is evident in this passage about dread:

> The real import of dread is to be sought in an infidelity to a personal demand of which one is at least dimly aware; the failure to meet a challenge, to fulfill a certain possibility which demands to be met and fulfilled. The price of this failure to measure up to an existential demand of one's own life is a general sense of failure, of guilt.[9]

It was this vague sense of guilt, this dread of failing to be, that led Merton to a balance and perspective about his own importance. At a time when he was receiving many honors, he notes one that was as important as any of the others: the honor of having a very small gold-winged moth settle lightly on his hand, remaining with him in its delicate perfection until he blew it away.[10] Such reflections brought Merton back to the important realities of simple living. That kind of living, he believed, was the only way to avoid the guilt for not being fully and emotionally engaged in his day-to-day existence. Living completely in the present moment was all he eventually saw as important.

Merton was once asked to contribute a statement about how he became such a success for a book on the subject. His response shows the humor of his later perspective on this issue when he says:

> If I had a message to my contemporaries, I said, it was surely this: be anything you like, be madmen, drunks, and bastards of every shape and form but at all costs avoid one

> thing: success. I heard no more from [the book's editor], and I am not aware that my reply was published with the other testimonials.[11]

Eventually success became almost irrelevant to Merton. By remaining faithful to his true self, he moved from egoism with its comparison and contrast to the deeper level of being where one is nether better nor worse than anyone else.

Despite the sense so many people had that Merton was almost transparent in encounters with them, he himself saw it otherwise. It is characteristic of 4s to appear revelatory, and in many areas they are; they often communicate, however, about everything except what is most significant to them. Merton admitted that when he revealed most he hid most, a 4 way of expressing this dynamic. The tendency often includes a feeling of specialness and uniqueness. At least this was so for Merton, who realized he needed to look for his identity not only in God but in others. He recognized this withdrawal as a trap, saying: "I tend to isolate myself from the rest of mankind as if I were a different kind of being."[12] Merton knew that such an attitude could not lead into genuine interior solitude, but only into "the false sweetness of a narcissistic seclusion."[13]

Merton learned to distinguish between true solitude and temptations to withhold himself from people. The latter are lifeless rather than life-giving, since they are not founded on the most important of virtues: love.

> Solitude is necessary for spiritual freedom. But once that freedom is acquired, it demands to be put to work in the service of a love in which there is no longer subjection or slavery. Mere withdrawal, without the return to freedom in action, would lead to a static and death-like inertia of the spirit in which the inner self would not awaken at all. There would be no light, no voice within us, only the silence and darkness of the tomb.[14]

This kind of withdrawal is imprisoning rather than liberating and cuts off a person's self from contact with the true self of another. It is this kind of withdrawal, based in false "specialness," that contributes to the isolation and alienation felt by Merton and many 4s.

Merton grew over his lifetime in the realization that he might well fall into narcissistic posturing in his pursuit of contemplative solitude.

In yet another part played on his personal life's stage, Merton the contemplative might turn out to be nothing but a role. In speaking about this temptation and possibility, Merton describes what a merely exterior contemplative looks like:

> He will assume varied attitudes, and meditate on the inner significance of his own postures, and try to fabricate himself a contemplative identity: and all the while there is nobody there. There is only an illusory, fictional "I" which seeks itself, struggles to create itself out of nothing, maintained in being by its own compulsion and is the prisoner of its private illusion. The call to contemplation is not, and cannot be addressed to such an "I".[15]

In contrast to what might be called this "ego-contemplative," the genuine contemplative is hidden from others as well as from self, no longer on any stage, even his or her own.

> [The contemplative] is, in fact, delivered from subjection to appearances, and cares very little about them. At the same time, since he has neither the inclination nor the need to rebel, he does not have to advertise his contempt for appearances. He simply neglects them. They no longer interest him.[16]

Such a simple existence is what Merton sees as redemptive in itself and as witness against sinfulness in the world.[17]

We see the influence in later life of Merton's 5 wing. His honest awareness in the midst of his fame that he could be judged—and actually was—imperfect, became his joy. He found happiness in hiddenness.

> To be little, to be nothing, to rejoice in your imperfections, to be glad that you are not worthy of attention, that you are of no account in the universe. This is the only liberation. The only way to true solitude.[18]

It was this 5 wing that was evident in Merton's vocation to monastic life. He was hidden away from others at least to some extent in the unnoticed and unnoticeable community routines. Something of this awareness may very well have figured in Merton's choice of Gethsemani Abbey. There he hoped to disappear silently among the other silent men. He seemed to sense that, for him, the essential road to solitude would lie in a contemplative monastery.

> [Contemplatives] have to explore these areas—because they are part of the general human experience, a part which is neglected by other people, a part which is necessary for a deep and fully valid human existence, and especially a deep and valuable religious development. We are called to make this exploration of this area—which is solitude, is the desert, is the desolate region—the region where man is alone with God.[19]

While we may detect something of an elite attitude in this passage, we also see that for Merton the monastery provided a situation where God was unavoidable. It is notable that it is imaged as a desolate desert, the other end of the continuum from the world of his rakish socializing.

Eventually even Gethsemani ceased to be solitude enough for Merton. The growing post-World War II community made for close quarters and necessitated busy and noisy building projects. Merton's formation work grew more time-consuming. Increasing numbers of men—many, ironically for him, drawn to the monastery by Merton's own writings—entered the novitiate. Changes in the Cistercian order made his hermitage dream realistic at last. In some ways, he saw the hermit life making him more than ever a monk of Gethsemani, and even more, of the world.

> [My monastery] is not an environment in which I become aware of myself as an individual, but rather a place in which I disappear from the world as an object of interest in order to be everywhere in it by hiddenness and compassion. To exist everywhere I have to be a No-one.[20]

Merton realized he was shaping monasticism for his and future generations, and that to do so with authenticity he would have to embrace solitude. The word *monk* means "alone one." Merton, however, was a cenobitic monk, a monk who lives in community. He would never be completely detached from the monastic family, nor did he want to be, it seems. There was something purifying for him in what he called the "relative inefficiency" of a life which produced only "some milk, some cheese, some bread, some music, a few paintings, and an occasional book."[21]

Place and product eventually became of no consequence for Merton. He realized that these things are not part of the substance of peoples' spiritual lives. Fame and success he saw as illusory early on; later he saw that achievements of any kind, especially spiritual ones, bear no fruit except that of inviting the mercy of God.

> What is the use of knowing our weakness if we do not implore God to sustain us with his power? What is the value of recognizing our poverty if we never use it to entreat his mercy? . . . The value of our weakness and of our poverty is that they are the earth in which God sows the seed of desire. And no matter how abandoned we may seem to be, the confident desire to love him in spite of our abject misery, is the sign of his presence and the pledge of our salvation.[22]

The answer to the 4 sense of abandonment, as Merton came to realize, is the necessity of removing barriers and entering into community with everyone in the Divine family. Merton saw monastic renewal taking place in the recovery of this deep desire for God that makes life with others "totally new."[23]

Rather than withdrawing into a narcissistic self-concern and self-protection, Merton plunged himself into his monastic community, where the need to balance solitude and solidarity led to a kind of desert he had not anticipated. Even in later years he never quite succeeded in living completely the life of a hermit; his brothers would never allow that, insisting instead that he join them for some meals and weekly conferences, at least. They perhaps saved him from the trap of role-playing the solitary. This and some other very concrete factors in his life kept Merton's feet on the ground. His later public recognition and lessened monastic restrictions about socializing also brought him back to center. He began to live more of what most of us would call a "normal life" in his last years. At this stage people did feel they knew the real Merton, probably because he was freer and more genuinely vulnerable in his maturity. Even then, however, his deepest struggles were private ones, as his journals testify.

In many ways, Merton never could have been anything other than a solitary. It was a vocation handed to him along with his personality as a 4. He was destined continually to reach out to others because he saw relationship as the essential backdrop to existence, as the way to meaning. More simply, he knew no view of life that did not include other people. He was destined as well, however, to experience a poignant separation from those he most wanted to allow into his life. That poignancy could become either a trap to melancholy or an instructive indication that he was distant from his own person and, therefore, from the persons of others. It proved both for Merton, depending on his stage of spiritual development and life's changing circumstances.

Probably the pull between social and solitary lessened in significance for Merton. As he became more honestly self-present, he seems to have become more immediate in his relationship and more natural both in living and in speaking about his life to other people. He relaxed into who he was: a highly gregarious man who never felt anyone knew him. Ultimately, he seems to have relaxed even deeper to a more authentic self where he no longer paid much attention to either dynamic. Even as a young man he seems to have had some sense of this call of his. He puts these words into the mouth of God. They are words that spring up, it seems, from the heart of his own being.

> And when you have been praised a little and loved a little I will take away all your gifts and all your love and all your praise and you will be utterly forgotten and abandoned and you will be nothing, a dead thing, a rejection. And in that day you shall begin to possess the solitude you have so long desired. And your solitude will bear immense fruit in the souls of men you will never see on earth.
>
> Do not ask when it will be or where it will be or how it will be: On a mountain or in a prison, in a desert or in a concentration camp or in a hospital or at Gethsemani. It does not matter. So do not ask me, because I am not going to tell you. You will not know until you are in it.[24]

Merton speaks here in words from that center where he and God and all people are one. In doing so he tells himself and his readers that life's social and solitary struggles are, after all, not very important. What is important is to let God, let life/Life, lead wherever it will. Abandonment to that God makes one truly solitary, absolutely alone with the Absolute. In that solitude there is no loneliness, no alienation, no abandonment. Whether all alone or in contact with other people, there is nothing but unity with self and others in the Divine.

The Temptation to Despair

It has proven interesting in my work with the enneagram to ask people to look at the circular figure and speak about what it is like to live at any one of its points. Nearly everyone asked has an immediate sense of what that question is about and can put words on what it is to see the world from a particular view. When we look at the 4's position, we note that it is toward the bottom of the figure on the right side across from the 5, the number that begins the rise again to 9 at the top. All of the other numbers are surrounded by a closed mesh of lines joining in a regular pattern. The 4 and 5, however, are open.

One might say that these points are precariously poised; they seem to be in danger of falling off the figure, slipping down from it. Many 4s speak of this life stance in terms of depression, a pressing on them by life and its circumstances. This position contributes to the insecurity of 4s, who fear at any moment to lose their balance and to disappear into some dark abyss. It has been said that we can never know a 4 without being aware of some depression.

There is always a search, and the search is for meaning. It is a grim and intense one. When meaning seems present, or at least possible, 4s can be positive and hopeful, even exuberant. When doubts or questions arise, however, 4s are inclined to slip from their sense of security, tenuous at best, into isolated and hopeless fear that all is meaningless.

Thomas Merton talked about this phenomenon in terms of dread and despair. These feelings seemed to lie just on the other side of the friendly, enthusiastic qualities Merton sometimes exhibited. People who knew him often commented on how an apparently light and carefree moment could suddenly become clouded, sometimes hostile and defensive. The man seemed to change in an instant, a fact that contributed to Merton's often being called a complex, even contradictory, character.

We do know that the struggle with dread and despair was a consistent dynamic in Merton's life. It had for Merton a palpable quality that he was able to communicate to his readers. Descriptions of this spiritual vertigo, the panic at the possibility of falling into nothingness, are graphic and concrete.

Nevertheless, Merton left largely to our imagination what he personally went through in the circumstances of his own life. We hear—as we have already noted, and as one often does with 4s—his philosophical summary of such experiences and how they are meant to be integrated into the spiritual journey. These discussions take place, for the most part, in his books and articles on spirituality. The details of his own dizziness as he stood over the abyss go unrecorded even in his poetry. He probably did not consciously withhold this information; more likely he assumed that it was impossible to communicate an experience so close to his very being.

As 4s so often determine, there are no words that can let other people know the most significant realities of their lives, and so they abandon attempts to do so. It is not that they try to hold back from self-revelation; there simply are no words for the depth of their experience, even for themselves. While this may lead to elitism in 4s, it can also result, when they are enlightened and free, in respect for and sensitivity to the unique joys and pains of every person's life.

For Merton, as for many 4s, the way to some security lay in carrying out the tasks of life, performing life's various roles competently and efficiently. Here we see the influence of the 3 wing. As Merton developed his ego around his self-image of student, writer, monk, contemplative, or whatever else took the stage at any given time, he knew what to do and what was expected of him. In other words, he knew what part to play. The postures of these changing roles made expectations clear. They also delivered him from being faced with his real, flawed, limited, and sometimes boring self.

One enneagram theory calls the 2/3/4 triad the feeling people. I would say instead that this triad is the one where people have the greatest problem with feelings. While 2/3/4s can readily name or label their experiences, they seldom appear "taken" by them. They may look like they are living out their emotional life, but they are more likely to be imitating the feelings of those around them or acting in ways they think immediate circumstances call for. This adaptation is instinctive. It leads 2/3/4s away from their own experience and replaces it with experience stimulated by the outer environment.

This reaction is not conscious, of course; it is as automatic an instinct as breathing and digesting. As an instinct it never stops, no matter how enlightened 2/3/4s become. Awareness can—and, where growth happens, does—enable 2/3/4s to recognize, eventually accept, and finally be at peace with this issue. When all of these progressive steps have occurred, the instinct is unmasked. Only then can a free response of choice be theirs.

This is what happened in Merton's case. We often hear him name being out of touch with his feelings and, therefore, incapable of an immediate, spontaneous response to the moment. His clue to the phenomenon of imitating others rather than living out of his personal reality was what he called *dread*. Dread occurs, says Merton, when we are not truly one with our experience, when we do not correspond with what we see and hear and feel and think at any given moment.[1] When this awareness of living a lie, of being distant from our own truth, becomes conscious, all of our usual ways of carrying out our familiar roles must be unlearned in the consequent confrontation with our falsity and self-deception. Where we might have been able to fool ourselves once, when this dread is present we can no longer find solace in the false self that Merton calls the ultimate role each of us plays.[2]

While all 2/3/4s speak of an interior poverty, for 4s the experience has an added dimension of this falsity. More than mere emptiness, 4s find an inner deceit. This deceit for Merton, as for many 4s, takes the form of alienation from genuine living. The parts played, the roles taken, the postures assumed, separate one from life. For Merton, as for many 4s, life and God are seen to be synonymous; therefore, to be distant from one's present experience is to be distant from God.

We see the influence of the existentialists in Merton. For him existentialism always held a Christian shading. The way to true freedom and authenticity is a person's cooperative task with God and in imitation of Christ, who called himself the Truth.[3] On the spiritual path Merton sees it as essential to face this dread, offering as it does the opportunity for conversion. More than a mere awareness of limitation and creatureliness, dread also includes a profound sense of helplessness. Nothing we might do is able to bring about simple, honest, moment-to-moment living.

The 4 compulsion to distance self from the feeling response in the present cannot be eliminated by effort of any kind; in fact, efforts only exacerbate the problem. There is no way out. Self-redemption is an impossibility. The only thing any creature can fashion is falsity: roles, self-preoccupation, postures. Eventually, all efforts fail and struggling stops, not by choice but because there is no longer any energy or purpose for the struggle.[4]

At this point, we experience the taste of personal evil. Not only are we full of deception, but we try to take on the role of God for ourselves and force spontaneity and life. No effort is so distancing from God. This is the pride that pushes away the God of mercy and causes the sense of abandonment and alienation in a private hell. Remorse, turning to God in sadness, disappointment, and grief, would dissolve the barriers that form part of the falsity. Yet, it is precisely this insistence on making ourselves worthy and authentic for God that deepens the chasm between the self and God. In guilt we can be our own judge and deliver sentence; in remorse, we abandon all effort as fruitless.

At this stage, we fall into despair. We cannot remake ourselves into authentic persons, responding with spontaneous thought and feeling in the moment. Neither can we stop trying to do so. We have been unfaithful to genuine life, which takes place in immediacy; we are a living lie. Merton realizes that such despair is a necessary part of the conversion process. He also realizes that to bear fruit it must somehow be grounded in hope. Otherwise, we could not call ourselves Christian; we could not be faithful to some undeniable truth even deeper than the despair: a trust that all of this agony has some purpose.

> This, then, is our desert: to live facing despair, but not to consent. To trample it down under hope in the Cross. To wage war against despair unceasingly. That war is our wilderness. If we wage it courageously, we will find Christ at our side. If we cannot face it, we will never find Him.[5]

After living at this place of hope against hope, the gift of an unreflected, immediate life is given. For 4s, this consists in simply being. Where for someone else, as has been said, an unconsidered life is not worth living, for 4s an unconsidered life is the great contemplative gift. It is something impossible to fabricate yet essential to possess. It is given all at once and everywhere and beyond any linear cause and effect; it permeates reality.

> [God's mercy] is like a pure diamond, blazing with the invisible light of heaven. It is in everybody, and if we could see it we would see these billions of points of light coming together in the face and blaze of a sun that would make all the darkness and cruelty of life vanish completely. I have no program for this seeing. It is only given. But the gate of heaven is everywhere.[6]

For Merton, the monastery was the place of conversion. It was where he as monk was led to "confront his own humanity at the deepest and most central point, where the void seems to enter into black despair."[7] Such, he believed, was the purpose of his own and any monastic vocation. It was what he understood in the vow of *conversio morum*, the conversion of life he pronounced at his monastic profession.

In the course of his life in community this apparent destruction—really the death of illusions and delusions, the false self—tested his spirit in what he called a passive purification.[8] He came to accept the incomprehensibility of this situation. It was one he recognized, possibly more in retrospect than when he was going through it, as the climate of serious prayer. All he could do was continue in the daily routines of his life with no sense of when or where liberation would come.[9] Merton learned that life in community includes a wide variety of persons who, like himself, struggle with their falsity. It is precisely this struggle that unites monastics. It gave Merton the loving compassion beneath any irritable impatience in his relationship with his monastic brothers.

Paradoxically, this sense of nothingness and helplessness, this dread, Merton experienced as joy because it put him "in direct contact with God who is the source of all joy and all life."[10] Significantly, Merton sees God not only as the one who gives meaning, but also as the one who brings heart and feeling to existence. The 4, out of touch with the immediate emotions in a situation, is in search for precisely this experience of "heart." It is what makes the previously sterile desert of life's succeeding moments blossom.

From the point of view of the enneagram, we say that Merton's dread and despair resulted from the emptiness, the lifelessness, of someone distant from the emotional function and unable to do anything to change that characteristic limitation. At the lowest point of despair 4s must face the human helplessness Merton describes. Such admission of powerlessness plunges a person into what is everybody's reality: creatureliness and limitation, dependence on God, the mysterious source of life. This life/Life is nothingness and possibility, pain and fear, anger and frustration, and anguish lived out, experienced. The affective level, once merely acknowledged, begins to function. Hope is fulfilled in the presence of real feelings.

Merton names this process as the way to monastic humility. After salutary despair, which finally ends the futile struggle to make self into a "god," one plunges "through the center of his humility to find himself at last in the Living God."[11] It is interesting to note, from the point of view of the enneagram, how Merton realizes that this humility "ultimately demands the complete forgetfulness of ourselves."[12] No longer can we be in our own audience or anyone else's. What was once a mere reflection on reality ultimately gives way to simply being; there is immediate response to immediate experience. Any return to self-observation, noting that we "have arrived" at contemplation, leads back to dread; we taste the false once again in being next to and observing experience.[13] Narcissism, the very opposite of contemplation, creeps in once more and the ego replaces the self-forgetfulness of wonder and gratitude.

Radical despair like this does not lead to the victim or martyr role 4s can sometimes get caught in at the ego level. Inasmuch as this despair is real, it touches into life/Life and is, therefore, empowering. The source of energy is in the emotions. Finding our immediate emotional life is to find God in whom is all strength. In this regard Merton reflects:

> Perhaps I am stronger than I think. Perhaps I am even afraid of my strength, and turn it against myself, thus making myself weak. Making myself secure. Making myself guilty.
>
> Perhaps I am most afraid of the strength of God in me.
>
> Perhaps I would rather be guilty and weak in myself, than strong in Him whom I cannot understand.[14]

Here is the ultimate subtlety of the hope that delivers from despair. In what Mott calls a magnificent passage, Merton repudiates his repudiator. He refuses self-hate, the only thing that makes despair a dead-end. Without that self-condemnation, despair leads inevitably to hope.

> To love our "nothingness" in this way, we must repudiate nothing that is our own, nothing that we have, nothing that we are. We must see and admit that it is all ours and that it is

> all good: good in its positive entity since it comes from God: good in our deficiency, since our helplessness, even our moral misery, our spiritual, attracts to us the mercy of God.
>
> To love our nothingness we must love everything in us that the proud man loves when he loves himself. But we must love it all for exactly the opposite reason.
>
> To love our nothingness we must love OURSELVES.[15]

Lest we think for a moment that Merton's humility was wrought in some sort of ethereal, private arena, we need to remind ourselves that life for him centered around human relationships and community. Despair is linked with the inability to be with self and, consequently, with other people. This fact came home to Merton not so much in chapel as in the corridors and rooms and grounds of the monastery. Others made it impossible for him to deny that he was good, he was lovable, he was loved. In a journal entry ten years before his death, Merton remarked:

> One reason I am so grateful for this morning's sermon is that my worst and inmost sickness is the despair of ever being able truly to love, because I despair of ever being worthy of love. But the way out is to be able to trust one's friends and thus accept in them acts and things which a sick mind grabs as evidence of lack of love—as pretexts for evading the obligation to love.[16]

Trust in life, giving way to it as it genuinely is, finally comes down to trusting other people for 4s. Once the 4's own limitation is accepted, so, too, is the limitation of others. No one is a perfect art piece. Rather, the imperfection of the material used to create is precisely what shapes its perfection—its unique perfection, we might add.

Dread signals the emotionally evasive patterns that fear has built up to separate the 4 from life/Life, from just being in the day-to-day. Despair follows when this dynamic and the compulsive patterns it has shaped are admitted. Eventually, humility appears beneath despair and the self-concern, self-consciousness, and self-protection it led to. The 4 then falls free of the fear of imperfection into the sea of human reality. In that sea, which is God and Life and Love, everyone finally is discovered; this is where the 4 responds without self-preoccupation and posturing.

Of course, humility saves everyone and leads to contemplative living. For 4s, its special issues are around dismay over their lack of real feelings. When faced, there is a peace with their tendency to fabricate feelings and thus to seal themselves off from their own and others' experience. The resulting state brings shame and guilt, a genuine shame and a genuine guilt. These feelings may be hard and unpleasant to bear, but they are real and so they bring joy. Like a storm that may have been dreaded, it results in refreshment for a parched earth.

In a letter to Rosemary Reuther, Merton says it this way:

> I refuse in practice to accept any theory or method of contemplation that simply divides the soul against body, interior against exterior, and then tries to transcend itself by pushing creatures out into the dark. What dark? As soon as the split is made, the dark is abysmal in everything, and the only way to get back into the light is to be once again a normal human being who likes to smell the flowers and look at girls if they are around, and who likes the clouds.[17]

At this point, there is no more dread, no more despair. There is only the joy of living life's succeeding moments.

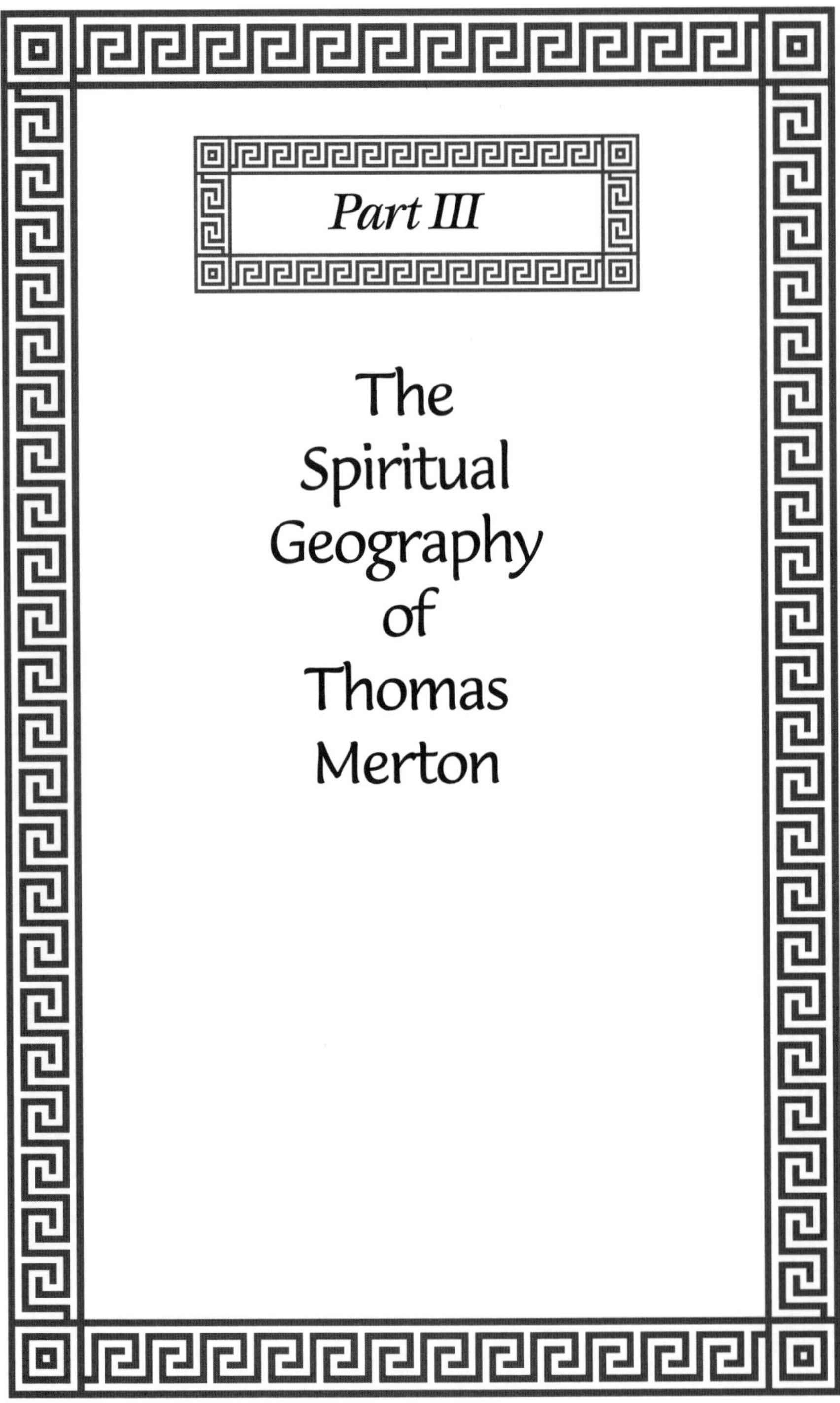

Part III

The Spiritual Geography of Thomas Merton

Spiritual Life as a Coming Home

Those readers who are familiar with Thomas Merton's writings will recognize geography as one of his images. For Merton, geography was much more than exterior terrain. The interior was also a landscape both rugged and smooth, marked with quicksands and deserts. It was a place hard to traverse because of its darkness, a darkness compounded by blindness caused by the lightning flashes when one gets close to the mystery of God.

The further along we travel on the spiritual journey, the more such lightning blinds us, according to Merton. Expressed another way, knowledge becomes someone/Someone felt instead of someone/Someone seen. Merton realized that, at least for him, the spiritual journey led to his personal, interior spirit, where the Divine Spirit dwells. He describes the journey of life as "interior: it is a matter of growth, deepening, and of an ever greater surrender to the creative action of love and grace in our hearts."[1]

Outer places are important for 4s. They were for Thomas Merton, as evidenced in the way he wrote about not only where but with whom he lived, especially in his autobiography and journals. Unlike the 5/6/7 triad, who surround themselves with symbols of their past and present and so honor their personal history, 4s see place as providing enough quiet and security to experience their own and the outer world's rhythms. Ultimately, however, these outer places are merely symbols of the inner place to which they lead. The journey may take in the outer home—and this place is symbolically significant—but more so the home of the heart.

For Merton, who often looked outside to classmates, family, friends, or monastic community for that place of belonging, life consisted in finding a belonging with himself. Rather than taking on the joys and sorrows of other people, which drown out a 4's inner messages, Merton eventually learned to hear his own genuine response underneath the anxiety to be approved and accepted.

Mott says, "It was Merton's very nature both to seek changes and to desire the unchangeable."[2] He was often on the move, if not geographically, at least in his thoughts and interests. Gethsemani Abbey slowed his body down until his mind could learn to stay home and rest. With some intuitive wisdom, Merton knew this was right for him. He sensed that home would only be found within. One wonders whether he would ever have come to the depths of spirituality he attained had his life sanctioned outer travels.

Not all guides in the life of the soul picture spirituality the way Merton does. For guides in the 5/6/7 triad it is a step-by-step outward journey that constitutes growth. For those 8/9/1s who are called to speak about the essence of the spiritual life, it is the holding of opposites from a point of unifying perspective that leads to peace and wholeness. Those who read Merton need to remember that his particular stance led him to formulate spiritual maturity in the way he did. Those people who find that Merton says what they need to hear about the essence of spiritual growth may well do so because he conceives of it in a way that fits their own life view. Many passages in Merton speak to everyone, but it is probably 2/3/4s who most resonate with his references to touching into feelings and desires and values as a necessary homecoming.

As it does for all of us, this view of Merton's about personal spirituality spills over into his image of God. In the prose poem "Hagia Sophia" Merton describes a God whose story is reminiscent of a man whose life spanned two continents and involved travel between them on several occasions.

> A vagrant, a destitute wanderer with dusty feet, finds his way down a new road. A homeless God, lost in the night, without papers, without identification, without even a num-

> ber, a frail expendable exile lies down in desolation under the sweet stars of the world and entrusts Himself to sleep.[3]

This homeless God accompanies Merton on his way to that interior place which offers enough centeredness to allow moving out to others in self-forgetfulness.[4]

Balance comes for 2/3/4s on the spiritual way when they realize their journey must take them inside themselves to their passionate hearts. It is important for them to move away from their instinctive pull toward activity and their preoccupation with the opinions and concerns of others. This is where their compulsions have been built up; exaggerated emphasis on what is outside them makes the genuine experience of their interior thoughts and feelings, needs and concerns, very distant. It is true that 4s, who appear more aloof and less outer-oriented than others in the 2/3/4 triad are off-balance in this outward direction. They grow to wholeness when they come to rest within, something very different from their tendency to attack their motivations and dispositions with analytical demands.

An inner quiet and reflectiveness, while essential for 4s, will soon send them outward again, refreshed and nourished. They will never need the amount of aloneness and privacy that 5/6/7s do; their energy, spent in finding their personal responses, over time brings them to their center and back to the social arena. Their temptation to stay long in the inner world is a small one. Once having found their authentic experience, they are soon out again to let others know what they have discovered from presence to their own reality.

It seems that Thomas Merton had this sort of rhythm. He craved quiet, mostly, it seems, to touch into himself and what he was experiencing. His journals testify to this fact. Nevertheless, he kept reaching out to others in his letters and writings as well as personally. If he could not go physically to people, he at least could invite them into his space, something he often did and frequently expressed ambivalence about.

One theme in the life of 4s is to desire to be with others and yet to be resentful when those they have encouraged to come into their world actually do so and take up too much time and space. As David Steindl-Rast puts it: "No one is outgoing unless he has a home to which he can return."[5] Merton handled this dynamic better than many 4s do because his rootedness in his solitary, contemplative life—which means his affective, human life—provided a base for his intense and frequent encounters with people.

While this base was symbolized in his hermitage, it went much deeper than any mere structure. One common image of the spiritual life is that of climbing a mountain. Jonathan Montaldo says that a turning point in Merton's life came when he realized that such a configuration of the way to God could never be his. Merton was most assuredly a poet. Having eventually found the way to his own genuine passions, he found the way to a self that was, of course, a self-with-God. Merton did not need to rise above the earth toward theories of ascetical theology; he was aloof naturally, even compulsively. What he needed was to plunge into what Montaldo calls "the muddled human paths of daily existence."[6] There he would find not only himself, but God as well. William Shannon speaks in Mertonian terms when he describes the encounter with the personal self and Divine Self as a single experience:

> Our awareness of God is a supernatural participation in the light by which He reveals Himself interiorly as dwelling in our inmost self. Hence, the Christian mystical experience is not only an awareness of the inner self but also, by a supernatural intensification of faith, it is an experiential grasp of God as present within our inner self.[7]

Shannon continues to paraphrase Merton as he further describes the self-in-God experience. Merton turns to the image of journeying home as this passage develops:

> By a paradox beyond all human expression, God and the soul seem to have but one single "I". . . To anyone who has full awareness of our "exile" from God, our alienation from this inmost self, and our blind wandering in the "region of unlikeness," this claim can hardly seem believable. Yet it is nothing else but the message of Christ calling us to awake from sleep to return from exile and find our true selves within ourselves, in that inner sanctuary which is His temple and His heaven, and (at the end of the prodigal's homecoming journey) the "Father's House."[8]

That Merton linked the inner sanctuary with his monastic home and, by extension, his hermitage testifies to the symbolic importance of place already mentioned. It was at Gethsemani that he learned who he really was, the angry, joyous, resentful, anxious, frightened, peaceful, limited man who was a monk. Montaldo says that "as much as Thomas Merton loved 'geography,'. . . (he) in the end realized that no place could be the right place for him if it was not 'right' inside."[9] Kept at home by Trappist rules and abbatial decisions, Merton had an abundance of opportunity to travel within. Montaldo submits that Merton's commitment to Gethsemani came from the deep self-knowledge he found through monastic stability.

> As insecure as his emotional life might personally have been, as fragile as his "con" of himself-as-hermit at Gethsemani might gradually have proven to be, Thomas Merton realized that to abandon his hunt for God at Gethsemani would have been to risk abandoning his hunt for God everywhere.[10]

This sense of the monastery as a place for homecoming was an early intuition for Merton. While a professor at St. Bonaventure College during his struggle with vocation, Merton heard in his imagination the bells of the monastery ringing out one night. The image was crucial in his resolution to enter Gethsemani; yet, like all of the symbolic elements of our life's myth, there is another, deeper meaning than we imagine at the time. "The bell seemed to be telling me where I belonged," says Merton, "as if it were calling me home."[11] Merton obviously realized there was importance in this symbol. Life was to tell him much more about the significance of his call to homecoming.

As his view of spirituality developed, the importance of finding his inner home grew until he could write of simple self-companionship with the humor and simplicity of a person relaxed and comfortable in his own good company.

> This is not a hermitage—it is a house. (Who was that hermitage I seen you with last night? . . .) What I wear is pants. What I do is live. How I pray is breathe. Who said Zen? Wash out your mouth if you said Zen. If you see a meditation going by, shoot it. Who said "Love"? Love is in the movies. The spiritual life is something that people worry about when they are so busy with something else they think they ought to be spiritual. Up here in the woods is seen the New Testament: that is to say, the wind comes through the trees and you breathe it.[12]

Merton eventually gave up the effort to explain his spiritual path. He no longer talked about what it was like to be so much one with one's self that there was no need even to reflect on that reality. He began to speak about this learning of his by recounting daily events of astonishing simplicity. These were peppered with a paradox that catches the reader—and probably also Merton himself—up short.

In some ways his journals are more poetry than his poems are. They tell of his unreflected time just at home with himself and however he was moment to moment. He speaks of this experience in many ways, especially in his later years. Doing so, he seems aware that there are no words to convey this aloneness with the being who is self. Because there are none, he stops trying to find any.

> It is necessary to be present alone at the resurrection of Day, in the blank silence when the sun appears. In this completely neutral instant, I receive from the eastern woods, the tall oaks, the one word "Day," which is never the same. It is never spoken in any known language.[13]

One thing that always interests people in the other enneagram triads is the 2/3/4 fascination with simply being. We see here an example of the distinction between instinct and learned experience and how instincts differ depending on our enneagram space. Merton shows us the joy and wonder that a 4 has around inner homecoming. To use Merton's own image of geography, 4s search the exterior countryside for persons and places to make them whole. They search, too, the interior countryside, applying analysis, evaluation, and criticism, only to find that these distance rather than help the process of coming to self-at-home-within. The only way to be with the self is to stop efforts to find the self. Other triads are born with this knowledge. For 2/3/4s, and especially for 4s, these anguished attempts at self-knowledge only alienate them from loving simplicity and self-acceptance. The wisdom of such awareness takes the better part of a lifetime.

Merton as poet best expresses what for at least a third of the human race is an amazing discovery. Merton the spiritual writer gets caught in the analysis that prevents not only the experience of self-companionship, but any adequate way to put words on it. Undoubtedly, this is the reason he avoided discussions about prayer and spirituality in his last years and turned, instead, to the problems and issues of ordinary living: politics, peace, monastic renewal. Some have said that the daily doing of life not only expresses the fact that 4s are present with themselves, but it helps that inner companionship to happen.

On his final pilgrimage at Polonnaruwa Merton finally pierced through "the shadow and the disguise." William Shannon asks and then takes back the question as to what it was that Merton found before those Buddha figures. He turns for his answer to Merton's final words, spoken to the monks and nuns at the Bangkok Conference. Wisely, it seems, Shannon realizes that Merton's learning of that experience only days before would be best expressed indirectly in how he acted and what he chose to tell that assembled group.[14] Significantly, Merton sums up the "whole purpose of the monastic life" as teaching people to live by love:

> The simple formula, which was so popular in the West, was the Augustinian formula of the translation of *cupiditas* into *caritas,* of self-centered love into an outgoing, other-centered love. In the process of this change the individual ego was seen to be illusory and dissolved itself, and in place of this self-centered ego came the Christian person, who was no longer just the individual but was Christ dwelling in each one.[15]

The balance, then, for Merton, was initially to go within, pulling to the solitude that prevented his fleeing from self-confrontation, an excuse busyness provides. It propelled him outside again, because it was in the outer world that Merton, like all 4s, needed to spend most of his time. If he did not he would imprison himself in the bonds of analysis. Merton's gifts around this dynamic are several. On the one hand, he helped people who run from their interior to face the demands of solitude. He also assisted people like himself, for whom solitude posed unhealthy self-examination and self-criticism, by gently and humorously urging them to relax. In the other direction, he took his learnings outside as teacher, writer, and spiritual and formation director, where he met those who struggled with their journeys, whether they might picture that journey as homecoming or not.

In fact, as Shannon points out, Merton was speaking about the inner home he found in the outer home of his monastery at the time he was about as far distant from that home as is possible for someone earthbound to travel. His last words were about his monastery and the way it had led him to "full realization."[16] Then he died alone, this man who had hardly left the monastery in nearly thirty years.[17] This was the monk who had written about his monastery home that

> When the full fields begin to smell of sunrise
> And the valleys sing in their sleep,
> . . . from the frowning tower, the windy belfry,

Sudden the bells come, bridegrooms,
And fill the echoing dark with love and fear.[18]

This man who belonged to the community of Gethsemani found what those bells had hinted at in his youth and finally revealed to him more fully. They were the "bridegrooms" that echoed love and the fear that comes when we know love will demand sacrifice. Ultimately, it is love that brings about the balance of inner and outer we all look for. For Merton, it drew him in only to send him out again. His instinct-turned-gift was presence to all those communities his monastic community had prepared him to be part of, even as it prepared him to face his essential solitude.

The Search for Meaning

We have already noted the position of the 4 on the enneagram circle and the felt sense of that position. One effect, as we noted, is the temptation to depression and despair with which nearly all 4s can identify. Falling into the abyss, falling out of existence, and plunging into nothingness are some of the ways 4s speak about their experience of being poised over a hole on a circle that one is always in danger of slipping through. One of the ways 4s deal with the profound anxiety of standing on the brink of annihilation is to search for some meaning, something testifying that creation has not only significance, but that it rests in some loving design.

When 4s enter their spiritual way in the second part of their lives, questions around these basic existential issues rise up with vengeance to terrify them. What they may have entertained earlier and then buried out of consciousness takes the shape of naked doubts that no longer can be put aside. As is their pattern, 4s attack the questions these doubts raise with analysis, but only when they can no longer silence them by a guilt for even asking. Once admitted, these elemental concerns about existence have to be carried to their limits if 4s are to be true to themselves. This is one of the ways 4s attempt to be their own gods, as we all attempt to do in our differing ways. They search within themselves for answers, expecting to find there the resources to account for mystery.

Like a dog chasing its tail, 4s go around a circle of question and unsatisfying answer that soon becomes a vicious one. The only solution to the dilemma is to break the circle by admitting creaturely limitation. No one can be all-knowing; no one can account for that which is beyond the merely human. This admission is the first and essential experience of humility that initiates conversion and the beginning of a genuine contemplative life.

Merton had always been a serious person, despite his ever-present sense of humor. He probably would have been so simply because he was poised over the enneagram abyss at the 4 position. Added to his basic instinct were both the circumstances of his life, which left him parentless while still a child, and the rootlessness caused by other events. The Catholic faith gave him surety. What he perceived as its definite answers soothed the questions which cut through religious doctrines to that existential place beneath. These questions, which were written in his flesh, could only be put to rest by denying that flesh. That was something Merton did rather successfully, if for only a time, after his conversion.

His autobiography provides an interesting study in this regard. Merton celebrates Catholic doctrine, even revels in the security of his newly found beliefs. Between the lines, however, the questions are felt perhaps even more than they are articulated. They will come up again, wise readers note with gratitude. Thomas Merton's gift was not to be a defender of the faith but a companion for all those who search. Merton tells us about what we must do and who we must be as searchers. Within a few short years we begin to hear Merton ask those consoling questions which make his readers know they are not alone. Were they present earlier and censored out by monastic superiors? Probably not. The exuberance of the autobiography's message that Merton had found his answer seems sincere, if naively so.

That the questions came alive again is obvious in nearly all of his later writings. It is also the reason Merton has survived times that have marked the demise of many other spiritual writers. In 1955 Merton, whose contemplative and community life had by now brought him home to his emotional and enfleshed reality, could write about questions and the anxiety they cause:

> Questions cannot go unanswered unless they first be asked. And there is a far worse anxiety, a far worse insecurity, which comes from being afraid to ask the right questions—because they might turn out to have no answers. One of the

> moral diseases we communicate to one another in society (and also in the church?) comes from huddling together in the pale light of an insufficient answer to a question we are afraid to ask.[1]

By this time in his life Merton realized that an optimistic view, as he says, is not necessarily a virtuous one.[2] Honesty, authenticity, is to admit the questions one has, even though one feels audacious and guilty about asking them. The part Merton's writing played in this search for meaning reveals one way in which he grappled to suppress his existential insecurity, only to have to face it again. It also says something of the mentality of his autobiography, which may have been part of the whistling in the dark he speaks about in this passage:

> To understand that one has nothing special to say is suddenly to become free with a liberty which makes speech and silence equally easy. What one says will be something that has probably been said before. One need not trouble about being heard: the thing that is being said has been heard before. One ceases to depend on being heard, or thought of. And then, suddenly, one realizes that he has spoken, in the past, as if speech and communication gave him a real existence. Speech has only served us as a protection against the secret terror of not existing![3]

Monastic life itself, Merton had hoped—and that hope pervades his autobiography—would take care of his terror of the meaningless abyss. This expectation failed him as well. He discovered what being a monk really means: the coming to humble silence before the mystery/Mystery of life/Life.

> The monk is the temple of the silent Spirit of God, and his work will therefore consist not so much in making and changing and unmaking things, or in repairing them, as in healing the world with the blessing of a silence that recognizes and fulfills, by its connatural sympathy, the silence hidden in all things.[4]

One place where we see Merton moving back and forth between the ordinary and concrete reality of his community life and the basic searing questions of existence is in the concluding chapter of *The Sign of Jonas*. As he goes around his everyday fire watch, and through his everyday experiences reflecting on the everyday people and events that make up his life, the instinct to search out a deeper, a larger, meaning breaks through. By the end of this walk, described in what may well be the best of his poetry, Merton reveals to us how 4s arrive at true peace. It may be only for a time that questions are reconciled with reality, but in life's growing wisdom, such times become more frequent for Merton, as for other 4s. Even when the experience of abandoning self to mystery may be lacking, the memory that such is the way to find peace becomes more and more sustaining.

As Merton walks around the monastery checking doors, locking up, securing the monastery buildings for the night, he reflects on the history contained in this familiar place. He feels like an archeologist going through Gethsemani "not only in length and height, but also in depth."[5] He notes that the geological strata covers many ancient civilizations, some of which he himself has lived through during his ten years in the community. The place is so much more than it appears; "the meanings are hidden in the walls. They mumble in the floor under the watchman's rubber feet."[6] He comments on the night, which makes the whole world seem like paper; the most substantial things either crumble, tear apart, or blow away. He turns to God with this awareness:

> O God, my God, the night has values that day has never dreamed of. All things stir by night, waking or sleeping, conscious of the nearness of their ruin. Only man makes himself illuminations he conceives to be solid and eternal. But while we ask our questions and come to our decisions, God blows our decisions out, the roofs of our houses cave in upon us, the tall towers are undermined by ants, the walls crack and cave in, and the holiest buildings burn to ashes while the watchman is composing a theory of duration.[7]

Merton starts to ask his questions at this anxious point. Not the least of his concerns is about the many people coming to his monastery who are searching for solitude and invading his own. One question he places to himself, which his unwillingness to open to new members causes him, is what kind of solitude he really wants, his own or that of the Christ of compassion?[8]

Another, deeper question has to do with his own death and whether some caring God will welcome him beyond this life "and set my feet upon a ladder under the moon, and take me out among the stars?"[9] This latter question calls from the depths of his existence and asks whether there is meaning in creation and a loving Being who has made it all. Merton wonders whether this God he is praying to remembers and holds in concern, the places and people and events of this simple life, which is all he possesses. He asks whether his existence matters, and the response is a silence he has learned to value: "There is greater comfort in the substance of silence than in the answer to a question."[10]

He recognizes as a trap even this dialogue, supposedly with God, but really with himself. This imaginary conversation with God is one in which he sees himself taking both parts. To pose questions and answer them is of human making, Merton has learned. It is the kind of script he as a writer—and a 4—is so facile at constructing. This does not mean that God has never communicated with him. On the contrary, his experience has taught him discernment between his imaginary fabrications and the spontaneous, unsolicited, and surprising messages from his true self/Self. The wise Merton says, "I do not wait for an answer, because I have begun to realize You never answer when I expect."[11] One might add that Merton has discovered God does not answer in the way one might predict; God's answer is not in words

> but in the emergence of life within life and of wisdom within wisdom. You are found in communion: Thou in me and I in Thee and Thou in them and they in me: dispossession within dispossession, dispassion within dispassion, emptiness within emptiness, freedom within freedom. I am alone. Thou art alone. The Father and I are One.[12]

Presence, existence, the direct experience of life/Life puts questions to rest. Nothing else can do so. The humbling thing for Merton to realize was that such presence and direct experience so often eluded him; his compulsion, his limitation, was precisely in the quality of his presence, his ability simply to be in the moment. This separation from himself and therefore from the Greater-than-self was the reason he raised his questions in the first place. He doubted because he so often failed to live really and simply.

The year before he died Merton talked about his own questioning and answering. He summed up life's questions as two:

> Can man make sense out of his existence? Can man honestly give his life meaning merely by adopting a certain set of

> explanations which pretend to tell him why the world began and where it will end, why there is evil and what is necessary for a good life?[13]

He tells his readers what life has taught him as an explorer and searcher of realms. From these realms he returns with the knowledge that only in the human heart—our human hearts and those of other people—will we learn that "explanations no longer suffice."[14] There "one learns that only experience counts."[15] Merton kept plumbing the depths of his physical, affective, and perceptual life in the present moment. There was no point, he discovered, in asking theoretical questions. Instead,

> if you dare to penetrate your own silence and dare to advance without fear into the solitude of your own heart, and risk the sharing of that solitude with the lonely other who seeks God through you and with you, then you will truly recover the light and the capacity to understand what is beyond words and beyond explanations because it is too close to be examined.[16]

William Shannon summarizes what life taught Merton this way:

> What counts ultimately is not what you say or think but what you experience. No one understood this better than Merton . . . no one knew better than he that life is not a matter of concepts or of words. . . . Life is opening yourself to experience . . . first to this experience and that; and finally to Experience Itself.[17]

It might be added that Merton had this realization and taught it so well and so clearly because he also knew its opposite. The very trap that he tended to slip into was what he was able to warn others about. The ability simply to live in the present moment was what he had learned through years of trial and error.

One of the animals associated with the dynamics of the 4 is the panther. In this poem by Rainer Maria Rilke, a poem which, significantly, Merton selected to teach his novices in his brief classes on poetry, we find a primitive expression of the questions, the doubts and despair, the answerless resolution Merton and other 4s know well. The panther he writes about is in the Paris Zoo, held in a captivity reminiscent of the compulsive prison 4s experience.

The Panther

From seeing the bars, his seeing is so exhausted
that it no longer holds anything anymore.
To him the world is bars, a hundred thousand
bars, and behind the bars, nothing.

The lithe swinging of that rhythmical easy stride
which circles down to the tiniest hub
is like a dance of energy around a point
in which a great will stands stunned and numb.

Only at times the curtains of the pupil rise
without a sound . . . then a shape enters,
slips through the tightened silence of the shoulder,
reaches the heart, and dies.[18]

Here we see the instinct of the 4 exaggerated into proud compulsion; a "great will" insists on circling its endlessly questioning energy until there are no questions left. Rather than yielding to the reality of human limitation, 4s insist on trying at least to understand why they must be limited, why they cannot be all-knowing. Again and again, something or someone slips through and "reaches the heart," offering the promise of an answer. Rilke's panther finds that this temporary distraction from anxious activity dies away and the compulsion returns. Merton found the same. He also found the only solution to this compulsion, temporary though it was, given Merton's instinct.

> Is there indeed a mysterious stream of reality and of meaning, running through the history of mankind? If so, who is called to discover it and travel with it? . . . What is the reality? The only answer is that it is Unknown, but that one knows it by unknowing.19

In the end, Merton's compulsive pride yields to humility. The search for answers can end only in caged futility. The thirst for meaning is only quenched when 4s set up their dwelling in the prison of their humanity, accepting that they are creatures.

Deaths and Births

I am aware of the need for constant self-revision and growth, leaving behind the renunciations of yesterday and yet in continuity with all my yesterdays. For to cling to the past is to lose my continuity with the past, since this means clinging to what is no longer there.

My ideas are always changing, always moving around one center, and I am always seeing that center from somewhere else.

Hence, I will always be accused of inconsistency. But I will no longer be there to hear the accusation.[1]

The life view of the 4 includes a panorama whose focus is on beginnings and endings, births and deaths. Because all of us assume, at least early in life, that everybody's way of looking at things is like our own, we often do not stop to put words on what our life view is, since we see it as the only one. Instead, we merely talk about experience within its framework. Learning to listen for clues to another person's angle on reality can make us more sensitive to concerns and issues other than our own.

When we listen to Thomas Merton and observe his life, we pick up subtleties that indicate how he scanned from past through present to the future. As he did so, he focused on endings or dyings. Doing so became the source of the melancholy we often detect in the words and even the voice of 4s. Indeed, for them all things do pass away, most of them never to return.

On the other hand, it is the awareness that when one thing ends another begins that is the root of the 4's hope. Without that hope, despair takes over—and for the compulsed 4, that is what happens—so that chronic depression follows. Some have said that 4s tend to clinical manic depression. This may be true. Probably 4s with a 3 wing are more prone to fluctuate back and forth between depression and the manic efforts to rise out of it. Those with a 5 wing may instead spend more of their lives on the depressive side.

Merton would probably have been in the former category. At least it seems that he built up his self-image and his persona in early life around a positive element, choosing to put forth for others as well as for himself that there was much in life to laugh at, even to be happy about. His letters and journals especially show the dynamic of this swing from cynical discouragement to its dismissal through humor. There are also strains of gratitude, always for the simple and natural, running through his autobiographical writings. In this more cheerful side of his life he moved out in relationship to community members and others with whom he was associated. The darker, less hopeful aspects—especially where these concerned attitudes toward himself—he kept in a more withdrawn privacy.

Merton knew he was considered inconsistent, as the opening quotation of this chapter from his journals indicates. Yet these apparent inconsistencies, these fluctuations of thought, feeling, and behavior, are very consistent when one understands his 4 personality. Feedback from persons who knew him well demonstrates a pattern of responses some might call unpredictable. Perhaps it could most accurately be said that Merton was predictably unpredictable. The enneagram provides an explanation for how and why Merton thought, felt, and acted as he did. It removes some of the mystery around certain events and relationships in his life which, although initially inexplicable, can be explained when one understands his personal dynamics as a 4.

The perception that life is a series of beginnings and endings seems to be a given for Merton. As a result, when we read him we need to look for subtle strains of that theme in his words; he would see little need to emphasize what, for him, was an obvious worldview. This assumption of the ever-repeated pattern of birth and death was woven into Merton's spirituality. It became for him, as it does for many 4s, an argument for life's significance.

Some of the 4 intensity and focus happens because events take on meaning in this rhythm; they are either initiating and new or they are summary and concluding. Either way, they are important. Another aspect of this dynamic follows: Each moment is special and unique; no moment is ordinary. Experience is but life and death, always and at every moment.

In *The Rule of Benedict*, the heart of Cistercian, Trappist spirituality, the Father of Western Monasticism tells us that the monk ought to keep death daily before his eyes.[2] This is a wholesome reminder for people who tend either to interior quietism or exterior overinvolvement. However, for Merton, as for other 4s, it can serve to increase compulsion, to accent something that needs no accenting. Put another way, for Merton, the instinct to see life and death everywhere could easily become compulsion and vice rather than the virtue Benedict was encouraging. It might be better advice for Merton and other 4s to be less intense, to get over the idea that everything is a life-and-death matter.

Such was the attitude that Merton eventually grew into. It involves following the old spiritual axiom, *Age quod agis*: do what you are doing. Toward the end of his life we find him heeding that advice. He described his periods of retreat in later years as just going about his daily existence, focusing on nothing more than carrying out what needed to be done with full attention.[3] He identified this attitude as a Zen approach.

What can be exaggerated in any one of us, however, can sometimes be a source of help for others. We see this with Merton when his grappling with life and death forced him to face the fears that come when distractions fall away and silence confronts.

> Those who love true life, therefore, frequently think about their death. Their life is full of a silence that is an anticipated victory over death. Silence, indeed, makes death our servant and even our friend. Thoughts and prayers that grow up out of the silent thought of death are like trees growing where there is water. They are strong thoughts, that overcome the fear of misfortune because they have overcome passion and desire. They turn the face of our soul, in constant desire, toward the face of Christ.[4]

The virtue that exists in carrying around a view of life's significance is caught in another passage. Once again it touches the 4 search for meaning, a search which ends for Merton in Christ.

> "Who are you when you do not exist?". . . When the question presents itself as an alien chill, it is saying something important: it is an accusation. It is telling me that I am too concerned with trivialities. That life is losing itself in trifles which cannot bear inspection in the face of death. That I am evading my chief responsibility. That I must begin to face the deepest of all decisions—the "answer of death"—the acceptance of the death sentence—and with joy, because of the victory of Christ.[5]

The rhythm of beginnings and endings was for Merton something more than mere preoccupation with swings from life to death and back again. He talks about the constant adjustment of thought to life and life to thought, and he sees it as an example of how we are "always growing, always experiencing new things in the old and old things in the new." He concludes that "thus life is always new."[6] Someone else might say that life is process and continual change. There is a nuance in the way 4s—and Merton—view and name process and change, however. The 4's perception of life as drama may specify his or her experience. On the stage of life, people and events have an entrance and an exit. They begin to influence the play for a time and then eventually stop doing so. Such comings and goings carry not only nostalgia for what has been, but also that pervasive melancholy characteristic of the 4 energy.

Correctly or incorrectly, Merton, like other 4s, projected his way of seeing things onto others. He wrote in 1962 about the nuclear age in which he was living:

> Surely one cannot feel comfortable or at ease in such a world. We are under sentence of death, an extinction without remembrance or memorial, and we cling to life and to the present. This causes bitterness and anguish. Christ will cure us of this clinging and then we will be free and joyful, even in the night.[7]

We see here again Christ as solution to the bitterness and pain, despair and discouragement of life.

Somehow Merton wrestled in his darkness until light came. Perhaps light triumphed because he could no longer struggle and so gave up efforts to do so; instead he waited for what he had learned through experience was an inevitable dawn. We do have some clue of the steps in Merton's personal process. It is found in his reflection on another fire watch, one written years after the first, which concluded *The Sign of Jonas*. This time he is novice master rather than in formation himself. He notes how so many of the men he had guided and was currently working with would move off-stage, as it were, out of the drama of his influence, even out of the monastery itself. He reminds himself that each one of these men is precious to God; that consideration suggests hope, not in the world around him, but once again in Christ.

Even though we have the power to destroy the whole world, life is stronger than the death instinct and love is stronger than hate. It does not make logical sense to be too hopeful, but once again this is not a question of logic and one does not look for signs of hope in the newspapers or the pronouncements of world leaders.[8]

Merton finds the hope that the world offers "so transparently hopeless that it moves one closer to despair."[9] Hope for him is clearly more than efforts to be optimistic. Death for Merton is a very real, a constant and palpable thing; it is an experience he cannot deny. There is no distraction for Merton, nor for other 4s, from this most terrifying and apparently final experience. The only option is to face the ultimate and walk into it with full consciousness. Merton found a surprise when, in the deaths of his life, he did just that:

> To "return to the Father" is not to "go back" in time, to roll up the scroll of history, or to reverse anything. It is a going forward, a going beyond, for merely to retrace one's steps would be a vanity on top of vanity, a renewal of the same absurdity in reverse.[10]

There was no running away from death for Merton because it was everywhere. There was only a need to find why death must be. More accurately, Merton found that death—personal, physical death—was just another beginning:

> Our destiny is to go on beyond everything, to leave everything, to press forward to the End and find in the End our Beginning, the ever-new Beginning that has no end.

> To obey him on the way, in order to reach him in whom I have begun, who is the key and the end—because he is the Beginning.[11]

Probably the most helpful solution to the ever-present problem of death which plunged Merton, as it does so many 4s, into heady analysis, was to be concrete. The rarefied atmosphere of hypothetical thinking evaporates in real life. To obey on life's way, Merton discovered, was all the reality he possessed. Finally, he learned that in fact he could only be in the present moment, living each successive one until that moment which would be his death.

Walking in the monastic graveyard served to conjure up for Merton more of the comings and goings of those he knew and with whom he had shared community life. Reminiscent of his fire watch reflections, we hear him consoling himself with the promise of the Christian message.

> Our dead rest in Christ. The cemetery is the symbol of Christ. To rest in Christ is to live (hence cypresses, green even in winter, are not supposed to suggest melancholy thoughts, as the Romantics imagined—just the opposite)! Yet the dead do not all live totally in Him. What Purgatory is we neither fully know nor fully understand. But why treat it as a preternatural reform school?[12]

Merton refused to get caught up in a reward-and-punishment type of Christianity, despite the prevalence of that attitude in his day. He simply did not know what the hereafter might be like, so he gave up trying to figure it out. Once again we see him abandoning analysis for mystery, acknowledging the limitation of his human mind. This theme of letting go is linked again with endings and beginnings in his introduction to *The Thomas Merton Reader*, a book he was somewhat reluctant to publish because readers might consider his thoughts on the subjects contained in the book finished ones. He handled his ambivalence this way:

> When a thought is done with, let go of it. When something has been written, publish it, and go on to something else. You may say the same thing again, some day, on a deeper level. No one need have a compulsion to be utterly and perfectly "original" in every word he writes. All that matters is

> that the old be recovered on a new plane, and be, itself a new reality. This, too, gets away from you. So let it get away.[13]

It is important to notice that Merton saw life's deaths and births developmentally; life did not have a linear movement for him but rather a spiral one. Dying and being reborn were progressive for Merton. They resulted in deeper wisdom, an increasingly more profound savoring of experience. For him, as for other 4s, there is consolation in this image, which gives meaning to life's pain. Death and birth as an enriching, descending spiral is a recurring image for Merton.

Probably no place more than in his poetry do we find Merton's search for the meaning of endings, especially those of a personal nature. Merton not only knew death concretely in the early loss of both parents, but also in that of his only brother, John Paul. Turning for consolation to Christ became an early theme; he saw his own and his brother's deaths as somehow one with Christ's: "Your cross and mine shall tell men still/ Christ died on each for both of us."[14] This response recurs as he grapples with the loss of friends, fellow monks, business associates, and even public figures. He may have expressed it best in the final chapter of *No Man Is an Island*:

> If, at the moment of our death, death comes to us as an unwelcome stranger, it will be because Christ also has always been to us an unwelcome stranger. For when death comes, Christ comes also, bringing us the everlasting life which He has bought for us by His own death. Those who love true life, therefore, frequently think about their death. Their life is full of a silence that is an anticipated victory over death. Silence, indeed, makes death our servant and even our friend. Thoughts and prayers that grow up out of the silent thought of death are like trees growing where there is water.[15]

It does not seem too remote a consideration to link Merton's Trappist vocation to his concern over and preoccupation with death and life. He tells us as much in the above passage. Monastic life forced his confrontation with this mystery. In the monastery he could not evade the issue; he had only a friendly silence in which to face not only death's terror but its apparent lack of meaning. Merton was too honest to walk away from what he found not only the ultimate, but the continually preoccupying question. On the last journey of his life, his Asian pilgrimage, Merton reflected:

> The marginal person, the monk, the displaced person, the prisoner, all these people live in the presence of death, which calls into question the meaning of life. He struggles with the fact of death in himself, trying to seek something deeper than death; because there is something deeper than death, and the office of the monk or the marginal person, the meditative person or the poet is to go beyond death even in this life, to go beyond the dichotomy of life and death and to be, therefore, a witness to life.[16]

Monastic life calls for faith, Merton continues. He also insists that there can be no faith without doubt. Some religions have called facing death, says Merton, the "great doubt." Fidelity to the search, once again in his last days, leads Merton to "a certitude which is very, very deep because it is not his own personal certitude, it is the certitude of God Himself in us."[17]

Merton returns once more to the present, the place of redemption for him as it is for everybody. For 4s, including Merton, that present moment between past and future is where they quiet their questions with the concrete and the simple and the sensory. Everything holds still in the silent reality that Christ is in that moment; the one who died and rose long ago also brings both death and life together in the individual's personal existence shared with his. In a small book published several years after his death, Merton talks about Christ, the God of all history, and of our personal history:

> Christ is the Lord
> of a history that moves.
> He not only holds
> the beginning and the end
> in his hands,
> but he is in history with us,
> walking ahead of us
> to where we are going.[18]

That Merton recognized how narcissistic and selfish his preoccupation with this issue could be seems evident in what he names as the solution for letting go of grappling with death:

So we are called not only to believe
that Christ once rose from the dead,
thereby proving that he was God;
we are called to experience the Resurrection
in our own lives by following Christ
who lives in us if we love one another.
And our love for one another means
involvement in one another's history.[19]

Once again we find Merton coming around to love as a solution to despair. The only way he knows of to break out of the cycle of death and life is to stay in the present and respond to it. Response needs to be made to the human beings one encounters. Only they can put to rest the struggle to find meaning that death and endings create. As Christ lives within a Merton who struggles, Christ lives as well in everyone else. The answer Merton found, because he was faithful to his life/death question and unwilling to run away from the silence that forced it, is loving presence here and now to the presence of others.

Merton never completely carried off the habitual practice of such presence in his own life. Indeed, for various reasons, no one ever does. Because he did not, he continually returned to issues of death and birth. His Christ was a risen one, but also a Christ who suffered on the cross of Merton's own never completely whole person and of other persons' limitations, too.

The risen life is not easy;
it is also a dying life.
The presence of the Resurrection
in our lives means
the presence of the Cross,
for we do not rise with Christ
unless we also first die with him.
It is by the Cross that we enter
the dynamism of creative transformation,
the dynamism of resurrection and renewal,
the dynamism of love.[20]

Merton tells us here how he cut through his compulsive preoccupation with death and life. Love was his final answer to his obsessive and persistent questioning. It was this love of Christ and of human beings that gave him sometimes rest, sometimes contentment with his lack of rest. Engagement with persons cut through analysis to prove to him that simple living is the resurrection that triumphs over death.

The Spirit of Jesus

According to enneagram theory, the Divine is manifested in the many different aspects of creation. Applied more personally, each human enneagram type especially incarnates something of the Creator. In Christian terms, each triad and each space within that triad, resonates in its energy with a different Person in the Trinity of Divine Persons. For 8/9/1s it is the Life-Giver and Nourisher, the Father/Mother/Creator God to whom they witness, each type in the triad nuancing that witness. The Son of God becomes the inspiration for the 5/6/7 triad and each space in it. The Spirit of Jesus alive in the here and now takes flesh in the flesh of 2/3/4s, a little differently depending on the number in the triad.[1]

These particular emphases do not mean, of course, that the two other Persons hold no significance. What they do mean is that there is not only a real affinity for one of the Persons, but that there is also apparent collaboration with the Person in the gift one offers. The individual's energy and the Divine Energy attributed to that Person are intertwined in ways that are evident. Each of us makes flesh in a special way an aspect of divinity in accord with that member of the Trinity especially described with characteristics like our own.

Thomas Merton was steeped in the Christian view of Trinity from his earliest days. He translated life into those terms because, whether living as a non-Catholic or Catholic Christian, God in three Persons had always been the way the Divine was presented to him. When he talked about his life, his call, and his mission, therefore, he did so relating not so much to the theoretical doctrine of the Trinity as to the personal God it describes. Over and over again in his writings we hear him speak about both the spirit within the individual person and the Spirit of Jesus alive in the present times within all creation.

The 2/3/4 journey is a journey home, as we have already said. That means for them that the inner spirit or self or world must be found in order to find God, however God is named. Karlfried von Durckheim describes the felt sense of this union with God:

> Just as Divine Being, striving to manifest itself, is present within us, so the experience of union with it becomes at the same time an experience of our own being. And, equally, the experience of our own being is an experience of our oneness with Divine being. If we have once become conscious of ourselves in our own essence, we have become conscious of our union with Transcendental Being. We must, therefore, search for that Being which liberates us and inwardly determines our form, and thus discover within ourselves an "immanent transcendence" far beyond the frontiers of our little ego.[2]

Merton used similar, if particularly Christian, words to describe that felt sense:

> According to St. Paul, the inmost self of each one of us is our "spirit," or "pneuma," or in other words the Spirit of Christ, indeed Christ himself, dwelling in us. "For me to live is Christ." And by the spiritual recognition of Christ in our brother, we become "one in Christ" through the "bond of the Spirit." According to the mysterious phrase of St. Augustine, we then become "One Christ loving himself."[3]

The experience of this oneness with the divine in the depths of the self, as Merton says, is truly "mysterious." He cannot explain it any more than Augustine can. Undeniable as this experience may he, he knows it defies analysis or articulation. True to form, he asks his questions:

> The Holy Spirit has a name which is known only to the Father and the Son. But can it be that when he takes upon himself, and unites us to the Father through the Son, he takes upon

> himself, in us, our own secret name? Is it possible that his ineffable name becomes our own? Is it possible that we can come to know, for ourselves, the name of the Holy Spirit when we receive from him the revelation of our own identity in him? I can ask these questions, but not answer them.[4]

At that time, Merton displayed boldness in even admitting he thought about the possibility of being merged with God. By stating these considerations in the form of questions, Merton avoids any accusation of heresy. Mystics before and since—especially, perhaps, mystics from the 2/3/4 triad—sometimes make theologians wonder just what they mean by union with God. Another description of this characteristic 4 emphasis on the inner spirit/Spirit may serve to clarify. The position and role Christ holds for Merton, as for others in this space, add a dimension to the experience of God within.

> [The Resurrection and Ascension of Christ] meant that in each one of us the inner self was now able to be awakened and transformed by the action of the Holy Spirit, and this awakening would not only enable us to discover our true identity "in Christ" but would also make the living and Risen Savior present in us. Hence the importance of the Divinity of Christ—for it is as God-Man that he is risen from the dead and as God-Man that he is capable of living and acting in us all by his spirit, so that in him we are not only our true personal selves but are also one Mystical Person, one Christ.[5]

This Christ of both Merton and the 2/3/4 life view differs from the inspirational model. It is not drawn from the past memory of the God who walked the earth two thousand years ago. Merton's Christ, the Christ of his enneagram stance, is alive now within the spirit of those who live and breathe today. While he is careful to maintain that the Divine and human natures are distinct, he adds that "the gap between God and man has been bridged by the Incarnation, and in us the gap is bridged by the invisible presence of the Holy Spirit."[6] The Incarnate Son is one with the Spirit in each person. The effect of this union is that "Christ is really present in us, more present than if He were standing before us visible to our bodily eyes."[7] It is this Spirit of Jesus who lives now in our own time, in every time.

The Spirit is the source of the love Merton keeps coming around to as the only answer to life's questions. Living in love for him is something concrete, particular, and very real. It is the fruit of contemplative awareness, and as such it is neither detached nor distant. He says that love is guided by the Spirit of Christ. It "is not something pale and without passion, but a love in which passion has been elevated and purified by selflessness, so that it no longer follows the inspiration of mere natural instinct."[8] It dissolves boundaries between people by dissolving boundaries of judgment within the self. It is a compassion, a suffering with others, that is the fruit of living one's own life with the passion of honest humility and self-acceptance.

> The man with the "sacred" view is one who does not need to hate himself, and is never afraid or ashamed to remain with his own loneliness, for in it he is at peace, and through it he can come to the presence of God. . . . Such a man is able to help other men to find God in themselves, educate them in confidence by the respect he is able to feel for them . . . helping them to put up with themselves, until they become interiorly quiet and learn to see God in the depths of their own poverty.[9]

One of Merton's favorite topics is mercy. He walks around Old Testament stories describing the Hebrew *chesed* or mercy that melts guilt away and leaves only innocence, innocence within other people and one's own self. Here is the place of peace to which the Spirit leads us. It is here that oneness in Christ's body becomes something real.

> [God] has also given us his *chesed* in the Person of his Spirit. The Paraclete is the full, inexpressible mystery of *chesed*. So that in the depths of our own being there is an inexhaustible spring of mercy and of love. Our own being has become love. Our own self has become God's love for us, and it is full of Christ, of chesed. But we must face it and accept it. We must accept ourselves and others as *chesed*. We must be to ourselves and to others signs and sacraments of mercy.[10]

Pouring ourselves out indiscriminately to those God has placed in our lives is the unselfish and unself-conscious folly "which is the work of his Spirit."[11] Only helplessness and need, our own and that of other people, are to govern the mercy we offer self and neighbor. The result of letting God claim us in this way Merton calls new life, new light, and the passage from death to life. It takes place because of the intervention of the Divine Spirit.[12] Thus, the Spirit is alive and active in every age, not only in human beings as a whole, but in the individual spirit, the true self of each person. Merton insists that each member of "the church" possesses this Spirit "to open his eyes to the mystery of God's presence and action in his own life."[13] This is not a collective experience, but a deeply individual and personal one.

When asked to deliver a final prayer to the Calcutta Conference, Merton chose this same theme, obviously one which came to his mind in ecumenical settings. He prayed:

> Oh, God, in accepting one another wholeheartedly, fully, completely, we accept you, and we thank you, and we adore you, and we love you with our whole being, because our being is in your being, our spirit is rooted in your spirit. Fill us then with love, and let us be bound together with love as we go on our diverse ways, united in this one spirit which makes you present in the world, and which makes you witness to the ultimate reality that is love.[14]

Awesome as this gift is, life in the Spirit is not exempt from the need for thoughtful discernment. Merton reminds us that "to judge by an entirely new and hidden criterion: by the unseen life of the Holy Spirit" is "fraught with great risk."[15] How does one distinguish what is illusion and what is grace? How does one know that one is not involved in the work of darkness? Merton suggests that the Holy Spirit's interventions are seldom completely at variance with traditional norms. Nevertheless, the life of the contemplative is radical and honest, and tension rises from that fact. He finds it unfortunate that "the modern tendency in the West has been to completely equate the 'will of God' and the 'action of the Holy Spirit' with the common and universal standard."[16]

When prophetic persons—and surely Merton must have been thinking of himself—examine whether their personal energy is coming from darkness or light, the criteria include manifesting more self-effacing characteristics than proud, disobedient ones. "If a person is really guided by the Holy Spirit, grace itself will take care of eccentricity, self-will, and vain show, for exterior simplicity and obscurity are signs of grace."[17] Ultimately, the Spirit bows to community decision, and that is how one distinguishes genuine spirit/Spirit from egoistic willfulness.

For Merton, all of the time since Christ physically left the earth is "the time of the kingdom, the time of the Spirit, the time of 'the end.'"[18] This means for him that human rebirth transcends cultures and dissolves boundaries. Such a life involves experiential faith at the root of our lives. Connor quotes Merton's description of the metanoia that will be ours, individually and collectively; such metanoia is to "deliver ourselves utterly and totally into the hands of Christ and his love." When we do we find that metanoia, having let go, we will "be transformed in his time, in his way, by his Spirit."[19] This life is a silent one; it is a life of mystery, a wisdom "which is hidden, but revealed by the Spirit of God. And the Spirit Himself is hidden. Nor is His voice heard with the ears."[20] Only the heart can reveal this Divine Presence.

For Merton, it is the monastic life that provides the temple of the Silent Spirit of God, "whose work will . . . consist not so much in making and changing and unmaking things, or in repairing them, as in healing the world with the blessing of a silence that recognizes and fulfills . . . the silence hidden in all things."[21] In other words, unity with the Spirit is a contemplative task, one that calls a person to place hope and expectation in God rather than human solutions or situations, "in the Holy Spirit and not in laws." Any laws can and need to be under the guidance of the Spirit.[22]

Merton sees the monastery as a place where the Spirit rules in special ways. Depending less on the support of legislation in black and white, the community puts its trust in the love and grace of Christ. Believing that the Holy Spirit has granted to the community to be a source of light and life, and acting in a spirit of openness and sincerity, the brothers under their Father seek to work out together actual solutions to their problems.[23]

This may sound like an abstract or idealized picture of monastery life, Rather, it is yet another summary statement of what Merton had learned experientially. He was day after day at Chapter meetings; he shared his ideas and the feelings around them on committees and in one-on-one encounters with his brothers. Idealistically as it may be expressed, what he talks about here became the underpinning of his concrete monastic life. It sustained his conviction that monasticism had value, not only objectively, but for him.

Merton trusted that the unique depths of each monk's private contemplative life in the Spirit merge with the Spirit's action in the whole monastic community. He was grounded in the felt sense of that Spirit, discerning as he himself discerned, and as his fellow monks discerned, and as they did so together. Merton believed the Spirit's presence extended to everyone. He had confidence in the life with which the Spirit empowers all on life's journey. This life infused both personal and communal decisions. Late in his life he said:

> If we trust God to act in us, God will act in us. This is how our lives become prophetic. Prophecy is not technique, it is not about telling someone else what to do. If we are completely open to the Holy Spirit, then the Spirit will be able to lead us where God wants us to go. Going along that line, our lives will be prophetic.
>
> It's so simple, and it's never been anything else. Renewal consists, above all, in recovering this truth.[24]

It all came around for Merton to a genuine living of one's life, individually and as a member of communities. To do this is to enter the prophetic life of the Spirit in each person. This prophetic presence of the Spirit is as real now as it was in biblical times when tongues of fire symbolized spirit/Spirit in each and all on Pentecost. Rather than a one-time event, Pentecost recurs in every age. Jesus continues to live through his Spirit, says Merton, until the "end times" actually do end, once and for all. Until then, human beings are not alone on this earth.

Thomas Merton talks and writes to us about our individual spirit joined with the Divine Spirit because this reality best describes God's presence for him. Spiritual life makes the most sense to Merton looked at and expressed this way. It does so because of his 4 life view.

Oneness in the Spirit

> For the good person to realize that it is better to be whole than to be good is to enter on a strait and narrow path compared to which his previous rectitude was flowery license.[1]

In discussing Thomas Merton's openness to Eastern thought, Parker Palmer makes use of this telling quotation. It is significant because it links two aspects of Merton's spirituality: the interior personal boundaries dissolving into a single unity, and the openness to receive other people beyond boundaries of culture and belief. The two are inseparable in human transformation. Said another way, it is impossible to embrace one's own reality without embracing others with similar mercy.

Growth is natural to all living things; life demands that we grow. Human persons, however, can interfere with their development and flowering. They do so when they feel helpless and impotent, unable to manage their personal existence. The message of dependence is one all children learn. The struggle for independence and personal control becomes synonymous with the struggle for life. No wonder it is difficult as life continues to learn to let go into the rhythm and pull of a greater reality than the self.

It is as though every human being places boulders in the stream of life early on and then spends later years removing them. St. Paul describes this human process and what it leads to when he says that we are slaves to the fear of death (Heb 2:15). We resist yielding to a life experience we cannot predict. Since we do not trust life/Life, we attempt to control it, to shape it, and we shape ourselves into controllable people in the process. We are afraid to risk the unknown and the unpredictable.

Holding ourselves off from life in order to be in charge of it creates boundaries. We divide reality into good and bad depending on what in ourselves wins us belonging and what does not. We make an enemy of perceptions or feelings or behaviors we cannot control. We delineate an inner and outer world with sometimes opposing characteristics. We distinguish masculine and feminine and choose which we will identify with, to the exclusion of the other. We separate body from spirit and judge that these are in opposition.

In the process of judging, rewarding, and sentencing aspects of ourselves we also include people and circumstances. Soon there are at least enclosures, if not armed camps, all over our lives. There is comforting simplicity in this world we shape. A world of black and white reduces anxiety; we need only make the obvious choice. Ambivalence is at a minimum.

In adulthood life gets more complicated. Experience raises questions about what we saw as good and bad. We find we are not God, not in complete control. Even more so, we see the illusions and delusions that said we ever could be. Our enslavement to one point of view becomes impossible. We are drawn more and more into that stream where everything begins to flow together. In retrospect, when we look back from a freer place, we thank life/Life for this gift that makes us more one within ourselves and one with others.

The 4 is assisted in this process, as we all are, with particular gifts. For 4s these include a natural disregard for legality, an inability to dismiss—and an eventual taking comfort—in the sensuous and physical parts of themselves. There is a parallel conviction that at the core human experience is universal.

The first of these characteristics allows 4s to set aside those rules and regulations society has formed out of this divisive tendency we all initially possess. When experience signals something life-giving, 4s easily put aside restrictions against whatever seems to block what they would call growth. This instinct makes 4s feel little guilt about overlooking legislation or breaking laws, except those that allow this growth and change.

The second characteristic, accepting the physical part of their persons, opens 4s to a bodily response to reality. While they can be caught in analysis—working at perceptions—they rarely are governed by the detached or merely theoretical. What comes through the senses, especially through sexual response, speaks symbolically to 4s and so takes on spiritual significance. The sacredness of the physical is a given for 4s.

The third characteristic that breaks down boundaries as 4s move into the second part of life flows from increasing experience of the passion each person endures and cooperates with if growth is to happen. This passion moves to compassion, suffering with, that some have called a special fruit of 4 transformation. Human experiences are shared by all, 4s believe. No matter what words a person chooses to describe feelings, what vocabulary to explain beliefs, what ways to articulate discernment, the fundamental, underlying occurrence is the same for everyone.

It follows for 4s that cultures and religions create boundaries only when superficially viewed. Speaking from a deeper place all people are able to communicate because at the center human experiences are shared; we really can understand one another.

Merton, like the rest of us, drew boundaries in himself. The autobiography, written at a time when he was still very much involved in ego-development, has many themes along the lines of division. Body and spirit, good and evil, action and contemplation, world and monastery are a few of the dichotomies he sees. Already, however, he is questioning the degree to which it is possible and even wise to attempt such separation. Merton's 4 gift of allowing feeling and perception and action to come together in an entire organic response is already evident in this book. Like the disciplined new convert he is, Merton dutifully works within what he sees as the Catholic framework. His outlook is consciously other-worldly; he thinks it has to be now that he is both Catholic and monk. However, after only a few years at Gethsemani he can write these words describing his earlier dynamics:

> We drove into town . . . and all the while I wondered how I would react at meeting once again, face to face, the wicked world. I met the world and I found it no longer so wicked after all. Perhaps the things I had resented about the world when I left it were defects of my own that I had projected upon it. [2]

Yet, there is more here for Merton than merely becoming less fearful and broader in his views. He is convinced that openness to himself and the world are vital:

> There is something in the depths of our being that hungers for wholeness and finality. Because we are made for eternal

> life, we are made for an act that gathers up all the powers and capacities of our being and offers them simultaneously and forever to God.[3]

Already we see a Merton who realizes that placing reality into opposing categories not only will not work, but is contrary to nature and, therefore, counter-productive to genuine contemplation. The spiritual life is already showing Merton that the source of unity beyond division is God. In Jesus the most amazing thing happens: the boundary between Creator and creation is bridged.

> The Word, in the Father, is not only transcendentally removed at an infinite distance above us, but also and at the same time he is immanent in our world, first of all by nature as the creator of the world, but then in a special dynamic and mystical presence as the Savior, Redeemer and Lover of the world. The point is then to know how we enter into contact with this special presence of the Lord in his cosmos and in our hearts.[4]

Entering into this divine contact "is effected by the Holy Spirit," Merton tells us.[5] This is another way of saying that the contemplative life prepares us to see everything in God. Merton distinguishes between this contemplative attitude and an ascetical one in another passage:

> If we try to do things ascetically, we may do them, but it usually ends up as patchwork. . . . If prayer is something that we do, it's going to be patchwork, because I am a divided person, a divided being. . . . Self-conquest is something I'm going to do; I've made up my mind to conquer myself. Then I must fight myself. I'm divided.[6]

Clearly Merton sees the fundamental sin, Adam's sin in the biblical myth, as a loss of contemplative wholeness.

> The idea is that Adam was a contemplative before the Fall and that the essence of the Fall was a choice of a life of multiplicity over a life of unity. This may be Platonism and it may be all wet, but there's a certain psychological truth in it.[7]

It is a loss, too, of the sacredness of all things when they are seen as separated from rather than united in the divine.

Slavery to the fear of death for Merton, as for other 4s, includes facing apparent nothingness and finding being and therefore holiness there.

> The truly sacred attitude toward life is in no sense an escape from the sense of nothingness that assails us when we are left alone with ourselves. On the contrary, it penetrates into that darkness and that nothingness, realizing that the mercy of God has transformed our nothingness into his temple and believing that in our darkness his light has hidden itself. Hence the sacred attitude is one which does not recoil from our own inner emptiness, but rather penetrates into it with awe and reverence, and with the awareness of mystery.[8]

The journey into the darkness of contemplation results in seeing all that exists as a holy unity. This unity includes other people as conversion continues and boundaries created in egoistic pursuits fall away:

> The contemplative is not isolated in himself, but liberated from his external and egotistic self by humility and purity of heart—therefore there is no longer any serious obstacle to simple and humble love of other men. . . . The more we are alone with God the more we are with one another, in darkness, yet a multitude.9

In another place Merton states that "the true contemplative is not less interested than others in normal life, not less concerned with what goes on in the world, but more interested, more concerned . . . and [can] enter more directly into the pure actuality of human life."[10] Merton outlines clearly and simply the prelude to this contemplation:

> The first thing that you have to do, before you start thinking about such a thing as contemplation is to try to recover your basic natural unity, to reintegrate your compartmentalized being into a coordinated and simple whole, and learn to live as a unified human person. This means that you have to bring back together the fragments of your distracted existence so that when you say "I" there is really someone present to support the pronoun you have uttered.[11]

Even the boundary between nature and supernature dissolve; through the grace of Christ, nature in its very being is recognized to be "supernatural." The miracle of the Incarnation brings this union about.[12] All of human nature for Merton is good. Anne Carr notes that as Merton explored the meaning of self, he not only affirmed but embraced the world and its materiality and joyously accepted the body with its limits and contingencies.[13]

He moves even more deeply beneath the conviction that all things are supernatural to the realization that creation itself is a grace.[14] Merton did not need to baptize creation somehow to make it holy; he found, as Heschel has said, that being is its own blessing. Carr calls Merton's view of life without boundaries of nature/supernature—the fusion of religious and psychological language—his particular genius.[15]

From this profound base in contemplative simplicity Merton was able to dialogue with the East. His ability to do so was perhaps his greatest contribution to contemporary spirituality. He met the East from his monastic experience, seeing monastic life as providing "a real possibility of contact on a deep level."[16] He notes that as structures, as systems, and as religions, Zen and Catholicism mix no better than oil and water.[17] Elsewhere he uses another boundary-making image when he says that comparing Christianity and Zen "would almost be like trying to compare mathematics and tennis."[18] The secret, he says, in what we might call ecumenical dialogue is to approach such exchange contemplatively, from the realm of "mystical liberty" beyond egoism.[19]

This contemplative base explains the value of monastic interaction between East and West for Merton. A monastic approach is rooted in a common contemplative experience and avoids the trap Merton describes for us.

> Now the reader with a Judeo-Christian background of some sort (and who in the West does not still have some such background?) will naturally be predisposed to misinterpret Zen because he will instinctively take up the position of one who is confronting a "rival system of thought" or a "competing ideology" or an "alien world view" or more simply "a false religion." Anyone who adopts such a position makes it impossible for himself to see what Zen is, because he assumes in advance that it must be something that it expressly refuses to be.[20]

Merton does not dismiss complexities in East/West dialogue, however. He asks his characteristic questions courageously and finds that he has no sure answers for them. He warns lest we view the East/West exchange as more than an attempt to better mutual understanding and a means to provide significant clues about the interior life its mystics put into words.[21] Perhaps his most important contribution to this East/West dialogue is precisely his 4 awareness that human experience is universal. At the experiential level unity can take place.

Such an attitude was simply a given for Merton as a 4. He realized, however, that not all people shared his view. Consequently, he made no assumptions but carefully explained his own outlook, notably in relationship to Zen.

> It cannot be repeated too often: in understanding Buddhism it would be a great mistake to concentrate on the "doctrine," the formulated philosophy of life, and to neglect the experience, which is absolutely essential, the very heart of Buddhism.[22]

Despite the fact that Christianity is a religion of revelation and delivered to us in words and statements, Merton reminds his readers:

> This obsession with doctrinal formulas, juridical order and ritual exactitude has often made people forget that the heart of Catholicism, too, is a living experience of unity in Christ which far transcends all conceptual formulations . . . Catholicism is the taste and experience of eternal life.[23]

Merton the artist is fascinated by the symbolic presentation of unity found in Japanese art. There is "no divorce between art and life or art and spirituality." Instead, they "are brought together and inseparably fused."[24] Merton the monk sees "the art of tea," a highly formalized ritual for presenting and drinking tea, of superlative interest to monks everywhere. "It depicts a monastic style of life in which art, spiritual experience and communal, personal relationships enter together into an expression of God in this world."[25]

Once again we find Merton coming back to the concrete experience of love as the greatest unifier. He remarks how profoundly moved he was when he heard Dr. Suzuki's words at the end of the conversation on which much of *Zen and the Birds of Appetite* was based: "The most important thing is love!" Merton adds: "Truly *prajna* and *karuna* are one (as the Buddhist says), or *caritas* (love) is indeed the highest knowledge."[26]

In an essay about East/West dialogue, Merton outlines what he sees as the four great needs of the human person. As he puts words on what he calls the third need we hear quite clearly expressed his distinctly 4 worldview.

> Third: Man's need for a whole and integral experience of his own self on all its levels, bodily as well as imaginative, emotional, intellectual, spiritual. There is no place for the cultivation of one part of human consciousness, one aspect of human experience, at the expense of the others, even on the pretext that what is cultivated is sacred and all the rest profane. A false and divisive "sacredness" or "supernaturalism" can only cripple man.[27]

It seems to have been that need for whole and integral experience and the search to satisfy it that led Merton to Eastern dialogue. Eventually he traveled there physically as well as in perception and affection. Final wholeness was facilitated by this call and desire. It was executed by the curious death that completed Merton's personal unity and plunged him into the love beyond the search. Some have pointed to the irony of Merton's dying so far from his monastery. Perhaps there was a simple appropriateness about it as well as symbolism for monastics of the West. Merton seems to have hinted at that when speaking in Calcutta two months before his death.

> I think it is above all important for a Westerner like myself to learn what little they can from Asia, in Asia. I think we must seek not merely to make superficial reports about the Asian traditions, but to live and share those traditions, as far as we can, by living them in their traditional milieu. . . . I believe that some of us need to do this in order to improve the quality of our own monastic life and even to help in the task of monastic renewal which has been undertaken within the Western Church.[28]

Merton himself never had a chance to do any extended living in that traditional milieu of Asia. By his final journey, however, he has prepared the way for others to do so. Even more, beyond the monastic tradition he has opened the East to countless persons who are willing to meet Asians as he did, beneath doctrine and at the level where people live out their beliefs day to day.

The Way to Hope

Hope is born out of despair. Despair comes to us when all the avenues of possibility and plan have been explored and are dead-ends. For 4s, script writers and organizers of the future by instinct, despair is accompanied by an additional dimension; it tells them that what they do best fails them in the long run. The future cannot be controlled, and that future includes relationships, work, and ultimately sickness and death.

There is only the present moment, 4s come to realize, and it is a realization that leaves them feeling trapped and enslaved. No longer can the now be made more interesting and energizing and possible by embellishing it with future fantasies. Eventually 4s must face that there is nothing to do but face the moment. No longer can they delude themselves by looking back at what was or forward at what might be. There is only the straightforward—and therefore the contemplative—encounter with the only life any of us has: life in the present.[1]

The fact that one lives in time and that time is a sequence of moments from past into future forces 4s to seek life the only place it truly exists. Rather than seeing the present as a narrow crack between that past and future, 4s who grow in contemplation learn to savor the simple, ordinary realities of now with the result that each successive moment takes on dimension. For Merton, tasting with his senses and relishing what his eyes and ears and nose and skin surface and taste offered held him in the moment and prevented him from flying off into optimistic or pessimistic possibilities of life down the line. His personal littleness and limitation became more and more evident to him as this contemplative practice deepened. He tasted his creatureliness in this way; he discovered that, were he to open to all of the present moment, he would have all of life he was capable of processing.

At the same time he learned a dimension beyond the temporal. He found that each small thing, if one honors and respects its existence, is more than linear. A deeper dimension of reality replaces the more superficial one which is all a panoramic view of past/present/future affords. Another way of saying this is to acknowledge that Merton grew into a personal contemplative life, as distinct from merely being a member of a contemplative community. The journey by which he arrived at contemplation resulted in a breakthrough from the surface elements of each moment to their deeper significance.

There is a nuance describing this triadic reality for the 4 space. Hope is the conviction that if one is faithful to the apparently empty, trivial, meaningless experiences of the day-to-day, one discovers what is so; one discovers one's being; one knows what it is to be alive. It is not that 4s need to spend their lives looking for significance. To do so for them is a trap which only feeds their compulsive seriousness and intensity. It is rather that they need to relax in the trust that to respond as each moment calls for is what life is about. Such trust in life is hope. It relieves 4s from pumping up every minute with dramatic or romantic significance. It puts them in touch with reality. Only the contemplative 4 knows this experience, and Thomas Merton was one such contemplative.

This dynamic is the heart of Merton's teaching on the true and false self. For him, the challenge of human beings—and he says this from a 4 perspective—is to face the depths of their poverty as creatures. In their humanity they find not only nothingness, but even more shockingly, falsity. The "word of God,"[2] which each person is, becomes covered with overlays of self-creation. For 4s—and for Merton therefore—these overlays include characteristic illusions and delusions of romanticism and drama. Life is not only a stage, but one on which fantasy plays are enacted about deprivation and self-exaltation, among other things. Someone else, writing from a different worldview, would say all of this differently, of course. Building up a larger-than-life caricature of positive and negative circumstances adds flavor to the lies 4s tell themselves and others.

Merton talks about the dread that comes when one fails to accept one's inner truth, a dread that is a "hell of mercy" because it reveals the nothingness, the poverty we cannot embrace but God has always known and embraced.[3] Littleness and hiddenness, perhaps his ways to talk about the simple and ordinary, look like ignorance and despair. In fact, they are a despair that is the mask of perfect hope. Hope is only found in a silence beyond life's apparent significance.

> To be banished from the world of men by the silence of God means, in the end, not that one finds a new and mysterious universe to live in, but that the old, ordinary universe, with all its shabby poverty, while remaining perfectly ordinary, perfectly real, perfectly poor, becomes transfigured from within by a silence which is the supreme and infinite "poverty" of an infinitely rich and generous God![4]

Donald Grayston notes the change in Merton's image of contemplation from that of a citadel to a wide, impregnable country.[5] Grayston sees both images representing security in the Spirit's life, what we might call hope. The first suggests an enclosure; the second, openness and freedom. The first indicates separateness; the second, a widening out to our environment.[6] We seem to find here once again that dynamic in Merton where moving away from self-concern offers a promise of life. The more Merton grovels in anxious narcissism, the more he becomes depressed and despairing. When he lets go into each moment's promise, allowing himself to be taken up into its experience, his personal limitation is forgotten in the overwhelming power and energy of the Creator of all.

In the colloquial French expression *point vierge* (quite literally the virgin point), Merton finds his answer about his personal value, that of other people, and the rest of creation. Beyond one's efforts, no matter how noble, rests the reality of simply being. He speaks of the birds near his hermitage who open their eyes with "an awakening question"; their condition asks if it is time for them to "be." The Creator answers simply, "Yes." Each morning, he notes, is like the first morning of creation.[7] One might add that he saw each moment as a new creation, saw the eternal in the temporal, the timeless in time. At the point of pure truth, where God sparks and disposes of our lives and which we can never touch, there is life. Out of this place, therefore, hope springs.

> This little point of nothingness and of absolute poverty is the pure glory of God in us. . . . It is like a pure diamond, blazing with the invisible light of heaven. It is in everybody,

> and if we could see it we would see these billions of points of light coming together in the face and blaze of a sun that would make all the darkness and cruelty of life vanish completely. . . . I have no program for this seeing. It is only given. But the gate of heaven is everywhere.[8]

It is a short path for Merton from this point where life and Life coincide to the place of compassion. Still again we hear a Merton who moves out from narrowed despair, through self-forgetfulness to the loving, free embrace of others:

> "*Temps vierge*"—not a blank to be filled or an untouched space to be conquered and violated, but a space which can enjoy its own potentialities and hopes and its own presence to itself. One's own time. But not dominated by one's own ego and its demands. Hence open to others—compassionate time, rooted in the sense of common illusion and in criticism of it.9

If growth in contemplation is growth in truth—in no longer needing to be lied to about anything, as DeMello has put it— Merton finds confrontation with the once hidden, once denied, a possibility. The mercy of God, the *chesed*, makes such confrontation endurable. As we experience this embrace of the loving Creator, we can be more open and free, because we are delivered from the threat of facing what we cannot bear. Despair loses its power. Nothing and no one can instill fear any longer. In God's gaze

> they see that it is love and that they are innocent. (Their flight and the confusion of their own fear make them guilty.) The *chesed* of God is truth. It is infallible strength. It is the love by which he seeks and chooses his chosen and binds them to himself.[10]

This *chesed*, this mercy, is linked for Merton with hope: "*Chesed* (mercy) . . . is the power that binds us to God because He has promised us mercy and will never fail in his promise. For He cannot fail."[11] For Merton, God the Creator of life breaks through time's limitations and the limitations of all who live in time. This is so because God's fidelity lies in the very act of creating us and everyone else; the fact that we exist gives rise to hope.

On the last page of *The Sign of Jonas* Merton closes his Fire Watch prose/poem with the Voice of God, who says:

> What was vile has become precious. What is now precious was never vile. I have always known the vile as precious: for what is vile I know not at all.
>
> What was cruel has become merciful. What is now merciful was never cruel. . . . Mercy within mercy within mercy. I have forgiven the universe without end, because I have never known sin.[12]

Here we find the source of Merton's hope. It is the bottomless poverty of himself and all creation that empties itself out for the Creator to fill. Everything is possible from such a perspective, such a faith.

> What was fragile has become powerful. I loved what was most frail. I looked upon what was nothing. I touched what was without substance, and within what was not, I am.[13]

Lest so transcendent a realization remove Merton from the here and now, he closes this chapter and the whole book with this next sentence: "There are drops of dew that show like sapphires in the grass as soon as the great sun appears, and leaves stir behind the hushed flight of an escaping dove."[14] There is poetry here to be sure, but it is a poetry grounded in the sense experience of the moment. In the "I am," the very existence of everything that is, there is hope. Better put, the "I am" is, in itself, where life/Life is found.

It is a small step—and Merton took it—between this interior confidence and the confidence to be extended to other people. He talks about the "sacred" view, the contemplative view, life lived where time and eternity intersect in the present. The person who lives fully in the moment opens up fearlessly and

> in his dealing with others he has no need to identify them with their sins and condemn them for their actions: for he is able, in them also, to see below the surface and to guess at the presence of the inner and innocent self that is the image of God . . . [God] is capable of allaying some of their fears and helping them to put up with themselves, until they become interiorly quiet and learn to see God in the depths of their own poverty.[15]

There can hardly be anything written about Merton that does not include the experience he had days before his death at Plonnaruwa. The direct, uncomplicated experience of reality/Reality he had, before the large Buddha figures there, blended sense experience, one simple moment, and life/Life. It stirred in him his characteristic response: compassion. It is as though, when he could be fully in the present, something of God's creative mercy infused him. He tells us that looking at those figures he was "suddenly almost forcibly jerked clean out of the habitual, half-tied vision of things, and an inner clearness, clarity" was undeniable.

In that moment he saw why he had set out for Asia, possibly why he had made his whole life journey. Finally, as never before, being-in-the-now has fully occurred. He says, "I have now seen and have pierced through the surface and have got beyond the shadow and the disguise." His disembodied heart has become an enfleshed one, and the feeling he is aware of is compassion. Indeed, "everything is compassion"; he is swimming in it.[16]

Shortly after, on the day of his death, he tells other men and women, monastics like himself, what it means to live in hope.

> The monk is a man who has attained or is about to attain or seeks to attain, full realization. He dwells in the center of society as one who has attained realization—he knows the score. Not that he has acquired unusual or esoteric information, but he has come to experience the ground of his being in such a way that he knows the secret of liberation and can somehow or other communicate this to others.[17]

Thomas Merton has continued beyond his life to communicate what he learned in monastic living and what was brought together for him in Ceylon. It is the simple reality that life is. Life needs—can have—no "refutation," as he puts it. When we touch genuine being/Being, despair fades away and we know only life/Life. Merton did not look into the future at Polonnaruwa. Neither did he look back at all the other contemplative moments of presence-in-the-now that preceded it. He just saw what is so. He speaks about the experience: "It says everything; it needs nothing. And because it needs nothing it can afford to be silent, unnoticed, undiscovered. It does not need to be discovered."[18] Merton loses himself in what he has earlier referred to as the innocence of pure presence. Soon after, in one more of those innocent moments, he moved past time never to return to it.

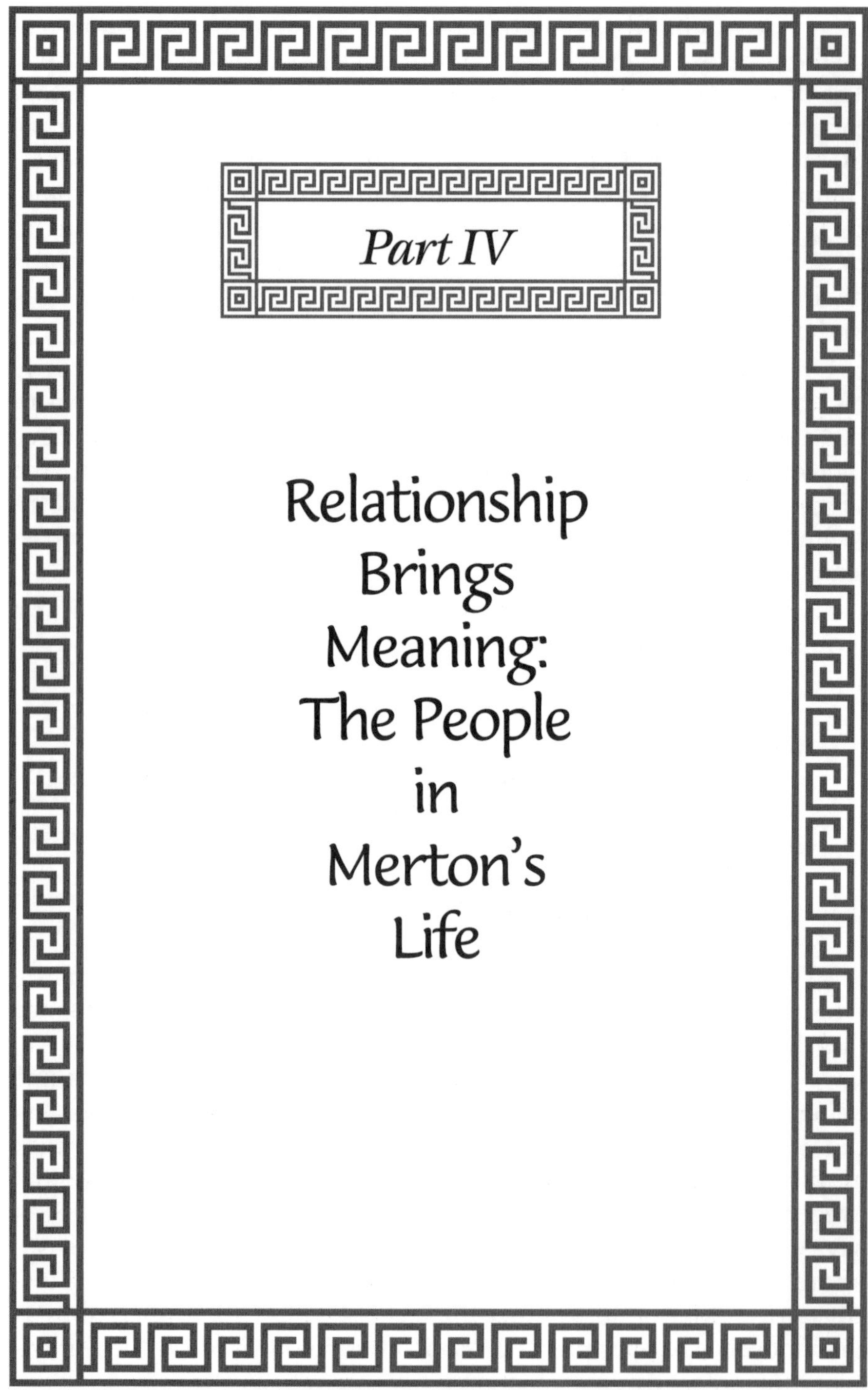

Part IV

Relationship Brings Meaning: The People in Merton's Life

The Monastic Community

The 4 personality type is an interesting combination of deep and private solitude and the social instinct of the 2/3/4 triad. When the 5 wing dominates, 4s seem especially aloof and often distant, even remotely detached. When the 3 wing is more prominent, they are warmer and more outgoing. There is something in addition for 4s about the security of feeling at home that allows them to let down their guard and open up. Real issues and concerns are not only allowed to be seen but are freely revealed and explained. Long association with people offers 4s the testimony of fidelity through life's changes.

Over years of experience 4s find out that conflict, misunderstanding, and even division need not end relationships. There is always the suspicion in 4s that if others were ever to come close enough to see who they really are they would be abandoned. In life's inevitable situations of stress, the "good face" they feel obliged to put forward, the harmony they feel personally responsible to maintain or create, fails. In such circumstances, when people who are consistently in their lives continue to relate to them and to care for them, they are amazed. For this reason long-standing relationships pose problems for 4s even though they are, of course, essential, as they are for everyone. It is not unusual for 4s to move from person to person, from group to group, in what looks like fickleness. This dynamic is sometimes about avoiding the ordinary; at other times, however, it is about leaving others behind before they themselves can be abandoned. Probably the deepest and most real kind of hope 4s can experience is based on the testimony of a lifetime of commitment to the same people. This is one of the reasons Merton's monastic vocation held such significance for him. The monks knew him in all of his limitation and loved him nonetheless.

It is not always easy to see in 4s the social instinct of their triad. They often seem to seek aloofness rather than community. Solitariness, often aloneness that becomes loneliness, seems stronger than affection and concern. The group is less valuable for them than the search for uniqueness. Running with the pack is not an image one thinks of with 4s. Nevertheless, beneath their holding themselves away from the group, there is a basic instinct to connect with it. Even more so, there is the envy they have of people who are able to be together in unself-conscious relationships.

While it may not be as obvious for them as for other 2/3/4s, they are prone to lose touch with their own truthful response to people and circumstances and take on the issues and values of those with whom they live and work. Often their apparent aloofness is a defense against losing their boundaries by assuming as their own the concerns of others. Their withdrawal is frequently an attempt to pull away far enough to find that interior body sense that tells them who they are and what their authentic response is.

Early in his vocation Thomas Merton embraced—even grabbed onto—the customs and values of Gethsemani Abbey. Much of his later life was spent discerning between what constituted his appropriate collaboration in monastic life, calling for mature sacrifice of his will and wishes, and what was the denial of his very person. Like all of us, he undoubtedly made mistakes in that discernment. Much of the tug-of-war between Merton and his monastic superiors comes from his struggle around being interiorly free and yet willingly collaborative.

Anne Carr notes that Merton saw the monastery primarily as "a 'school of liberty' meant to release its students to the spontaneity of interior growth and the independence of maturity."[1] It is undoubtedly this view of monasticism that inspired Merton's last comment in Bangkok: that monks need, ultimately, to stand on their own feet.[2] Surely by this he meant that they needed to be authentic, community persons, not rebellious, ego-engrossed monks.

Merton was committed to finding this true freedom. He realized that relationship in monastic community was his school for that liberation. Life there led him beyond mere following rules and regulation to the heart of monasticism, that humility Benedict outlined in his *Rule*.

Struggles around what was mere compliance and what was loving sacrifice for the good of his brothers became less an issue as he grew in self-knowledge. Confronted with his tendency both to withdraw and to sell himself out in order to be acceptable both to the group and himself, he faced illusions and delusions around day-to-day choices in community. He found it hard to refuse demands on his time, both for ordinary things and in order to accept positions of responsibility. His social instinct and his creative interest in all manner of possibilities led him to volunteer ideas and time, sometimes unrealistically. He was often irritated at being over-involved in others' needs, but eventually he learned that his instinct created many of the situations about which he complained.

Even his desire for the hermit existence became purified over years of growing to humble honesty about his limitations. He wrote about humility toward the end of his life:

> The desire in us is not only to be, but to be our own idol, to be our own end. It sounds nice on paper but it is a bit sickening in reality. Do pray for me, and don't go and tell me I am humble, because that is not true except on a superficial, exterior level. Pray for me to be humble, and really humble. Not with the fake, inert sort of humility that excuses all kinds of hidden pride and prevents us from doing God's word. But with humility that is deep and afraid of nothing, of no truth, and which is completely abandoned to God's will. How hard that actually is. [3]

In a letter to Rosemary Reuther Merton calls himself "a non-monk and an anti-monk, as far as the 'image' goes;" he goes on to insist, however, that he is "certainly quite definite about wanting to stay in the bushes" of his community life.[4] Matthew Kelty, one of Merton's fellow monks, remarks how exasperating and disappointing it was for Merton that many had no confidence in his perseverance in the monastery. Those who lived daily with him experienced his commitment, a dedication that allowed him the assurance of acceptance. He could be himself, caring and railing both.

> He was an obedient monk and in this relationship to the Abbot he saw the elemental structure of the monastic life. If we do not read this lesson in his life, we have not read him well. But let no superior rest comfortably in his seat with the blessings of Father Louis on him, for the man could burn

> with a prophet's ire against those who misused authority and threw their weight around with reckless abandon.[5]

John Eudes Bamberger, Merton's monastic brother, physician, psychiatrist, and friend, acknowledges that Merton's twenty-seven years of perseverance as a monk and his fidelity until death might seem unlikely considering his temperament.[6] When word of Merton's cynical remarks about his monastery leaked back from his Asian trip, his brother monks were not surprised. Such comments were consistent with what he had said when he was home. On the other hand, two days before his death Merton wrote a note to his community tinged with homesickness. He ends it with a warm and familiar greeting and title: "Best love to all. Louie." The sincerity of that greeting was obvious to his brothers.

Bamberger, however, asks the valid question as to when Merton's complexity, even contradiction, became ambivalence.[7] Probably the best answer to that question comes out of the depth of the 4 dynamic. Merton allowed himself complete exasperation, total frustration, only because he was increasingly trusting of the basic commitment within which he ranted. As he grew in confidence that he was committed to his brothers and they to him, he relaxed enough to reveal his hope and despair about the people with whom he lived. He knew they were and would remain his monastic family, even when they found out the depths of his disillusionment with them. Even more, he knew in his better moments that this disillusionment with his brothers was really disillusionment with himself, lack of self-acceptance, and exaggerated self-criticism.

As he recounts the numbers of monks who were touched by Merton, whether abbots, peers, or formation persons, James Connor acknowledges that personally Merton was "one who touched our own lives in a special way," not so much through his instructions or even his spiritual direction, "but primarily through his living and animated presence among us."[8] Connor acknowledges that Merton could be "unedifying" at times, but goes on to say that "beyond that, he was a man who obviously had a deep and strong love for this place and for his brothers—for us."[9] Genuineness, if not always wholeness, seemed everybody's experience of Merton.

Kelty describes the rare impact Merton's death had on the community. It made the monks aware of what he calls the "dimension" of Merton's relationship with his brothers, the intensity of Merton's commitment to them and they to him.

> The comings and the goings, the agreements and the differences, the gives and the takes, the brightness and the dullness, the stupid and the silly as well as the brilliant and the accomplished—the whole fabric of the life of day to day was laid bare, and there for all to see was the glorious presence of love behind it all, beneath it all. It was evident that the man loved us. And it was evident that we loved him. And this love is the evidence of the presence of Christ.[10]

One of the most controversial relationships in Merton's life was the one with Abbot James Fox. With his abbot, as with his brothers, Merton seems to have been confident and trusting enough to express his feelings. It must have cost Merton much to volunteer to act as novice master. He would need to give up his hermit desires if his offer was accepted; on the other hand, he risked feelings of rejection if his offer was refused. He did volunteer and was accepted for the position by the abbot, who also chose Merton as his confessor through a fifteen-year period. Their relationship, while fraught with conflict, was affectionate. More important for a 4, it was honest and trusting. Merton could write from Asia: "Be sure, that I have never changed in my respect for you as Abbot, and affection as Father."[11] Obviously, whatever else they may have been, Merton's encounters with Abbot James were more than the authority struggles some have interpreted them to be.

Merton always tried to break through that false monastic mystique which greeted him whenever he dealt with people outside his monastery, even those who might be expected to have a more realistic view of community life. Writing to Rosemary Reuther he comments:

> Your view of monasticism is to me so abstract and so in a way arbitrary (though plenty of basis in texts can be found) that it is simply poles apart from the existential, concrete, human dimension which the problem has for us here.[12]

Even as a hermit Merton sees himself as part of this human community "which has seen fit deliberately and consciously to afford him liberty."[13] Out of his hermit life he sees himself able to "fruitfully serve my brothers."[14] Speaking further about this hermit vocation he writes to Reuther:

> This condition of mere humanity does not require solitude in the country, it can be and should be realized anywhere. This is just my way of doing it. What would seem to others

> to be the final step into total alienation seems to me to be the beginning of the resolution of all alienation and the preparation for a real return without masks and without defenses into the world, as mere man.[15]

Merton the hermit—though the word as applied to him always had limited dimensions—never left the family of Gethsemani. Upon his profession he spoke about "the deep and warm realization"[16] of immersion in the monastic community: "I am part of Gethsemani. I belong to the family. It is a family about which I have no illusions."[17] He adds that he is "glad to belong to this community, not another, and to be bred flesh and bone into the same body as these brothers and not other ones."[18] This gratitude never left Merton, despite his deepening realization of the limitations of his brothers, accompanied as these were, and in fact preceded by, his sense of his own limitations. Again to Reuther he writes:

> Problem: unrecognized assumption of my own that I have to get out of here. Below that recognition that life here is to some extent (not entirely) a lie and that I can no longer just say the community lies and I don't.[19]

Endearingly, yet with his characteristic tinge of cynicism, he adds:

> The people are not idols, they are real, they are my brothers though they are also for the most part idiots (my Karnap friend told me last week, without any opposition from me, "you live among idiots").[20]

Merton the novice master and writer, with significant responsibilities both inside the monastery and publicly, often felt the strain along with the value of being pulled into the common stream of community life. He gives trivial and very concrete examples of the annoyances of community living: of not being able to get a book he wants to read; of sawing wood with someone whose poor work indicates that he doesn't really care about the job; and of having that same person cough down his neck in choir, take the library book Merton is looking for, and fail to give him his dinner portion. When that same person accuses him in Chapter, Merton's patience is tested to its limits.[21] In the midst of such annoyances he talks about

> the profound consolation from the mere fact of being with the other monks . . . a profound happiness in just being there together, sitting in the same room and reading or writing, in the presence of God Who is the only possible reason for their unity.[22]

Merton seemed to need that physical togetherness at times in order to forestall feelings of abandonment. He spoke of the great suffering of being a hermit as the feeling "out there in solitude and seclusion" that "the Community has disowned you—scorns you—ostracized you, for good."[23] While this may have been a somewhat paranoid reaction, it also expresses his own ambivalence about abandoning, in a way, his fellow monks. Along the same lines, when he became irritated and judgmental about the cellarer's apparent ignoring of his requests for a private room, he later accused himself of rash judgments and uncharitable thoughts when this same cellarer ultimately offered a place for privacy and solitude even more satisfying than Merton had anticipated. He admits that he "just sat on the edge of my bed and cried" over "that concrete expression of love and affection for me."[24]

Bamberger comments on Merton's judgmental and impatient manifestations of what may well have been his style of oblique anger when he writes:

> He did not hesitate to make use of his considerable powers for criticism—the force of which had to be experienced to be believed—upon his own community, his beloved fathers and brothers. . . . We learned that living with a prophet was usually profitable, often interesting, and occasionally exasperating.[25]

Noise, especially of machinery, irritated Merton like the proverbial fingernail dragged along a blackboard. It nearly made him irrational, and he was not quiet about the sleeplessness that resulted for him from night harvesting, though whether that insomnia was due to the farm machinery or his intense reaction to it might be matter for discussion.[26]

This is not to say that Merton separated himself from community tasks or the rhythm of life in common. Kelty notes how very interested Merton was in community life, not as a busybody or gossip, but "he knew what was going on and kept his eyes open, missed little."[27]

This touchiness about life's little grievances was probably in large part due to what we might call Merton's artistic temperament. Much of the purification community living afforded him was also around this characteristic. Kelty very sensitively and with profound understanding both of Merton and the community remarks:

> He was the son of artists, was himself a poet, had all the romantic tendencies of the artistic temperament. His dreams, plans, ideas were manifold. He would submit them one after another as they came up, and watch the original interested response gradually cool and settle at last into the usual negative reply. It was almost a ritual with him. Under it he sometimes chafed and no doubt suffered much, but he knew what he was about. He had feelings that perhaps this after all was the best thing for him and these feelings in later years grew into solid convictions. If on the one side we say that the Abbot held the reins tight, there is small doubt that there was any other way to do it with such a man.[28]

This picture of Merton the poet and prophet—undoubtedly, as time bore out, decades ahead of his times—seems to have been a common one. Kelty describes it as Merton's habitual role. While it led him to frustration, it probably urged the community beyond itself in many ways; certainly it resulted in growth for Merton himself. Kelty adds, "Even Father Louis, in the end, was grateful for the guidance given him and realized that submission to the rule and to the Abbot had been his salvation."[29]

Merton's style as he re-enacted the community scene Kelty describes was one of "withering directness."[30] He "let it be known when he thought something was stupid."[31] which was obviously quite often. The following description of Merton's position among his brothers indicates that, while he had definite ideas, he was in his own mind and in the minds of others just one of the monks.

> No one made anything of him. He neither expected special handling nor got it. This does not mean that he adopted some sort of humble manner by which he managed to hide his own importance. On the contrary, he was very much himself, very alive and very real. . . . He did what he thought he should do and that was all there was to it.[32]

Somehow Merton was able to cut through his obvious importance in society and remain "a monk among monks."[33] "No one . . . ever thought of him as famous, a great author, a renowned personality. The basic reason for that was that he did not think of himself that way."[34] Never, Kelty goes on to say, did the monastic community make a cult of Merton. Perhaps, knowing him so well—because he came to the decision to reveal himself so candidly and completely—the monks couldn't do so.

Flavian Burns, for a time Merton's fellow hermit and friend, and at the end his abbot, summed up Merton's life in a homily to the community a week after his burial. His words indicate who Merton was for this group, but remain a reminder that only an individual concern for each monk made Merton so significant for them all.

> To me, personally, he was one of the most helpful and lovable men that I have ever had the pleasure to meet. I owe him more than words can say. His passing is a great loss. . . . He has left his mark deep in this community, and it will be with us for years to come, for he has planted it in the hearts of a generation, and God willing, it will be planted again for generations to come.[35]

Merton always wanted to be planted in the soil of Gethsemani until the end of time. Despite his death so far from home, his desire was respected and his body returned to his home, his monastic family, his brothers. John Eudes Bamberger describes Merton's burial beneath the cedars and in the shadow of the monastic church. He tells us: "He rests there now, beneath the trees that for him were living symbols of a transformed world and of the power of the cross of Christ."[36] This cross, a cross of contradiction to be sure, buried him through his fidelity deep in the heart of his monastery and the hearts of its members.

17

Friends and Colleagues

Many of Merton's associates comment that his personality was filled with contradiction. However, from an enneagram standpoint his responses are quite consistent with his 4 stance, even predictable. Merton fluctuated between friendliness and privacy, trust and mistrust, rebellion and obedience, shyness and openness, collaboration and aloofness, snobbery and ordinariness. Such fluctuation characterizes 4s and is their peculiar mix of the social instinct on the one side and the perceptual on the other.

Any Merton study yields an enormity of material from his own self-description and the comments of those who dealt with him. This chapter attempts to highlight and pull together an overview of this man whom some found puzzling and others quite understandable. His best friends, those he came to trust, were rarely surprised by his responses. Instead, they learned to expect Merton's variety of reactions and to know the impetus was usually not revealed despite his verbosity.

It would seem that, like many artists with words, Merton created a verbal smoke screen that covered his deepest feelings. Only by crafting his expression into the written form of letters, journals, poems, essays, and books was he able to clear away the layers that covered his intense emotions and account for his responses, even to himself.

Just before Merton died, John Balfour wrote about meeting him in India:

> He had that "washed" face only those people usually have who have just been through an L.S.D. experience of some major dimension. I did tell him that he did have that cleaner than clean, serenely open, quite halo-like face that I only saw on people after a deeply-moving psychedelic experience.[1]

The Dalai Lama noted something similar at their meeting.

> I looked in his face. I could see a good human being. I don't know how to explain but . . . you can tell people who have some deep experience. And of course this is special. He was not the type of person who was cheating other people, or looking down at other people. Not like that kind at all. Honest. Truthful.[2]

This sense of openness and spontaneity seems to have been a frequent impression when meeting Merton. Rabbi Silberman notes that from their first encounter in the monastery guest house he realized he "was in the presence of someone who lived with an inner center of calm—of peace—not in any static, self-satisfied way, but in a dynamic, open, sharing way."[3] One of Merton's novices, Richard Loomis, echoes this impression.

> When I would go to him for spiritual direction what I remember chiefly is the candor, the openness, and the tact, with which he would conduct those sessions. For example, you could talk to him about emotional turbulence. Ordinarily, you didn't go into a confessional in a Trappist monastery and say, "Emotionally, I'm distraught." But you could talk very directly to him about that, and one reason was that he would say, "Yeah, yeah, I've had that too."[4]

A number of assessments of Merton include this combination of flexibility and openness with an experience of deep centeredness. Loomis describes him as "deeply balanced and easy," and remarks how impressive that had been to him, considering Merton's unusual life. He marveled that Merton was able to keep that balance, noting that "it doesn't stay there unless you have a very good gyroscope."[5]

This inner peace seemed to flow and make whatever he did look easy, if not haphazard. When Brother Michael Casagram entered Gethsemani, he remarked to John Eudes Bamberger that Merton seemed the most disorganized monk in the monastery, to which Bamberger replied that Casagram could not have make a bigger mistake; Merton was the most organized man in the monastery. [6]

As a teacher Merton was scrupulous about not showing favorites. Possibly the 4 tendency to envy had made him, as it tends to do with 4s, compassionate toward someone's feeling left out of the social circle, a situation he would not want to contribute to by any actions of his own. He was strict and fair and in charge of his classroom. Ready as he was to appreciate a joke, it was usually one he himself deemed appropriate that was rewarded with attention. He stopped a seminarian's humming of "Begin the Beguine" during a lecture on the Beguines, indicating that he decided what was and was not funny.[7] It would seem that even his classes were shaped and formed into what he determined made for a rhythmic art piece. While he was not an intellectual snob, he sometimes was amazed at his students' lack of knowledge about what he judged to be general information.

Merton had the 2/3/4 social propensity to make acquaintances—and sometimes friends—very quickly. In this matter he leaned more to his 3 than his 5 wing, perhaps over-using the word *friend* in his enthusiastic responses to those he had just met. Commenting on this dynamic in himself he says:

> Ever since I was sixteen, and traveled all over Europe . . . I have developed this . . . trick of getting along with strangers and chance acquaintances—this complete independence and self-dependence which turns out to be, now, not a strength, but, in any big problem, a terrific weakness.[8]

One result of this "trick" was that people he encountered—as he himself also initially judged, it seems—considered their relationship deeper and more binding than it really was. Expectations of continued relationship on the part of those who met Merton seem the cause of that crowded, one might almost say imprisoned, feeling he sometimes had, even during his years in the hermitage. It often did spell weakness for him; he found it nearly impossible to escape others when his work demanded he do so.

What attracted Merton to people was their open innocence. He named it as the quality his Aunt Maud, Jacques Maritain, Robert Lax,

Mark Van Doren, and Daniel Walsh possessed.[9] It drew warmth and affection from him when he encountered it and sometimes seems to have led to declarations of friendship short encounters would not normally have warranted. Did Merton mean what he said when, for example, he spoke of the Dalai Lama after spending a few hours with him:

> It was a very warm and cordial discussion and at the end I felt we had become very good friends and were somehow quite close to one another. I felt great respect and fondness for him as a person and feel too that there was a real spiritual bond between us.[10]

From the 4 perspective, the answer to that question is probably yes. The sense of being understood and accepted is immediate, often unexpected, seldom definable for 4s. It may give way to that later 4 feeling that no one will ever be able to understand them; when it does last however, it forges an enthusiastic bond that depends not so much on continued encounter as on the conviction that, wherever such persons might be, they stand in fidelity and support.

Opposite this social dynamic is privacy and withdrawal. There are probably two notable ways this is evidenced for 4s, and surely for Merton. The first has to do with unwillingness, cloaked as inability, to confront difficult issues with people. This is certainly manifested in Merton's lack of relationship with his guardian, Tom Bennett, whom he did not inform of his entrance into the monastery until four years after the fact.[11] The strain caused by Merton's refusal to accept Bennett's warnings about the young man's college escapades had forged a silence he never moved beyond.

It was this reluctance to address hard circumstances coupled with a natural shyness that may have led Mott to comment that, until his brother's visit to the monastery just before his own death, he and Merton had been little more than orphans of the same parents.[12] Even a friend as long-standing and intimate as Bob Lax would say after Merton's death that he had learned about his friend's interior life and struggles from his books, not from personal conversation.[13]

As a young teacher at St. Bonaventure College Merton was described by one student as knowing his material well, but being someone who "never gave much of it to us."[14] He was not a popular teacher there and seems to have made little mark on those he taught. Perhaps the "nagging sadness, which had to be hidden from others, and which had a certain dramatic quality to it," as Mott says,[15] indicated Merton's interior focus, his preoccupation with personal struggles he felt he could share with no one.

Merton avoided showing his darker moods. John Eudes Bamberger commented on his surprise at unexpectedly coming upon Merton looking dejected and crushed; others probably could have said the same. When Merton saw he was being observed, his mood immediately changed to his characteristic buoyancy.[16] Merton had the feeling, Mott comments, that it wasn't decent to inflict darker moods on others. Mott adds that some of Merton's journals and other writings may have been darker precisely because of the lack of expression of depressive feelings elsewhere.

That Merton carried off this cheerful exterior is evidenced by the characteristic impression many monks had that he was light and affable.[17] From Merton's own perspective he was haunted by loneliness; he even questioned his retreat to the hermitage and his entire quest for solitude, wondering whether it might be a lamentation over the impossibility of human love.[18] For many 4s, and one suspects for Merton, the issue that underlies their search for privacy is a conviction that their unique experience is incommunicable.

What seems to have been true of Merton, and many 4s, was his inability to endure always being observed by others, including himself. Experience cannot be communicated because spontaneity is lost. The view from the audience—one's own or another's—kills the natural. What comes out is less than real, is shaped by this cautious artist of human exchange. Whether going the rounds of the monastery, singing in choir, or interacting with people, what Merton called his morbid fear of making a mistake stalked him.[19] Even his confessions were a mess, concerned as he was with crafting even his honesty. Father John of the Cross, clearly someone Merton desired to have as a friend, for that very reason could not be in the presence of the genuine Merton. The more significant the person, the more pretense was likely to cloud interaction; the more important the relationship, the less possible it was for Merton to be present to the other. He described this characteristic 4 problem and some of its mental twists:

> When I talk to Father John of the Cross now, I act like a complete phony and he is aware of it and I guess embarrassed by it, for my sake as well as for his own. . . . But the phoniness comes from overanxiety and impatience. On paper I have time to compose myself, and I can be more "real." With another person, I am thrown into confusion and do not foresee

> the consequences of the next statement and am so busy trying to avoid a crisis that I do not really listen to the other person. This is only fully true of my relations with Father John of the Cross. With other people I am disinterested enough to be more detached, more serene, and relatively normal. [20]

When Merton preached that we are already one, he was preaching to himself. This reminder seems to have been comfort in circumstances like these just described. His most significant mystical experiences seem to have centered around unity with self and others. This was true both at Fourth and Walnut in Louisville and before the Buddha states in Polonarruwa. When such moments occurred he would speak of the happiness that resulted and manifest a spontaneous freedom. It was as though shackles of self-assessment fell away and he enjoyed an unreflected interlude. When Merton found this place of openness in the presence of another human being, he named it "a testimony of confidence and friendship."[21] Given these personal dynamics, it would seem he names it well.

We have already discussed Merton's complex relationship with authority figures, notably his nemesis, Dom James Fox. That Fox helped Merton grow is witnessed to by Merton's own statement that in many ways he needed Dom James.[22] On the one hand, Merton was an initiator, a prophet—a creative artist. On the other hand, he sought approval and in order to win it would choose subservience. Mott was able finally to describe Merton as a rebel who won and kept a reputation for obedience.[23] Such a reputation was perhaps largely wrung out of the guilt he felt for his brutal judgments of Dom James and expression of these to himself in journals and to others in letters and conversation. He could be savage and humbly uncritical in rather quick succession. Dom James never showed the trust in Merton that he offered others, probably due to Merton's own ambivalence. Whatever the cause of this lack of confidence, Merton was deeply disturbed by it.[24] It would seem that the disturbance was largely about being unable to settle within himself his issues with his abbot.

We see this dynamic still operating at the end of his life when he turned to Archbishop McDonough, supposedly for confirmation, but possibly for affirmation, of his own view on traveling outside the monastery.[25] While appearing to seek advice, he seems to have been looking for support from his archbishop for decisions he had already made. This looked like rebellion to observers. In fact, it may well have been a characteristic 4 insecurity that needed someone to validate the authenticity of personal feelings. Whatever went on for Merton in these and other such instances, Bamberger comments: "Father Louis was at all times an amazing amalgam of independence and obedience."[26]

We have previously noted that despite the mental labyrinths Merton got into around relationship with people, he, indeed, had faithful and intimate personal friendships. Merton admired Daniel Berrigan's warmth and was drawn to it. He honored Berrigan by adapting his manner of dress, a typical 4 kind of compliment.[27] He even allowed Berrigan to challenge him, a real testimony to true friendship, especially for one whose basic self-criticism and insecurity necessitated a strong defense.

When Flavian Burns became abbot, the authority issues seem to have dissolved into creative personal searching. There was no need to protect himself out of fear of losing freedom or self-esteem; there was no need to use the 2/3/4 weapon of vindictiveness to maintain dignity. Trust and relaxation led to an atmosphere of understanding. They were, in the deepest sense of the word, colleagues, and Merton knew it. Though Flavian Burns became his superior, he remained his brother.[28]

How did Merton see himself as a friend? Generally speaking, with his usual self-criticism and self-accusation. He criticized himself for talking too much, an appraisal which may account for his insistence on conversations having a point and ending when they ceased to serve a purpose, whether of good fun or communication.[29] Perhaps this also ties in to his artistic sense, which instinctively felt the pulse of beginning, middle, and end. Merton's psychiatrist, Dr. Jim Wygal, judged him capable of proper self-assessment and self-correction.[30] John Eudes Bamberger echoes this thought.[31] Apparently by the end of his life Merton had grappled through trial and error to the gift beyond the compulsion; he had learned to be honest without being brutal to himself. Earlier, his assessments had manifested themselves in an aloof stance and critical cynicism bordering on snobbery.[32]

Merton named as his own the dynamic of "specialness" characteristic of 4s when he spoke of "above all the insistence on being different from other people."[33] He was always embarrassed by his Grandfather Jenkins, surely a man who carried the shadow of Merton's 3 wing. His boyhood memory of his grandfather casting showers of coins to the poor in the French villages where the family was traveling remained with him, possibly as a symbol of his own propensity for grand performances.[34] Many years later John Eudes Bamberger spoke about Merton's over-effusiveness when asking for prayers for the Berrigans in Chapter. Merton also tended to make absolute statements that were sometimes tinged with drama; like many 4s, there was truth in them that he honestly experienced, if only for the moment.[35] He could later apologize with equal drama for his fervor in making such remarks. Yes, he was his grandfather's grandchild, and he seems to have recognized that early in his life.

Flavian Burns comments that self-knowledge and the acceptance of God's mercy make a saint. According to that definition, he finds Merton qualifying:

> He was a person who was very conscious of his need for God's mercy, his sinfulness, his weakness. And I don't think he was in for any surprises when he came before the Lord on Judgment Day. Most of us, I think, have a little surprise in store for us when we come before the clarity of God and see ourselves. We'll have some experience of chagrin. But I suspect that Merton had already seen that and had placed that before the Lord and depended on him to take care of it.[36]

Here again we see the virtue or gift that was an outgrowth of his compulsion of self-analysis. Beyond the bitter, withered poison of self-preoccupation, Merton found a flowing and flourishing humility. Brother Maurice Flood says it simply:

> I called him a wholesome person . . . some call people like that saints and mystics, but they're really earthy persons, down to earth, they radiate wholeness. They have this integration of the universe within them.[37]

It was this quality that led so many to see Thomas Merton, imperfect as he was, as friend.

18

The Feminine

> Our first need . . . is to live the contradictions, fully and painfully aware of the poles between which our lives are stretched. As we do so, we will be plunged into paradox, at the center of which we will find transcendence and new life. Our lives will be changed. Both our beliefs and our actions will be more responsive to God's spirit. But this will happen only as we allow ourselves to be engulfed by contradictions which God alone can resolve. With Jonah, we will be delivered. But first we will be swallowed into darkness.[1]

A man's anima needs to be incorporated into his personality for his journey of individuation to become complete. Since "spiritual way" is but another phrase describing this individuation process, the wholeness that comes from incorporating the feminine aspect is part and parcel of a man's holiness. Both of these ways of expressing human growth and maturation—the psychological and the spiritual—form the basic assumptions of this chapter. My purpose here is to take this basic Jungian premise into the concrete of Merton's history, particularly as a 4.[2]

At the beginning of Merton's life we meet his formidable mother. She must have been an enigma to herself; surely she was for Tom. On the one hand, she adored him, treasuring and recording every word from his mouth, every action of his developing personality. On the other hand, she worried about this independent, creative little boy who so soon set off on his own path. She could not control him for long. She could not shape him into the perfection she was always seeking as an artist, whether with paint and palette or in human relationships.

One may well wonder whether Ruth Merton was also a 4. Many of her issues, at least as perceived by Tom, were ones we find him striving to master. She was lacking in deep affect and aloof, showing her love in little connecting actions, in writing, in words. She was anxious and ill-at-ease when things were flawed or went unfinished. She withdrew when faced with her death, probably not wanting to inflict her fear and pain on those she loved, especially her children, who could not, she must have assumed, understand such things. Perhaps she was a bit of a snob; Merton describes her as demanding intellectual perfection. He tells how he saw his mother's dream for himself, her firstborn:

> Mother wanted me to be independent, and not to run with the herd. I was to be original, individual, I was to have a definite character and ideals of my own. I was not to be an article thrown together, on the common bourgeois platter, on everybody's assembly line.[3]

In fairness to Ruth Merton, we need to remember the enneagram theory that we process our life experience from the particular stance that is ours from birth. We translate what we say and do into the terms of the world of that instinct into which we are born. Maybe Ruth was in reality the woman Merton describes, but maybe she was described as she was only because Merton saw her that way. We know that, like all children, he took to heart the judgment of himself he thought he saw her making. He says that in her anxious, worried attitude she communicated to him that "the imperfection of myself, her first son, had been a great deception."[4] He construed himself at his worst, and so committed his fundamental sin in a characteristic 4 way by doubting the goodness of his intrinsic being.

By whom did Merton think Ruth saw herself deceived in having been given such a son? Probably by some unfair Fate or Providence or Deity—some Creator, at any rate—who had botched up this bit of creation. Such an appraisal, whether it was truly Ruth's or Merton's translation of Ruth, became a familiar refrain in his life. He returned to it again and again, either explicitly or indirectly in his attitude toward himself as well as his actions around relating to other people. It found articulation in his writing about the false self.

That his contemplative vocation was entwined with his relationship with his mother and through her with other women seems evident. Like all men, he had to pull away assertively from his mother and what she stood for. He had to create a sensitive, reflective, positive personality to counteract the view he had of himself as a disappointing lie. This attractive persona could only be a cover; underneath was this other picture of himself that the most important person in his life had, at least from his perspective, declared by her actions and affect to be the *real* Tom. He had to keep that worrisome child out of sight. He could not let any people get too close lest they see the ugliness under the mask.

It is small wonder, then, that Merton remarks in his later years: "In the natural order, perhaps solitaries are made by severe mothers."[5] A more accurate statement of the dynamic might be that solitaries are made because they perceive themselves judged severely by their mothers and accept that judgment. Applied even more specifically, 4 solitaries result only after judging that their basic worth is a lie and that the people they encounter need to be kept from knowing who lives beneath the engaging surface they try to maintain. A friendly, nonconflictual mask is worn for people to see, but there is an interior alienation; the 4 solitary cannot even acknowledge, let alone accept, his or her self.

The journey from that externally affable, interiorly desolate self-isolation to loving, humble self-embrace constitutes the 4 spiritual path. It is the way home to the place of rest and peaceful mercy. As long as people alternately are pushed away in disgust and hungrily grabbed at in efforts to cover over basic worthlessness, there is loneliness. True solitude comes when 4s tire of these varied efforts and let in the reality of imperfection and the experience that another can love them just as they are.

According to Jung, it is the feminine dimension that fleshes out all this theory. The feminine is concrete, specific, physical, primitive. Only an actual woman, according to Emma Jung, can bring a man to wholeness, just as it is a real woman who leads to his original division. The lonely Merton, perceived as rejected by Ruth, had to put an accepting woman in her place to become whole. An actual feminine person had to mediate and model acceptance so that Merton could become his full self. As a 4, this translates into Merton's very real need for bodily contact with some woman who would not push him away, who would hold him in her arms and not leave him as his mother had left him, affectively at first and later on physically in death.

Merton knew all of this instinctively as a man and as a 4. He lived out of it long before he ever heard of Jungian psychology. We know he did so from the relationships he attempted, characterized in his own words as coming from "deep shyness and need of love." He talks about his "efforts to get complete assurance and perfect fulfillment" from these relationships.[6] The way he tried to do so was through sex. On the eve of his fiftieth birthday he could still say that sex was something he "did not use well, something I gave up without having come to terms with it."[7] His younger years involved a series of named and unnamed women. His relationships with these women seem to have held that rhythm of clutch and abandon, so characteristic of 4s, which flowed from his need to be connected and his despair of ever being so. It seems significant that in this journal entry, written at the time a young nurse named Margie, whom he met while in a Louisville hospital, was entering his life, he acknowledged his unfinished business around this phase of development.

Robert Lax says Merton frightened women by rushing at them. Perhaps, says Mott, he did so as a way of ensuring that he would not get too involved.[8] It would be part of the 4 dynamic to set up such inevitable unfulfillment. Whatever the reason, each failed encounter deepened the conviction that he most surely was unable to relate to a woman. This conviction deepened a sense of the lie of his own goodness, the worthlessness of his very being. There were some women who were just friends, among them Jinny Burton, but there were those with whom physical intimacy became a frantic symbol for union—with himself and another—unconscious as the search probably was.

He learned quite young the emptiness of such pursuits and the injustice involved; his fathering a child revealed the second- and third-party consequences both to partner and offspring. By his mid-twenties he talked about "a burden of desires that almost crushed me with the monotony of their threat, the intimate, searching familiarity of their ever-present disgust." Shortly after he added, about an adulterous relationship: "The experiment was terrible, unpleasant, not deliberate, half-conscious passionate. Above all, it wasn't necessary."[9]

Merton never seems to have lost the tantalizing fascination of being in the presence of a woman, at least a young and attractive woman. Friends noted up to the time of his death how a beautiful girl often drew his aesthetic appreciation. Early in life he had used this consciousness and its accompanying self-consciousness as his excuse for not signing on at Friendship House; he said he would be working with a staff of women and could never forget that fact. It would complicate things too much and deprive him of the freedom to be himself and compel him to perform for this audience. We see him at that point in his life shelving the whole question of women, leaving them without concrete reality. He reveals his thinking in this matter:

> If I am with women, I know they are women, every minute: and when I was in the world altogether, that was what I liked to be aware of. Now I cannot dare to. When I am away from women, I do not think about them, however, and can be at peace to pray.[10]

Denial is in this statement. It is the denial of self-gratification, to be sure. It is also the denial of women, earthly and physical women. More so, it is the denial of the necessary human encounters that would erase Ruth Merton's perceived severity and replace it with the experience of a merciful interior mother/self/Self. Merton suspended his search, or rather took a long detour on his way. He probably needed to do so at that point in his development. But a detour it was, and one which he left only by returning to the way in his last years through his relationship with Margie, whom he met at a time when he was physically, and, it seems, psychically vulnerable.

This is not to say that Merton had no significant feminine relationships throughout his lifetime. In many ways those he did have were probably as free as they were because he had successfully compartmentalized his life so that women no longer created a threat, at least not a sexual threat. Many of the women Merton collaborated with in one or another way were strong women, women we would call feminists today. Surely Catherine de Hueck, Mary Luke Tobin, and Rosemary Reuther fit that category. They met Merton in his 5 wing, at his perceptual level. There were other women who took on the task of caring for one or another of his needs. Both groups caused him some discomfort. To engage Thomas Merton demanded a strong woman, and strong women perhaps reminded him of his mother. He said in a letter to Rosemary Reuther:

> I am not mad at you for being an "intellectual woman" but only for seeming to reject me. I don't take to rejection, I tell you. I need and value your friendship and I will also on my part be more or less grown up about it and try to give you

> what I can in my turn, once I know what you want. And now I think I do.[11]

This is a very 4 remark, not only from the aspect of fearing rejection, but also in Merton's promise to give what he finds Reuther wants. The 4 adaptability, the need to know what a person is looking for and then supply it, followed Merton to the end of his life, at least where women were concerned. He seems to have had some sense of this dynamic, because he comments to a group of contemplative nuns to whom he gave a retreat:

> Many men and a lot of clerics are really women-haters. They're afraid of women and they deal with women as if they were enemies, in a tricky or dishonest way. We've all met men who will not talk straight to a woman and who always have a special routine for women. They'll talk straight to another man, but for women they've got a lot of flim-flam, or they beat around the bush.[12]

That Merton was envious of the women he knew who were also friends of someone else, at least when that someone else was Dom James, was played out for a time in Merton's relationship with Naomi Burton, one of his publishers. The two got beyond that phase, but the problem may well have been caused by his longing for a quality of relationship he saw others had and that as a 4 seemed unattainable.[13]

As did many men in the religious life of his day, Merton directed his idealized feminine energy toward Mary, the Mother of God. This woman symbolized the wholeness that the feminine promised and offered a man in the safest of ways. For much of his time in the monastery, Mary seemed to satisfy his need to grapple with the feminine. In speaking to his novices about Mary, he notes: "I was talking about grace and it would be foolish to talk of grace without talking of her."[14] Undoubtedly, his devotion to Mary was not only genuine but important for the development of at least the theoretical framework of his contemplative life. She provided the softer, forgiving attitude he needed to find toward himself. She began the reversal of Ruth Merton's severity, "gracing" her monastic son with an acceptance no real woman had ever provided him. There were other women he met along the way in his readings about the spiritual life, notably Julian of Norwich, whose approach to Jesus was boldly to call him Mother. This gentle yet daring woman attracted Merton to the point where he came to prefer her to John of the Cross, an earlier hero.[15]

The search for the feminine did not stop when Merton entered the monastery, therefore, but it took on dimensions of the contemplative, of the mystical life. Others have spoken in detail about Merton's anima dreams in which he encounters a wisdom figure named Proverb. That he would have such dreams is expected, considering his commitment to the conversion/individuation process with its call to wholeness through including the countersexual aspect of his personality. As someone who respected and addressed his interior experience, Merton dialogued with the Proverb of his dreams. He noted "a great difference"[16] in their ages, just one foreshadowing of his own life myth to be lived out concretely in his relationship with Margie, nearly thirty years his junior. Another intimation he drew as he continued to journal about this dream was that Proverb was leading him to greater incarnation. This is evidenced in the link he made with this dream and the experience of union with humanity on the corner of Fourth and Walnut. Both experiences held for him an energy that welcomed human weakness and limitation. Until Margie came along, however, it was largely this universal aspect of incarnation that impressed Merton.

The prose poem "Hagia Sophia" seems an expression of Merton's personal grappling with the feminine during his mid-forties. Centered around the canonical hours, it includes a section about an unnamed nurse waking him in a hospital. We find Merton reaching again for his myth. As a 4 who grapples with the feminine, he seems in the writing of this poem to have arrived at the peak of what the theoretical can offer. He had painted the backdrop of what the feminine means in general and what it needed to mean in particular. There remained only to live it out. In a later poem to Margie, "Certain Proverbs Arise Out of Dreams," Merton surely was making a connection with this earlier dream image. There was no longer any question that he had made this feminine quest concrete, nor does he seem to have enduring regrets for doing so. Whatever the pain and impossibility of permanent relationship with Margie, Merton decided that to open himself to her was part of his growth.

Some see Merton as "using" Margie, and perhaps he did. In some ways all explorations into intimate, sexual encounters are, in their early stages, self-seeking, inspired by pleasurable learning. This reality was probably the ultimate reason for what seemed their mutual decision both to accept the growth their relationship had proven to be for them and, finally, to end it. They both seemed to have come to the realization that what they determined had been, in some way, right for them both in its immediacy and physicality, was, in the long term, not right. They both came to acknowledge another overriding destiny, which they eventually accepted.

In this relationship with Margie do we find the Merton described earlier: the man who clutched and let go? Undoubtedly his instinctive 4 dynamic was still alive. Nevertheless, the man whose compulsions had been burned away through decades of genuine sacrifice for the people in his life came to this relationship with a newly discovered dignity and a compassion born out of self-respect earned through suffering. Merton himself could never reconcile why he and Margie seemed to need the physical aspects of their encounters. Perhaps one reason they did was because as a man Merton's feminine needed to become focused on a particular person.

Still further, Merton as a 4 carried the life view in which bodily experiences become essential symbols for spiritual growth. In no other space on the enneagram circle is it so necessary physically to act out the meanings one has theoretically discovered. As a 4, Merton apparently determined that he could never come to the full experience of union with all creation, all human beings, without knowing union in the flesh.

Merton was a great contemplative, ever stretching toward the darkest contemplative paradox Palmer speaks of in this chapter's opening quotation. Merton had to resolve the ego struggles of his earlier years, as we all do, on the road to conversion. As a young man he had sought to symbolize his personal value through being accepted by another in brief, aborted encounters. Later, he shelved the physical aspects of the search for the life of the spirit. In doing so he tried to eliminate his instinctual sense that the physical, especially the sexual, symbol of incarnate wholeness needed to be allowed. In later life he bowed to some inner direction about looking for the incarnate compassion he judged he must discover through incarnate passion.

We do not know what this relationship meant for Margie; we do know that Merton saw it as the final and necessary step to become a contemplative master. Because of his time with Margie, Merton's life came full circle, as all lives must. His self-severity and its mirror of severity toward others died when he allowed Margie to love him. We know this is what happened: Mott tells us that, after Margie, Merton never again talked of the inability to love and be loved.[17]

As surely as it had to take place, Merton's relationship with Margie had to end. He had trusted the experience, and he trusted it to its completion.[18] Merton was called to profound contemplation and nothing short of this living symbol could have made it possible as he saw things. In the monastery Margie was seen to be a "problem," but Merton judged otherwise. Mott tells us that Merton considered their relationship the solution to much that had been lacking in his life.[19] It was just as true, however, that this relationship had to end. Marriage was not the vocation to which Merton saw himself called. He writes wisely during this time:

> When I got home I called her and we were talking again, foolishly, of possibilities, of living together, my leaving here, "marrying" her, etc. But it is all preposterous. Society has no place for us and I haven't the gall it takes to fight the whole world particularly when I don't really want married life anyway, I want the life I have vowed.[20]

Here is the impulsive, rebellious Merton, blaming the church for not allowing married monks at the same time that he acknowledges he himself is not made for marriage. He kicks at the goad of celibacy while acknowledging he wants it in the deepest existential sense of that desire. He knows his monastic life is a fit, even though he longs to have Margie and decides that, somehow, at least temporarily, she is also a fit. It is this double admission the two of them seem to have come to: both that the relationship was meant to be and that it was only temporary.

Another symbol occurs after the relationship has ended. Merton burns Margie's letters without even glancing at them.[21] This may seem a callous action, one devoid of sensitivity. Rather, it may well have been another and necessary symbolic statement saying that Margie had been who she was meant to be, and now life had moved on. This may have been Merton's way of dealing with the pain of not being able to live what he so desired. He was finally becoming a celibate, one who knew what he embraced and the sacrifice it called for.

In talking to a group of contemplative nuns not long after the Margie experience, Merton said about a sexuality that is not part of the married vocation:

> It takes all you've got. There's no time or energy for anything else. It seems to me that anyone who knows what that involves would be delighted to be released from it. To feel free again, to be able to pray if you want, to have a sense of being all one, are things we value in our life. Some people can give themselves to another in married life and still have something similar. But there are people called to this kind of

> freedom as a way of life, and they appreciate it. There is something telling them, "This is for me, this is my choice."[22]

"This kind of freedom" that Merton describes as the celibate life he shares with the contemplative nuns to whom he speaks. He talks calmly and objectively, but his journals and his poems of the Margie period indicate how this peace was wrung from passion. In typical 4, cool summary, he quietly tells what he has learned after the fact and when he has discovered the meaning of the events. The passion, once so burning, is gone, replaced by what he has learned from it.

In another place, Merton spoke of the unromantic and ordinary life which was his as a celibate. It is perhaps this aspect of the life that added to its fittingness for him, as he eventually realized.

> All monks, as is well known, are unmarried, and hermits more unmarried than the rest of them. Not that I have anything against women. I see no reason why a man can't love God and a woman at the same time. . . . One might say I had decided to marry the silence of the forest. The sweet dark warmth of the whole world will have to be my wife. . . . So perhaps I have an obligation to preserve the stillness, the silence, the poverty, the virginal point of pure nothingness which is at the center of all other loves. I attempt to cultivate this place without comment in the middle of the night and water it with psalms and prophecies in silence. It becomes the most rare of all the trees in the garden, at once the primordial paradise tree, the *axis mundi*, the cosmic axle, and the Cross. . . . There is only one such tree. It cannot be multiplied. It is not interesting.[23]

How paradoxical and appropriate that as Merton entered upon his at least partial hermit existence, Margie came into his life. She made him a true celibate, whole within himself, embraced by his own compassion. That compassion now spills over in an incarnate rather than abstract mysticism. His journals and poems testify that this incarnation indeed led to the cross, the *axis mundi*. Merton was meant to be a great spiritual guide; therefore, he had to plumb the depths of passion. Everyone called to a deep mystical life must become passionate in his or her characteristic way. Mott summarizes the Margie story by a quotation from Merton's journals and his commentary on Merton's own conclusions:

> "We can no longer love wisely. . . . " With all the suffering, all the damage to two people—and to others—the story has a moral beyond morals. "The love of creatures" (to use a phrase from Merton's old style) is seldom wise. Sometimes we learn great wisdom in loving unwisely.[24]

The little boy who was a 4, who had tried to find his worth through grasping and leaving others—and so egoistically grasping and cruelly leaving himself—had learned that love is possible. The man who was a 4, who accepted himself through being physically, tenderly, gently accepted by another, found a peace within. This is the monk who could write to Margie;

> I will no longer burn your wounded body. We do not need to weary ourselves grasping anything, even love: still less the bloody jewel of desire.[25]

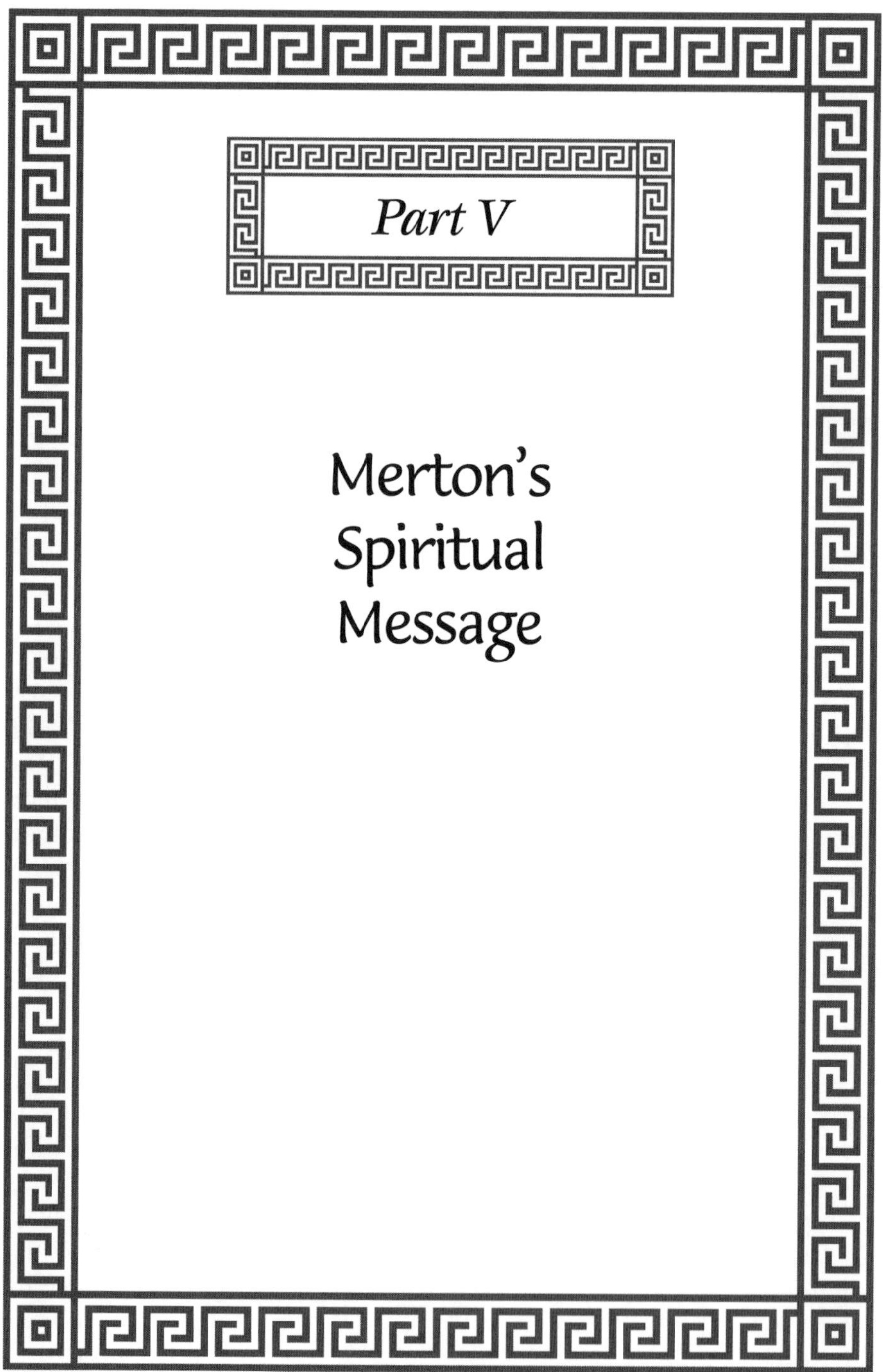

Part V

Merton's Spiritual Message

19

The True Self

A person's spirituality is part and parcel of who that person is, and since we have looked so closely at Thomas Merton, we already know his spiritual legacy. The last section of this book, therefore, serves as something of a reprise of all that has gone before.

For Merton, the whole spiritual life came to be a unity, a fact which makes these last three chapters hard to pull apart from one another. The experience of the true and false self is dependent on the contemplative attitude we possess. Our prayer becomes simply who we are through ego struggles and beyond them to reconciliation. Our life is our prayer. To the degree that we have seen and grown to accept the necessary self-deceptions of early times and the humbling reality of limitation, we are living prayers.

Thomas Merton learned these lessons, as everyone must, through trial and error. He was not afraid to risk making mistakes, which is why his faults were so numerous, and yet people were so fond of him. He was real; or rather, in the course of life he became real. His gift to us is that he kept telling us whatever it was he came to all along his way. In enthusiasm for some new awareness he often spoke confidently, even though a few years later he might contradict the very statements he had once proclaimed. For this reason it is very important to read Merton to the end. He himself was embarrassed by some of his earlier spiritual insights, inevitably based on a less whole, more dichotomizing period of his development.

One thing is certain: the spiritual heritage of Thomas Merton is experiential. When he talks about the division between action and contemplation, he does so, not theoretically, but from his felt sense of what that separation means. When he tells us that everything is one, is holy, is prayer, he does so because he found that out. Over time his discussion on spiritual realities became based less and less on definition and more and more on descriptions rising out of his experience. What Merton tells us is what he personally came to.

It would follow that whatever it is Merton talks about, it describes the 4 perspective. His view follows from and encompasses his own issues and dynamics, rising from his particular stance in the world. What are vices for him may be another person's virtues; his suggestions may be counterproductive for some. He is not a good guide for everybody. There are, no doubt, many people for whom he has no appeal. Others may think they understand what he is saying when, in fact, their personal issues may hardly be analogous to his own. As much as possible, we need to suspend our own worldview in order to enter Merton's. It is uniquely his, of course, but it is also filled with the recurring issues of his 4 stance.

With all this in mind we look at Merton's theme of human journey as moving from a false to a true self. Another way to put his teaching, if such it can be called, is to say that in the course of spiritual development a person needs to move from self-observation of self-performance to true and unreflected experience. We need to get off our personal stage and stay out of our personal audience. This is a theme 2/3/4/s can readily identify with. That being so, they are probably the ones who most find Merton a helpful mentor.

When Merton describes the spiritual life he uses typical vocabulary from his own triad. He says the experience of self is not a fabrication of our imagination, something or someone placed alongside the Divine Being. Rather, the self and the Divine Self are one, almost coextensive, at least as known and felt by a person. He adds that there is no need to seek God; there are no spiritual projects to embark on in order to be united with the Divine Being.[1] Nothing initially appealed more to Merton, a 4, than to have a spiritual task to perform; the security of working at holiness was a trap promising to relieve anxiety and engage the doing function he already tended to overuse.

He discovered that there exists in the relationship of the human being and the Divine Being a secret dynamic. It is an energy that only God can know. Merton urges people to forget about the connection and how it takes place. Instead, any movement depends on getting beyond accomplishment or desire of accomplishment. When this happens, a person finds freedom. Merton personifies the experience, calling it Freedom itself, the Divine Being. [2]

Merton tries for the concrete by using images to speak of the inner self, the true being. A lifetime lay behind his description of this inner self as beyond manipulation, "like a very shy wild animal that never appears at all whenever an alien presence is at hand."[3] Surely, for Merton, the alien presence is the false self, which, he goes on to say, troubles the true self by trying to lure it out.

He uses another, more static, image: the true self is not like a motor in a car. It is not a thing resting at the center of the human machine that "turns over" and propels it into action. It is not like life; it is life itself. He insists that there is no way to hold or study or even describe the self. Only the interior silence beyond fussing about the spiritual life allows it to manifest itself. One can only imagine how many times Merton must have become excited by this experience of self only to have that awareness immediately send the self scurrying away.

Merton struggled, as we have seen throughout these pages, with a lack of self-worth; the experience of his existential goodness came and went, undoubtedly dependent on whether or not he was, as we say today, in touch with his reality. His very search for meaning pushed the experience of meaning out of reach. Only when he could see himself as the "word of God" could he stop looking for justification and relax.[4]

Instead of worrying about making a case for his right to exist, Merton eventually realized that he needed to forget about the whole issue and use his freedom "in order to love."[5] This has often been said to be the 4's redemption: to let go of interior activity and respond to what is going on outside the self. Especially for 4s, this kind of self-forgetfulness moves the interior task from an endless and fruitless self-analysis to being taken up into a wider world. Note, however, that the intermediate stage of grappling with what is and what is not genuine interiority must be passed through before this can happen.

There is a kind of fascination with the experience of existential dread for 4s. Something in them thrills at looking into the face of meaninglessness, much as a person is drawn to the edge of a high precipice. They are compelled to look down into nothingness which in compulsion they see as *no* thing and, therefore, as *some* thing. The anguish of this empty terror tells them they must be about their spiritual life. Merton calls the bluff of such an experience when he says:

> "Dread" in this sense is not simply a childish fear of retribution, or a naive guilt, a fear of violating taboos. It is the profound awareness that one is capable of ultimate bad faith with (one)self and with others: that one is a living lie.[6]

It is important to underline that for Merton dread became that inauthentic, self-preoccupied self-search that postured a serious spiritual life rather than the fear of meaninglessness. This latter humiliation held for Merton, as for other 4s, a far more subtle dynamic rising out of the interior maze a compulsive doing function creates.

Neither does unity with the Divine suggest living out the role of solitary, romantic as that may seem for a 4. The prophet standing above the crowd, the mute who cannot convey to others a translatable message, might be appealing melancholy, but it is anything but the Christian good news. Merton discovered that he was no more special than anybody else. In fact, everyone else was one with him in Christ, not theoretically, but in their flesh and blood, their ignorance and a dirtiness, their vindictiveness and pettiness.[7] The freedom and emptiness Merton talks about are utterly simple and unreflected.[8] They are beyond the ego with its roles and masks, beyond the theater stage 4s find it so hard to exit from. It is with all of these dynamics in mind that we need to listen to Merton when he says:

> Contemplation is all the more pure in that one does not "look" to see if it is there. Such "walking with God" is one of the simplest and most secure ways of living a life of prayer, and one of the safest. It never attracts anybody's attention, least of all the attention of him who lives it. And he soon learns not to want to see anything special in himself.[9]

Merton names this attitude liberty and finds it buried in ordinariness. Such an experience, says Merton, is totally different from self-consciousness, the 4 trap. It is, rather, the felt sense of Being which, if reflected upon, ceases to be that experience.[10] Here again we see how Merton's instinct, his tendency to narcissistic self-examination, makes him especially helpful for people in our time. He describes "modern man" as needing

> liberation from his inordinate self-consciousness, his monumental self-awareness, his obsession with self-affirmation, so that he may enjoy the freedom from concern that goes

> with being simply what he is and accepting things as they are in order to work with them as he can.[11]

This simple formula saves a person from compulsion, at least it does so for a person like Merton. It is a profound absorption that is "clean and wakeful, with nothing strained or pathological about it."[12] There is much energy in this attitude; in fact, it is precisely this consciousness that releases pent-up energy, allowing it to flow through a person and out into action. Merton calls it "a direct grasp of life in its unity and concreteness" and says it is the Zen reality. No wonder that Merton was attracted to the East with its "grasp of what was always there, but not perceived, because an ego-subject cannot perceive it."[13]

Evil for Merton is about being separated from this pure experience. Spiritual death, rather than being a violation of some legal code, is "having separated myself from truth by complete inner falsity, from love by selfishness, from reality by trying to assert as real a will to nothingness."[14] Merton sees evil as the falsity of being, says Shannon. To take it to another level, it would seem that Merton sees being absorbed with one's being as something separate and observed from outside is what constitutes the existential lie.

Merton's life revealed increasing disinterest in his earlier distinctions between East/West views of self and God. Perhaps it was his 5 wing that initially drew him to the debate, but he moved to experience beyond such distinctions. It is still true that he carried to the last some need to insist on natural versus supernatural awareness in his writings, but[15] one wonders whether such theoretical categorizations were forced on him by censors. His journal entries suggest that they were; Merton seems hardly to be bothered with separating himself either from his own experience or his felt sense of the Divine.

Knowing and experiencing God and knowing and experiencing self, then became for Merton a single existential experience. Merton would probably call the merging of these two elements one "action," since simply being was beyond his ken.[16] Stillness was always still-movingness for Merton, as it is for others in the 2/3/4 triad. Life remained an active flow, cascading an individual into unreflected, loving concern for others. The more true the self, for Merton, the more self-forgetful and sacrificial he became. The true self swam in charity and responded to the call of life from whatever source it cried out. No wonder Merton took time to address the many requests from the many persons who approached him.

The search for the true self must be a lifelong one. This is so not because searching leads directly to finding, but because searching leads to seeing the deception of a search. Trials and errors that reveal the lie in looking for what we already possess provide necessary learning. Because Merton sought for his true self, his compulsions around that search were uncovered. Better such mistakes and illusions than a trance-like allowing no failure! The simple wisdom that life taught him in this hard and humbling way led to the gift of presence in the moment.

> As soon as a man is fully disposed to be alone with God, he is alone with God no matter where he may be—in the country, the monastery, the woods or the city. The lightning flashes from east to west, illuminating the whole horizon and striking where it pleases and at the same instant the infinite liberty of God flashes in the depths of that man's soul, and he is illumined. At that moment he sees that though he seems to be in the middle of his journey, he has already arrived at the end. For the life of grace on earth is the beginning of the life of glory. Although he is a traveler in time, he has opened his eyes, for a moment, in eternity.[17]

For Merton, the forgetfulness of self, of that character that walks across life's stage, is the essence of the contemplative attitude. Better put, perhaps, not only does the stage empty, it disappears. The 4 is no longer in any audience or observing anyone. When this becomes so—and it does in the present life only at the most contemplative of moments—the eternal present is.

The Contemplative Life

Thomas Merton is undoubtedly a great master of spirituality and prayer. He wrote about both extensively and lived them intensely—as he came to see, too intensely. Again, we need to follow his thought from his earlier to later years to find out just what he meant when he talked about this contemplative life. What he termed contemplation changed as he changed. Like the rest of what he spoke and wrote, contemplation became a simpler, less complex, more unified reality. His later statements carry the wisdom and the humorous perspective we have already noted throughout this book. They are summarized in this chapter for the purpose of clarifying their characteristically Merton, and therefore, 4 themes.

Merton distinguished between active and passive contemplation, writing about both extensively in his series of pamphlets titled "The Inner Experience." These were worked over many times during a period of years. About these writings Merton says to Sister Therese Lentfoehr:

> I was much too superficial and too cerebral at the time. I seem to have ignored the wholeness and integrity of life, and concentrated on a kind of angelism in contemplation. That was when I was a rip-roaring Trappist, I guess. Now that I am a little less perfect I seem to have a saner perspec-

> tive. And that too seems to be not according to the manuals, doesn't it?[1]

Merton would say, as probably most monastics would, that it was the spirituality of the *Rule of Benedict*, centered in and revolving around the Rule's chapter on humility, that describes the contemplative. In this section we see a person whose sense of the presence of God surrounds and permeates him or her like a seamless garment. Whether in a private, personal situation or celebrating the liturgy of the hours or eucharist or living side by side with community members, the person's awareness is increasingly that of creature before Creator with the ever-deepening consequences of such an attitude.[2]

It was this fifteen-hundred-year-old Benedictine spirituality that lay at the heart of Merton's spiritual formation and his twentieth-century articulations of what the contemplative life means. Merton most assuredly has shaped contemporary attitudes about presence to self, others, and the Divine; he has done so out of his monastic tradition. Based in that heritage he could write:

> The contemplative mind today will not normally be associated too firmly or too definitively with any "movement," whether political, religious, liturgical, artistic, philosophical, or what have you. The contemplative stays clear of movements, not because they confuse him but simply because he does not need them and can go further by himself than he can in their formalized and often fanatical ranks. [3]

Such assurance of rootedness and stability amid changing spiritual fads was the gift his monastic legacy gave the sometimes fickle, fascinated, 4 Merton. It was also, perhaps, his participation in this monastic universe, alive also in the East, that enabled him to share understandings with spiritual leaders from those backgrounds. There is something archetypal about the monk, which monastics from whatever tradition recognize. It becomes, often unconsciously, part of a common experience they instinctively recognize in one another.

What is more, the monastic spirit, founded as it very concretely is, on working and living in community, is a mirror of all human living. We recognize that to be the case when we read Merton and find him as applicable to the contemporary marketplace as he is to the monastery. He notes that contemplation is "not something general and abstract, but something on the contrary as concrete, particular and 'existential' as it can possibly be."[4] A prophet in so many ways, Merton was surely at the forefront of monastic revival. The universality of the call to contemplative life became, after he had long struggled to that awareness, his message. William Shannon notes what an immeasurable gift this revelation was for our times. He tells us to remember that Merton's intuitions came not from his reading—because no one was writing such things in his day—but from his own experience of contemplation.[5]

The natural unity of all life is the heart of the monastic reality. Simple, uncomplicated, holistic, and experiential, the contemplative life is what everyone not only can, but is meant to attain. This means, as Merton says in many places, that we become increasingly ourselves; someone dwells behind and looks out from our eyes and speaks from our lips. If human beings are to have the depth and dimension they were meant to have as person, they need to become contemplatives. An existential urgency draws them to that destiny.

Earlier steps in the contemplative life are dark and confusing because they lead us to the wholeness we have given up for our partial, perceptual distinctions and judgments and our refusal to accept our organic unity. At the same time we experience being propelled along the contemplative way, we question the new experience. Shannon summarizes a person's contemplative questions as Merton would put them:

> How can he know he is on the right path, especially when he sees no path at all? How can he know whether this pain of separation from the God he once thought he knew is a real separation from God or the experience of a darkness wherein the true God is met more fully and deeply? How does he know whether what is happening to him is the beginning of infused contemplation or simply a growing distaste for the interior life that may signal an eventual return to a Christian life that is devoted largely to externals? [6]

Such questions assume that clarity of consciousness has dimmed. Merton himself talks about this dark knowledge as "an apophatic grasp of Him Who Is."[7] Paradoxically, this darkness is actually an experience of wholeness and fullness of living. However, we no longer recognize this growing openness to Being as our destiny, so long have we been involved in boundary-creating, in defining our limited selves. What is in reality more life, we experience as less. Said another way, so much life and light blinds us. In Merton's words:

> The "death of the old man" is not the destruction of personality, but the dissipation of an illusion, and the discovery of the new man is the realization of what was there all along, at least as a radical possibility, by reason of the fact that man is the image of God.[8]

For Merton, "the Gift of the Spirit is the gift of freedom and emptiness."[9] In the darkness there is peace and strength,[10] a sense, it would seem, of the rightness and fittingness of this dark path. Since, in fact, there is nothing else to do about what is going on, Merton advises, "Leave nothingness as it is," adding the hopeful comment, "In it, he is present."[11]

Anne Carr remarks that only when one has developed a healthy ego is this journey beyond ego to the self, the unique word, possible. What she terms authentic autonomy is the only appropriate self-gift; only a self who possesses itself is capable of the austere loss of self essential for any spiritual way.[12] In Christian terms Merton says, "Contemplation is the awareness and realization, even in some sense experience, of what each Christian obscurely believes: 'It is now no longer I that live, but Christ lives in me.'"[13]

To his credit, and more easily perhaps because he was a 4, Merton was able to hear and respond to the contemplative experience in whatever terms people talked about it. He turns to Zen to show how some of life's earlier questioning attitudes eventually dissipate:

> Zen living shows that all the questioning is useless. But you have to have questioned everything in order to see that there's no point in questioning anything. Because everything is unquestionable, it's right there. But we put questions in between what is there and ourselves. Underlying Zen is a great awareness of what reality is. It includes a respect that doesn't analyze but takes reality as it is. It helps us to be content with things as they are and go on from there.[14]

We see in this passage how Merton both faced and put to rest two of the 4 compulsions: overanalysis and the restless, discontented envy that always wants whatever one does not have. While these instincts would remain, and his life would always include grappling with them, Merton—as seems obvious here—had unmasked them for what they are. No longer could these instincts blindly control him. Once discovered, the power of his compulsions was weakened by this awareness.

One way Merton seems to have underlined what the contemplative attitude meant in a very concrete way was by using the camera. Brother Patrick Hart talks about this hobby of Merton's:

> While walking in the woods, Merton photographed the images of his contemplation as he saw them, as they really were, in no way manipulated to create an artificial effect. He photographed whatever crossed his path: a dead tree root, the texture of weather-beaten clapboards on an abandoned barn, a rusted distiller, or the play of light and shadow on dry leaves in the woods. His contemplative and incarnational vision of reality was quite simply "things as they are." As such, they spoke eloquently to him of their creator. The camera was for Merton a potential catalyst for contemplation.[15]

Perhaps the most significant part of this quotation is that Merton did not arrange or pose any of the things he photographed. There is no part or role for anything to play, as he might once have thought there was in his instinctual 4 stance.

Toward the end of his life he comments in a similar vein on the personal artificiality of positioning in society. He imagines, as well he might out of his 4 view, that someone might say "'As a religious who is a dentist, I hope to exemplify the Christian life at the professional level.'" He responds to this imagined statement out of the wisdom of his 4 experience: "Instead, I would say, just be a dentist. . . . Just go ahead and do what you have to do."[16]

In this very simple remark Merton outlines the human being's personal responsibility: to be who one is. That he links this universal human mission with his own monastic vocation is clear in this excerpt from the final presentation in Bangkok:

> The monk is a man who has attained or is about to attain, or seeks to attain, full realization. He dwells in the center of society as one who has attained realization—he knows the score. Not that he has acquired unusual or esoteric information, but he has come to experience the ground of his own being in such a way that he knows the secret of liberation and can somehow or other communicate this to others.[17]

For Merton, freedom would always have the feel of activity about it. The idea of simply being would, for him, always remain an idea rather than an experience. We hear him speak further about his monastic, contemplative life in the instinctive doing terminology of his triad:

> Not that I must undertake a special project of self-transformation. Or that I must work on myself. In that regard, it would be better to forget it. Just go for walks, live in peace, let change come quietly and invisibly on the inside. But I do have a past to break with. An accumulation of inertia, waste, wrong, foolishness, rot, junk. A great need of clarification, of mindfulness, or rather, of no-mind. A return to genuine practice, right effort. Need to push on to the great doubt. Need of the spirit. Hang on to the clear light.[18]

This, one of Merton's final statements about contemplation, reveals the only kind of contemplative Merton could ever be: one whose instinct would always remain activity. In becoming such a contemplative he mirrors for each of us that we, too, can only become fully our creaturely potential. Merton became fully himself, fully a 4, aware of who he was, not denying his instinct but living it.

There are imperfections we, like Merton, possess because of our compulsions. There are those consequent on our creatureliness, which means that by definition we have only a partial view of reality, one of nine possibilities. Thomas Merton learned to live his imperfections without fear of failure. That fearlessness to be human led to his freedom, as it does to our own, whatever our enneagram stance. This is the only way any of us can fulfill our human destiny.

21

Prayer

Last, we look at Thomas Merton the pray-er, the living prayer. We will continue to address the contemplative experience expressed in prayer from a monastic standpoint of private and liturgical prayer, because such was Merton's life. He says of the prayer life of the monk:

> Meditation, psalmody, prayerful reading of the Scriptures (lectio divina) and contemplation are all part of a unified and integrated life in which the monk turns from the world to God. Monastic prayer is, therefore, the ensemble of these varied ways of finding God and resting in his presence.[1]

Merton's life in the monastery had shown him the value of doing the ordinary, human thing rather than trying to be an angel.[2] David Steindl-Rast says that Merton equated finding his true self with living a life of prayer.[3] This approach to prayer is marked by a Benedictine lack of methodology.

> O.K., now, pray. This is the whole doctrine of prayer in the Rule of St. Benedict. It's all summed up in one phrase: "If a man wants to pray, let him go and pray." That is all St. Benedict feels it is necessary to say about the subject. He doesn't say, let us go in and start with a little introductory prayer, etc., etc. If you want to pray, pray.[4]

When a person prays, Merton tells us, it is as though he or she circles around the present reality, delving ever deeper into its significance.

> In prayer we discover what we already have. You start where you are and you deepen what you already have, and you realize that you are already there. We already have everything, but we don't know it and we don't experience it.[5]

It all became so simple for Merton, so non-analytical, so lacking in drama and romance. Prayer involved no posturing of any kind:

> I refuse in practice to accept any theory or method of contemplation that simply divides soul against body, interior against exterior, and then tries to transcend itself by pushing creatures out into the dark. What dark? As soon as the split is made, the dark is abysmal in everything, and the only way to get back into the light is to be once again a normal human being who likes to smell the flowers and look at girls if they are around, and who likes the clouds, etc.[6]

Merton's propensity for making connection with others, usually verbally, may have led him to say of prayer:

> It's not necessary to talk to God in order to develop this awareness, although we do this sometimes . . . and that's fine. But it's not essential. Are we going to say "I love you"? The more we talk, the more foolish it sounds.
>
> This is where silence comes in. We listen to the depth of our own being, and out of this listening comes a rich silence, the silence of God, which just says "God" or "I am." Now, this is something![7]

We can almost feel in these words the "holy awe"[8] contemplation always includes. Is it the awe of our own or of the Divine Being? By the end of his life Merton seems not to bother about this question, let alone its answer. To experience the self includes an experience of the Greater-Than-Self, as many spiritual guides have told us, among them Thomas Merton. The opposite is also true for him. When we are lacking in contemplation we are not present to our true self and are in misery.

> The dimensions of prayer in solitude are those of man's ordinary anguish, his self-searching, his moments of nausea at this own vanity, falsity and capacity for betrayal. Far from establishing one in unassailable narcissistic security, the way of prayer brings us face to face with the sham and indignity of the false self that seeks to live for itself and to enjoy the "consolations of prayer" for its own sake. This self is pure illusion and ultimately he who lives for and by such an illusion must end either in disgust or madness.[9]

These illusions—and delusions as well—cover the true self, our genuine reality where we are one with the Divine. Merton dismisses even an I-Thou relationship with God, noting that the experience of ourselves and God is of one entity. He says elsewhere that there is no need to talk about this experience of unity with Being—one of his ways of describing prayer—with anyone. If we find a friend who understands, we might allude to it vaguely. Surely it is not to be talked about in any detail.[10] He is not manifesting here the melancholy theme that no one can understand. Rather, he is content with the realization that genuine understanding has very little to do with telling anybody anything. His 4 verbosity has finally yielded to silent self- and other-presence.

Merton does let us in on his prayer life indirectly when he talks about the way he goes about making a retreat:

> I go out on a hill or into the woods and just do nothing for as long a time as possible. After a while I have to go back and do something. But I think this is the most obvious way to make a retreat. Sometimes I take a little book and read about three sentences in a week. I say the office and do the things I'm supposed to do. That's all.[11]

He adds a summary of a California trip, when he spent the entire day on the shore "doing absolutely nothing except sitting there watching the waves come in and the clouds piling up over the hills."[12] Many of Merton's journals contain similar examples of the utter simplicity of his personal prayer. Even reading, something he had turned to from an almost insatiable 5-wing need for information, became of little importance. It would seem that his days often were the constant experience of being creature with Creator. He had, indeed, become Benedict's humble monk.

It may be that toward the end of his life Merton's only formalized "statements" to the Divinity took place during the liturgy of the hours, the divine office, the monastic work of God. In the mysteries of this liturgy and of the eucharist, he states, a person's inner awakening is signified and the myths of his or her life expressed. He acknowledges that "all genuine revivals of fervor attempt a renewal and purification of the interior life generated by symbolic rites, mysteries and prayers."[13] He adds, however, that in liturgical rituals revised after Vatican II, one needs to be aware of "emotional, sentimental, erotic and even bacchanalian substitutes for the awakening of the inner self."[14] Knowing how many reservations Merton had about liturgical renewal in the 1960s, one can read between the lines here. There were many times when he was obviously offended by some of the monastery's modernized ceremonies. In his mind they may well have seemed at least a bit overdone if not orgiastic. Romantic 4 nostalgia for the Latin liturgy never left Merton, who as an artist, retained an understated style that was echoed in the strains of Gregorian Chant. Liturgy as imperfectly ritualized in community, whether in the old or new church, demanded much from Merton. He gave it, sometimes willingly, sometimes not.

Monastic spiritual tradition has never seen a conflict between public and private prayer. As Shannon notes, Merton shared this monastic view.[15] For him, the liturgy, with its theology expressed in scripture, music, art and poetry, became the point of transition between what he called active and passive contemplation. From liturgical statement to interior silence was a natural transition for him. One could even say that his doing compulsion might well have been kept at bay by the repetitive ritual of liturgy. There was just enough action involved to remove the top layer of anxiety and analysis to which purely private and personal prayer might have led. He wrote along those lines:

> The true vocation of the monks of the Benedictine family is not to fight for contemplation against action, but to restore the ancient, harmonious and organic balance between the two. Both are necessary. Martha and Mary are sisters.[16]

Merton the artist always found the performance of liturgy with its human limitations annoying. Such annoyance provided him with an important opportunity not only to practice penance, but to get beneath the ritual to the contemplative essence of it. Hard as it was for him to tolerate substandard artistry, he followed his difficulty to the place where liturgy is meant to take the worshipping community, individually and corporately.

> The value of the monks' Public Prayer is therefore not drawn so much from its sound as from the deep silence of God which enters into that sound and gives it actuality, value, meaning. The beauty of Gregorian chant, and that which distinguishes it from every other kind of music, lies in the fact that its measured sound, in itself beautiful, tends to lead the soul, by its beauty, into the infinitely more beautiful silence of God. Chant that does not have this effect, no matter how great its technical perfection, is practically without value. It is empty of the silence of wisdom, which is its substance and its life.[17]

Here we see the love of beauty and harmony followed to a level beneath the merely artistic presentation which 4s—and Merton—see as desirable. The more important harmony, a harmony which can tolerate something less than aesthetic perfection, is the place of contemplation, that harmony of creation as it really is in relationship to the Creator. The wisdom and silence and life of that kind of rhythm make peace with the less-than-beautiful.

Clearly, for Merton, the liturgical ritual was, as Joseph Campbell has said, the enactment of the myth. It was not only his personal myth and story that he celebrated, but that of his community and the whole of creation as well. Liturgical prayer was far beyond mere performance for him; it was his life which he expressed in the seasonal recurrences of the liturgical year. In this regard he writes:

> Unless the Christian participates to some degree in the dread, the sense of loss, the anguish, the dereliction and the destitution of the Crucified, he or she cannot really enter into the mystery of the liturgy.[18]

One might also add other experiences besides anguish and dread that take on life in the liturgical celebrations. It would be characteristic of Merton to discover the link between his life and that of Christ and all people in those liturgies that were more painful and, one might say, more melancholy and dramatic.

This dramatic quality of the liturgy could have become Merton's focus. He might have become lost in performance. Perhaps that is a bit of what happened when he grew so irritated at the imperfections in liturgical production. Such an attitude never took over for very long, however. Merton realized that, indeed, Christ's mysteries were his own mysteries. Liturgy was about those personal pains he so recognized and identified with. But the liturgy was also about his other realities of thought and body and emotion.

Contemplation for Merton was the perfection of worship.

> Without contemplation worship tends to remain lifeless and external. The mere existence of the church's liturgy is then a call to active contemplation. To remain withdrawn from the liturgy and outside it is to exclude oneself from possibilities of active contemplation that the church offers to all, with many graces and lights that she alone is privileged to distribute to her children.[19]

For Merton, personal contemplation and liturgical celebration fed one another. This was true for him not only in theory; he experienced it to be so. It may well have been precisely this balance and harmony between the two that made him the contemplative he was. He never got swallowed up in narcissism; neither did he lose the deeper meaning of liturgical celebration, which was silence and contemplation. In his rhythm of stillness and still-movingness, Merton's instinctual doing, exaggerated to compulsion, was burned away and purified.

As much as Merton may have hankered for the pure hermit life, he remained a monk all of his days. St. Benedict calls the monk who lives in community "the strong kind."[20] Not only did the common life and its liturgical expression address Merton's need for ordinary, incarnate living, but it fed his contemplation and brought it to fullness.

Conclusion

On his retreat at Gethsemani Abbey in 1941 Thomas Merton wrote: "I feel like a thief and a murderer who has been put in jail and condemned for stealing and murdering all my life, murdering God's grace in myself and in others, murdering Him in his image."[1] At twenty-six, Merton recognized that he was, indeed, God's word. He also was aware of his falsity, of the illusions and delusions that led him to deny his own worth, to eliminate the very life of God he was made flesh to witness. This appalling awareness propelled Merton on his way and led him to face the compulsions he had developed in futile efforts to wipe out who he really was.

We have benefited from his grappling with all of this in his personal life. We find parallels to our own existence, because something of this blindness and search and rediscovery of our value is part of all of us, is also our Way. Some of us struggle with the same sort of issues Merton had; some of us know other ones. We all follow some analogous path to awareness, because such is the human destiny.

In a matter of a few years we will know much more about how Thomas Merton traveled his Way. Now that twenty-five years have passed since his death, journals never before available to the public are being published. It has been tempting to wait for these before writing this book, because new and possibly more appropriate examples of his dynamics will abound. There is something to be said, however, for a project's readiness, and for me that readiness had arrived.

This means that readers who have followed me through these developments—those of Merton's life story and those outlining 4 characteristics—will have further work to do to bring these two considerations together. I am confident that what those who do so will discover will only substantiate these hypotheses.

My previous books have ended with a reference to the ongoing nature of enneagram studies. This one will, too. The enneagram is a developing tradition we are all creating. Were Merton alive today, the enneagram would probably interest him. Who knows what he might have contributed to its tradition. In his personal absence we nonetheless find him a continuing companion through his forthcoming publications, from which we will continue to learn more about his spiritual way and our own.

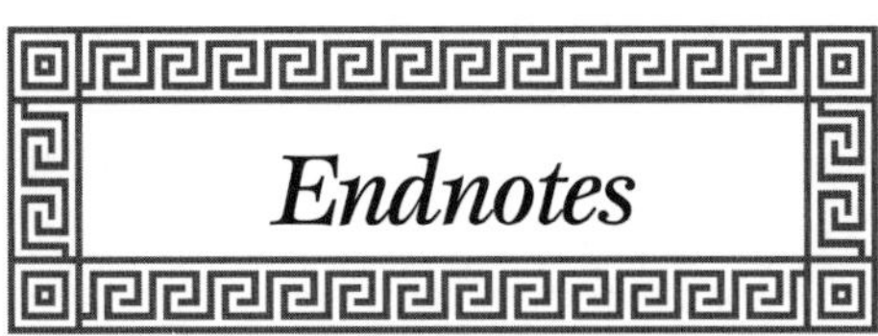

Endnotes

Introduction: Continuing the Dialogue

1. Two books that develop basic descriptions of the enneagram spaces are *The Enneagram* by Helen Palmer (San Francisco: Harper and Row, 1988) and *Personality Types: Using the Enneagram for Self-Discovery* by Don Richard Riso (Boston: Houghton Mifflin, 1987).

2. In his stories about the contemplative attitude, Anthony de Mello attributes to a "master" a number of statements about the spiritual life. Many of these are found in *One Minute Wisdom* (Garden City, NY: Doubleday and Company, Inc., 1986) and *The Song of the Bird* (New York: Image Books, Doubleday, 1984).

3. Suzanne Zuercher, O.S.B., *Enneagram Spirituality: From Compulsion to Contemplation* (Notre Dame, IN: Ave Maria Press, 1992) and *Enneagram Companions; Relationship and Spiritual Direction* (Notre Dame, IN: Ave Maria Press, 1993).

4. The fullest treatment of Erik Erikson's developmental theory applied to a specific personality is found in *Gandhi's Truth* (Norton, 1969).

1

The 4: Ego-Romantic, Ego-Melancholic, Over-Dramatizer

1. A brief summary of the history of the enneagram can be found in Riso, *Personality Types.*

2. *The Rule of St. Benedict* (Collegeville, MN: The Liturgical Press, 1981). The Prologue.

3. William Shannon, *Thomas Merton's Dark Path* (New York: Penguin Books, 1982).

4. Since new publications by Merton are still forthcoming, I refer you to The Thomas Merton Studies Center at Bellarmine College in Louisville, Kentucky, to obtain a current listing.

5. Merton's official biography, *The Seven Mountains of Thomas Merton* by Michael Mott (Boston: Houghton Mifflin, 1984) is my source for detailed information about Merton's life.

6. Some authors who write about Merton were personally acquainted with him and provide information in this regard. Mott's official biography and Paul Wilkes's *Merton by Those Who Knew Him Best* (San Francisco, Harper & Row, 1984) afford additional views of how Merton appeared to others.

7. I refer you to the Thomas Merton Studies Center for a complete listing of audiovisual materials and where these might be obtained.

8. The use of these terms came to me from notes taken by Robert Ochs, S.J., who originally studied with Claudio Naranjo at the Esalen Institute.

9. Wilkes, *Merton by Those Who Knew Him Best*, pp. 118-19.

10. Ibid., p. 98.

11. Ibid., pp. 81-82.

12. Ibid., p. 88.

13. Ibid., p. 118.

14. Ibid., p. 105.

15. Ibid., p. 118.

16. Mark 1:13.

17. James Connor, O.C.S.O., "Merton as a Spiritual Director," an address delivered at the International Thomas Merton Conference, Colorado Springs, CO, June 1993.

18. Quoted in Wilkes, *Merton by Those Who Knew Him Best*, p. 69.

2

The Fundamental Sin: A Figure on His Own

1. Mott, *The Seven Mountains of Thomas Merton*, pp. 18-19.

2. Thomas Merton, *New Seeds of Contemplation* (New York: New Directions, 1961), pp. 72-73. Although each chapter seems to be on an independent topic, this book in fact provides a summary of the spiritual journey and so has been my source for many references in this chapter.

3. Ibid., p. 32.

4. Parker Palmer, *The Active Life* (San Francisco: Harper and Row, 1990), p. 21.

5. Merton, *New Seeds of Contemplation*, p. 15.

6. Ibid., p. 15.

7. Ibid., p. 112.

8. Ibid., p. 87.

9. Ibid., p. 181.

10. Ibid., p. 74.

11. Ibid., p. 74.

12. Ibid., p. 75.

13. Quoted by Shannon, *Thomas Merton's Dark Path*, p. 133, from the fourth draft of *The Inner Experience* by Merton.

14. Merton, *New Seeds of Contemplation*, pp. 76-77.

15. Ibid., p. 180.

16. Jolande Jacobi, *The Way of Individuation* (New York: Meridian Books, New American Library, 1967).

17. Merton, quoted in Shannon, *Thomas Merton's Dark Path*, p. 41.

18. Ibid., p. 133.

19. Merton, *New Seeds of Contemplation*, p. 280.

20. Ibid., pp. 195-96.

21. Ibid., p. 293.

3

The Fear That Conflict Will Destroy

1. Merton, *New Seeds of Contemplation*, p. 123.

2. Ibid., p. 123.

3. Riso, *Personality Types*, p. 111. This chapter on the 4 dynamics affords the best description I have found, especially regarding the guilt and self-deprecation Merton names as the source of violence in our world.

4. Merton, "A Signed Confession of Crimes Against the State," in *A Thomas Merton Reader* (Garden City, NY: Image Books, 1974), p. 116.

5. Thomas Merton, "War and the Prayer for Peace," in *A Thomas Merton Reader*, p. 277.

6. Thomas Merton, "Christian Culture Needs Oriental Wisdom," in *A Thomas Merton Reader*, p. 295.

7. Merton, *New Seeds of Contemplation*, pp. 74-75.

8. Merton, *A Thomas Merton Reader*, p. 344.

9. Ibid., p. 349.

10. Ibid. p. 366.

11. Thomas Merton, *The Hidden Ground of Love* (New York: Farrar, Strauss, Giroux, 1985), p. 294.

4

Merton the Doer

1. David Steindl-Rast, in *Gratefulness, the Heart of Prayer* (New York: Paulist Press, 1984), talks about this dynamic in the chapter "Hopes: Openness for Surprise."

2. Merton, *New Seeds of Contemplation*, pp. 273-274.

3. Merton, "Christian Culture Needs Oriental Wisdom," in *A Thomas Merton Reader*, p. 296.

4. Ibid., p. 298.

5. Jonathan Montaldo, "Stability and Continual Renewal: Thomas Merton's Commitment to Gethsemani," a presentation delivered at the International Thomas Merton Society Conference, Colorado Springs, CO, June 1993.

6. Thomas Merton, *The Sign of Jonas* (New York: Harcourt, Brace, 1953), p. 251.

7. Ibid., p. 201.

8. Thomas Merton, *Day of a Stranger*, ed. with introduction by Robert E. Daggy (Salt Lake City: Gibbs M. Smith, 1981), pp. 37, 39.

9. Thomas Merton, *Disputed Questions* (New York: Farrar, Straus and Cudahy, 1960), p. 160.

10. Thomas Merton, *Zen and the Birds of Appetite* (New York: New Directions, 1968), p. 53.

11. Thomas Merton, *The Climate of Monastic Prayer* (Kalamazoo, MI: Cistercian Publications, 1981), p. 48.

12. Thomas Merton, "Spiritual Direction and Meditation," in *A Thomas Merton Reader*, p. 328.

13. Thomas Merton, *The Asian Journal* (New York: New Directions, 1975), p. 90.

14. Thomas Merton, *The Springs of Contemplation* (New York: Farrar, Straus, Giroux, 1992), p. 184.

15. Ibid., p. 219.

16. Thomas Merton, *Conjectures of a Guilty Bystander* (New York: Image Books, 1989), p. 282.

17. Merton, *The Springs of Contemplation*, p. 219.

18. Merton, *Conjectures of a Guilty Bystander*, p. 131.

19. Thomas Merton, *A Man in the Divided Sea* (New York: New Directions, 1946), p. 141.

5

The Special and the Ordinary

1. Mott, *The Seven Mountains of Thomas Merton,* p. 229.

2. Merton, quoted in Mott, *The Seven Mountains of Thomas Merton*, p. xxiii.

3. Ibid., p. 362.

4. Merton, *The Hidden Ground of Love*, p. 510.

5. Gloria Kitto Lewis, "Merton as Teacher," a presentation delivered at the International Thomas Merton Society Conference, Colorado Springs, CO, June 1993.

6. Merton, *New Seeds of Contempation*, p. 49.

7. Merton, *The Seven Storey Mountain*, p. 285.

8. Mott, *The Seven Mountains of Thomas Merton*, p. 362.

9. Thomas Merton, "St. John of the Cross," in *A Thomas Merton Reader*, pp. 292-93.

10. Ibid., p. 293.

11. Thomas Merton, "Herakleitos the Obscure," in *A Thomas Merton Reader*, p. 267.

12. Thomas Merton, "The Inner Experience: Kinds of Contemplation (IV)," offprint from Cistercian Studies, vol. 18 (1983:4), p. 290.

13. Thomas Merton, "The Inner Experience: Prospects and Conclusions (VIII)," offprint from Cistercian Studies, vol. 19 (1984:4), p. 341.

14. Merton, "The Inner Experience: Kinds of Contemplation (IV)," p. 296.

15. Ibid., p. 296.

16. Thomas Merton, "The Inner Experience: Infused Contemplation (V)," offprint from Cistercian Studies, vol. 19 (1984:1), p. 68.

17. Merton, *Conjectures of a Guilty Bystander*, p. 157.

18. Ibid., p. 157.

19. Ibid., p. 157.

20. Ibid., p. 158.

21. Merton, *The Springs of Contemplation*, p. 212.

22. Mott, *The Seven Mountains of Thomas Merton*, p. xxvi.

23. Therese Lentfoehr, "The Spiritual Writer," in *Thomas Merton, Monk*, ed. Patrick Hart (Garden City, NY: Image Books, 1976), pp. 122-23.

24. James Finley, *Merton's Palace of Nowhere* (Notre Dame, IN: Ave Maria Press, 1978), p. 113.

25. Thomas Merton, "The Inner Experience: Some Dangers in Contemplation (VI)," offprint from Cistercian Studies, vol. 19 (1984:2), p. 150.

26. Thomas Merton, quoted by Tarcisius Connor in Hart, *Thomas Merton, Monk*, p. 191.

27. Thomas Merton, "The Inner Experience: Notes on Contemplation (I)," offprint from Cistercian Studies vol. 18 (1983:1), p. 9.

6

Life as an Art Piece

1. Anne E. Carr, *A Search for Wisdom and Spirit* (Notre Dame, IN: University of Notre Dame Press, 1988), pp. 110-11.

2. Merton on Dylan Thomas, "Poets," *A Thomas Merton Reader*, p. 249.

3. Mott, *The Seven Mountains of Thomas Merton*, pp. 211-13.

4. Merton, *The Sign of Jonas*, pp. 233-34.

5. Merton, *Conjectures of a Guilty Bystander*, p. 22.

6. Thomas Merton, *No Man Is an Island* (New York: Harcourt Brace, 1955), p. 36.

7. Merton, "Herakleitos the Obscure," *A Thomas Merton Reader*, p. 263.

8. Ibid., p. 268.

9. Merton, *No Man Is an Island*, pp. 34-35.

10. Merton, *Conjectures of a Guilty Bystander*, p. 149.

11. Thomas Merton, "Art and Spirituality," *A Thomas Merton Reader*, p. 412.

12. Lewis, "Merton as Teacher."

13. Merton, *The Sign of Jonas*, p. 238.

14. Merton, *No Man Is an Island*, p. 34.

15. Merton, "Art and Spirituality," pp. 413-14.

16. Ibid., pp. 414-15.

7

Life as a Drama

1. Anthony Padovano, *The Human Journey—Thomas Merton: Symbol of a Century* (Garden City, NY: Doubleday, 1982), pp. 42-43.

2. Merton, *The Seven Storey Mountain*, p. 111.

3. Ibid., p. 111.

4. Ibid., p. 114.

5. Ibid., p. 118.

6. Merton, *Conjectures of a Guilty Bystander*, p. 174.

7. Ibid., p. 157.

8. Ibid., p. 157.

9. Chrysogonus Waddell, O.C.S.O., "Merton and the Tiger Lily" in *The Merton Annual*, vol. 2 (New York: AMS Press, 1989), pp. 59-84.

10. Mott, *The Seven Mountains of Thomas Merton*, p. 297. It is important to an understanding of Merton's grappling with his dramatic tendency to read the entire section describing this encounter with Gregory Zilboorg and its consequences.

11. Ibid., p. 298.

12. Thomas Merton, "The Inner Experience: Some Dangers in Contemplation (VI)," p. 147.

13. Ibid., p. 148.

14. Mott, *The Seven Mountains of Thomas Merton*, p. 184.

8

Social and Solitary

1. Carmen Bernos De Gasztold, *Prayers from the Ark*, trans. Rumer Godden (New York: Penguin Books, 1976), p. 43.

2. Robert Waldron, *Thomas Merton in Search of His Soul* (Notre Dame, IN: Ave Maria Press, 1994), p. 51.

3. Robert E. Daggy, "Thomas Merton: The Desert Call," in *The Merton Seasonal*, vol. 18, no. 2 (Spring 1993), pp. 8-15. There are several examples in this article about Merton's rediscovered enthusiasm for eating out and drinking with friends.

4. John Eudes Bamberger, O.C.S.O., "The Monk" in Hart, *Thomas Merton, Monk*, pp. 41-42.

5. Mott, *The Seven Mountains of Thomas Merton*, pp. 363-64.

6. Lewis, "Merton as Teacher."

7. John Howard Griffin, *Hermitage Journals—A Diary Kept While Working on a Biography of Thomas Merton* (Kansas City: Andrews and McMeel, 1981), p. 57.

8. Lewis, "Merton as Teacher."

9. Thomas Merton, *Contemplative Prayer* (Garden City, NY: Doubleday Image, 1971), p. 97.

10. Thomas Merton, *Restricted Journals* (June 5, 1963) quoted in Mott, *The Seven Mountains of Thomas Merton*, p. 392.

11. Finley, *Merton's Palace of Nowhere*, p. 54.

12. Merton, *New Seeds of Contemplation*, p. 51.

13. Merton, "The Inner Experience," quoted in Shannon, *Thomas Merton's Dark Path*, p. 99.

14. Thomas Merton, "The Inner Experience: Society and the Inner Self (II)," offprint from Cistercian Studies, vol, 18 (1983:2), pp. 125-26.

15. Merton "The Inner Experience: Notes on Contemplation (I)," p. 5.

16. Merton, "The Inner Experience: Some Dangers in Contemplation (VI)," p. 141.

17. Merton, *Contemplative Prayer*, p. 113.

18. Merton, *The Sign of Jonas* (1953), p. 111.

19. Thomas Merton, *The Solitary Life* (Lexington, KY: Stamperia del Santuccio, 1960), p. 214.

20. From the Preface to the Japanese edition of *The Seven Storey Mountain.*

21. Thomas Merton, *Contemplation in a World of Action* (Garden City, NY: Doubleday, 1971), p. 229.

22. Thomas Merton, *Thoughts in Solitude* (New York: Farrar, Straus and Giroux, 1983), p. 55.

23. Merton, *Contemplation in a World of Action*, p. 23.

24. Thomas Merton, *The Seven Storey Mountain*, pp. 411-12.

9

The Temptation to Despair

1. Merton, *Contemplative Prayer*, pp. 102-04.

2. Carr, *A Search for Wisdom and Spirit*, p. 108.

3. Ibid., p. 113.

4. Ibid., p. 117.

5. Merton, *Thoughts in Solitude*, p. 21.

6. Merton, *Conjectures of a Guilty Bystander*, p. 158.

7. Merton, *The Climate of Monastic Prayer*, p. 38.

8. Carr, *A Search for Wisdom and Spirit*, p. 115.

9. Ibid., p. 117.

10. Merton, *The Climate of Monastic Prayer*, p. 96.

11. Thomas Merton, *The Silent Life* (New York: Farrar, Straus and Cudahy, 1957), p. 4.

12. Ibid., p. 7.

13. Merton, *Contemplative Prayer*, p. 102.

14. Merton, *Conjectures of a Guilty Bystander*, p. 146.

15. Merton, *Thoughts in Solitude*, p. 44.

16. Merton, *Restricted Journals*, March 30, 1958, quoted in Mott, *The Seven Mountains of Thomas Merton*, p. 317.

17. Merton, *The Hidden Ground of Love*, p. 503.

10

Spiritual Life as a Coming Home

1. Thomas Merton, "Circular Letter to Friends, September 1968," in *The Asian Journal*, Appendix I.

2. Mott, *The Seven Mountains of Thomas Merton*, p. 205.

3. Thomas Merton, *The Collected Poems of Thomas Merton* (New York: New Directions, 1977), p. 371.

4. Thomas Merton, "Raids on the Unspeakable" in *A Thomas Merton Reader*, p. 365.

5. David Steindl-Rast, "Exposure: Key to Thomas Merton's Asian Journal?," *Monastic Studies*, pp. 181-206.

6. Montaldo, "Stability and Continual Renewal: Thomas Merton's Commitment to Gethsemani," p. 9.

7. Shannon, *Thomas Merton's Dark Path*, p. 119.

8. Ibid., p. 120.

9. Montaldo, "Stability and Continual Renewal: Thomas Merton's Commitment to Gethsemani," p. 13.

10. Ibid., p. 13.

11. Merton, *The Seven Storey Mountain*, pp. 364-65.

12. Merton, "The Day of a Stranger," in *A Thomas Merton Reader*, p. 433.

13. Ibid., p. 435.

14. Shannon, *Thomas Merton's Dark Path*, p. 216.

15. Thomas Merton, address delivered in Bangkok, Thailand, December 10, 1968.

16. Ibid.

17. Shannon,*Thomas Merton's Dark Path*, p. 217.

18. Thomas Merton, *Selected Poems* (New York: New Directions, 1967), p. 16.

11

The Search for Meaning

1. Thomas Merton, *No Man Is an Island*, p. xiii.

2. Ibid., p. xii.

3. Thomas Merton, *Silence in Heaven* (New York: The Studio Publication, 1956), p. 27.

4. Ibid., p. 27.

5. Merton, *The Sign of Jonas*, p. 354.

6. Ibid., pp. 354-55.

7. Ibid., pp. 356-57.

8. Ibid., p. 357.

9. Ibid., p. 360.

10. Ibid., p. 361.

11. Ibid., p. 358.

12. Ibid., p. 362.

13. Thomas Merton, *The Monastic Journey*, ed. Patrick Hart (Mission, KS: Sheed, Andrews and McMeel, 1977), p. 171.

14. Ibid., p. 171.

15. Ibid., p. 171.

16. Ibid., p. 173.

17. Shannon, *Thomas Merton's Dark Path*, p. 225.

18. Rainer Maria Rilke, *Selected Poems*, trans. Robert Bly (New York: Harper & Row, 1981), p. 139.

19. Merton, "The Inner Experience: Prospects and Conclusions (VIII)," p. 343.

12

Deaths and Births

1. Thomas Merton, *A Vow of Conversation* (New York: Farrar, Straus, Giroux, 1988), p. 19.

2. *The Rule of St. Benedict*, p. 185.

3. Merton, *The Springs of Contemplation*, pp. 188-89.

4. Merton, *No Man Is an Island*, p. 263.

5. Merton, *Conjectures of a Guilty Bystander*, pp. 262-63.

6. Thomas Merton, *Thoughts in Solitude*, p. 28.

7. Merton, *The Hidden Ground of Love*, p. 350.

8. Merton, *Conjectures of a Guilty Bystander*, p. 214.

9. Ibid., p. 214.

10. Ibid., pp. 171-72.

11. Ibid., p. 172.

12. Ibid., p. 41.

13. Merton, *A Thomas Merton Reader*, p. 16.

14. Thomas Merton, "For my Brother: Reported Missing in Action, 1943," in *Selected Poems*, pp. 12-13. This collection offers many examples of Merton's preoccupation with life and death issues.

15. Merton, *No Man Is an Island*, p. 263.

16. Thomas Merton, *The Asian Journal*, p. 306.

17. Ibid., p. 16.

18. *Thomas Merton, He Is Risen* (Niles, IL: Argus Press, 1977), p. 5.

19. Ibid., p. 8.

20. Ibid., p. 15.

13

The Spirit of Jesus

1. Zuercher, O.S.B., *Enneagram Spirituality*. See chapter 7, "The Meaning of the Incarnation," for a fuller development of these ideas.

2. Karlfried Graf von Durckheim, *The Way of Transformation* (London: George Allen and Unwin, 1985), p. 74.

3. Merton, "The Inner Experience: Society and the Inner Self (II)," p. 124.

4. Thomas Merton, "The Inner Experience: Christian Contemplation (III)," offprint from Cistercian Studies, vol. 18, (1983:3), p. 203.

5. Ibid., pp. 203-4.

6. Ibid., p. 211.

7. Ibid., p. 211.

8. Merton, "The Inner Experience: Society and the Inner Self (II)," p. 125.

9. Merton, "The Inner Experience: Christian Contemplation (III)," p. 215.

10. Thomas Merton, "The Good Samaritan," in *A Thomas Merton Reader*, p. 353.

11. Ibid., p. 355.

12. Merton, *No Man Is an Island*, p. 231.

13. Merton, "The Inner Experience: Christian Contemplation (III)," p. 210.

14. Thomas Merton, Special Closing Prayer offered at the First Spiritual Summit Conference in Calcutta, in *A Thomas Merton Reader*, p. 512.

15. Merton, "The Inner Experience: Infused Contemplation (V)," p. 66.

16. Ibid., p. 68.

17. Ibid., p. 68.

18. Merton, *Contemplation in a World of Action*, p. 216.

19. Tarcisius Connor in Hart, *Thomas Merton, Monk*, p. 180.

20. Thomas Merton, *Silence in Heaven*, p. 21.

21. Ibid., p. 27.

22. Thomas Merton, *The School of Charity*, ed. Patrick Hart (New York: Farrar, Straus, Giroux, 1990), p. 249.

23. Thomas Merton, Cistercian Studies 1 (1967), p. 8.

24. Merton, *The Springs of Contemplation*, p. 74.

14

Oneness in the Spirit

1. Thomas Merton quoted by Parker Palmer, "In the Belly of a Paradox: A Celebration of Contradictions in the Thoughts of Thomas Merton" (Wallington, PA: Pendle Hill Pamphlet 224, 1979), p. 22.

2. Thomas Merton, *The Sign of Jonas* , p. 91-2.

3. Merton, *No Man Is an Island*, p. 140.

4. Merton, "The Inner Experience: Christian Contemplation (III)," pp. 208-9.

5. Ibid., p. 209.

6. Merton, *The Springs of Contemplation*, p. 201.

7. Ibid., p. 260.

8. Merton, "The Inner Experience: Christian Contemplation (III)," pp. 213-14.

9. Merton, *New Seeds of Contemplation*, p. 66.

10. Thomas Merton, "The Inner Experience: Prospects and Conclusions (VIII)," pp. 340-41.

11. Merton, "The Inner Experience: Notes on Contemplation (I)," p. 3.

12. Merton, "The Inner Experience: Christian Contemplation (III)," p. 206.

13. Carr, *A Search for Wisdom and Spirit*, p. 145.

14. Ibid., p. 66.

15. Ibid., p. 130.

16. Merton, *The Asian Journal* (1975), p. 311.

17. Merton, *Zen and the Birds of Appetite*, p. 3.

18. Ibid., p. 33.

19. Ibid., p. 5.

20. Ibid., p. 35.

21. Ibid., p. 44.

22. Ibid., p. 39.

23. Ibid., p. 39.

24. Ibid., p. 90.

25. Ibid., pp. 90-91.

26. Ibid., p. 62.

27. Ibid., p. 30.

28. Merton, *The Asian Journal*, p. 313.

15

The Way to Hope

1. Zuercher, *Enneagram Spirituality*. These ideas are developed more fully in chapter 8, "The Present Moment."

2. Merton, *The Climate of Monastic Prayer*, p. 131.

3. Ibid., pp. 137-38.

4. Merton, *Silence in Heaven*, pp. 21-22.

5. Donald Grayston, quoted in Shannon, *Thomas Merton's Dark Path*, p. 146.

6. Ibid., p. 146.

7. Merton, *Conjectures of a Guilty Bystander* (1989), p. 131.

8. Ibid., p. 158.

9. Merton, *The Asian Journal*, p. 117.

10. Merton, "The Good Samaritan," p. 353.

11. Ibid., p. 351.

12. Merton, *The Sign of Jonas*, p. 362.

13. Ibid., p. 362.

14. Ibid., p. 362.

15. Merton, "The Inner Experience: Christian Contemplation (III)," p. 215.

16. Merton, *The Asian Journal*, pp. 233-36.

17. Ibid., p. 333.

18. Ibid., p.236.

16

The Monastic Community

1. Carr, *A Search for Wisdom and Spirit*, p. 134.

2. Thomas Merton, "Marxism and Monastic Perspectives," in Merton, *The Asian Journal*, p. 338.

3. Thomas Merton, Letter to Father Aelred Squire, O. P., August 29, 1966.

4. Merton, *The Hidden Ground of Love*, p. 511.

5. Matthew Kelty, in Hart, *Thomas Merton, Monk*, p. 35.

6. Bamberger in Hart, *Thomas Merton, Monk*, p. 41.

7. Ibid., p. 49.

8. James Connor, "Homily for the 25th Anniversary of the Death of Fr. Louis Merton," *The Merton Seasonal*, vol. 19, no. 1, (Winter 1994), p. 21.

9. Ibid., p. 22.

10. Kelty in Hart, *Thomas Merton, Monk*, pp. 35-36.

11. James Fox in Hart, *Thomas Merton, Monk*, p. 155.

12. Merton, *The Hidden Ground of Love*, p. 502.

13. Ibid., p. 505.

14. Ibid., p. 505.
15. Ibid., p. 508.
16. Merton, *The Sign of Jonas*, p. 32.
17. Ibid., p. 32.
18. Ibid., p. 32.
19. Merton, *The Hidden Ground of Love*, p. 509.
20. Ibid., p. 510.
21. Merton, *A Thomas Merton Reader*, p. 146.
22. Ibid., p. 147.
23. Merton, quoted by James Fox in Hart, *Thomas Merton, Monk*, p. 145.
24. Ibid., p. 146.
25. Bamberger in Hart, *Thomas Merton, Monk*, p. 46.
26. cf. Kelty in Hart, *Thomas Merton, Monk*, p. 25.
27. Ibid., p. 25.
28. Ibid., p. 33.
29. Ibid., p. 33.
30. Ibid., p. 24.
31. Ibid., p. 29.
32. Ibid., p. 28.
33. Ibid., p. 28.
34. Ibid., p. 29.
35. Flavian, "Epilogue, A Homily," in Hart, *Thomas Merton, Monk*, pp. 219-20.
36. Bamberger quoted in Hart, *Thomas Merton, Monk*, p. 60.

17

Friends and Colleagues

It is difficult to address the manifold relationships of a man so gregarious as Thomas Merton. In writing this chapter I have confined my sources to Mott's biography and Wilkes's small volume of Merton sketches written by a selection of his friends. His letters undoubtedly also provide a revealing picture of how he related to the people in his life; I recommend reading them.

1. Mott, *The Seven Mountains of Thomas Merton*, p. 555.
2. The Dalai Lama, quoted in Wilkes, *Merton by Those Who Knew Him Best*, p. 145.

3. Rabbi Silberman, quoted in Mott, *The Seven Mountains of Thomas Merton*, p. 387.

4. Richard Loomis, quoted in Wilkes, *Merton by Those Who Knew Him Best*, pp. 137-38.

5. Ibid., p. 138.

6. Mott, *The Seven Mountains of Thomas Merton*, p. 300.

7. Ibid., p. 263.

8. Merton, quoted in Mott, *The Seven Mountains of Thomas Merton*, pp. 161-62.

9. Mott, *The Seven Mountains of Thomas Merton*, p. 122.

10. Merton, quoted in Mott, *The Seven Mountains of Thomas Merton*, p. 549.

11. Mott, *The Seven Mountains of Thomas Merton*, p. 87.

12. Ibid., p. 221.

13. Wilkes, *Merton by Those Who Knew Him Best*, p. 70.

14. Mott, *The Seven Mountains of Thomas Merton*, p. 162.

15. Ibid., p. 54.

16. Ibid., p. 531.

17. Ibid., p. 387.

18. Ibid., p. 453.

19. Ibid., p. 386.

20. Merton, quoted in Mott, *The Seven Mountains of Thomas Merton*, p. 318.

21. Ibid., p. 433.

22. Mott, *The Seven Mountains of Thomas Merton*, p. 279.

23. Ibid., p. 279.

24. Ibid., p. 280.

25. Ibid., pp. 279-80.

26. Bamberger, quoted in Mott, *The Seven Mountains of Thomas Merton*, p. 531.

27. Mott, *The Seven Mountains of Thomas Merton*, p. 483.

28. Ibid., pp. 528-29.

29. Ibid., p. 387.

30. Ibid., p. 345.

31. Ibid., p. 405.

32. Ibid., p. 54.

33. Ibid., p. 449.

34. Ibid., p. 12.

35. Ibid., p. 462.

36. Burns, quoted in Wilkes, *Merton by Those Who Knew Him Best*, p. 111.

37. Flood, quoted in Wilkes, *Merton by Those Who Knew Him Best*, p. 141.

18

The Feminine

1. Parker J. Palmer, "In the Belly of a Paradox," p. 10.

2. Robert G. Waldron, *Thomas Merton in Search of His Soul: A Jungian Perspective*. Jungian developmental concepts as these applied to Thomas Merton are thoroughly discussed by Waldron; I have no intention of adding to his insights.

3. Merton, *The Seven Storey Mountain*, p. 11.

4. Ibid., p. 5.

5. Merton, quoted in Mott, *The Seven Mountains of Thomas Merton*, p. 363.

6. Ibid., p. 83.

7. Ibid., p. 83.

8. Mott, *The Seven Mountains of Thomas Merton*, p. 142.

9. Merton, quoted in Mott, *The Seven Mountains of Thomas Merton*, p. 1162. [?]

10. Ibid., p. 198.

11. Merton, *The Hidden Ground of Love*, p. 510.

12. Merton, *The Springs of Contemplation*, p. 171.

13. Mott, *The Seven Mountains of Thomas Merton*, p. 266.

14. Merton, *The Sign of Jonas*, p. 262.

15. Mott, *The Seven Mountains of Thomas Merton*, p. 362.

16. Ibid., p. 313.

17. Ibid., p. 438.

18. William H. Shannon, *Silent Lamp* (New York: Crossroad, 1992), pp. 200-1. In his brief summary of Merton's relationship with Margie, Shannon expands on the ideas expressed here. Shannon's work constitutes the most sensitive—and, I believe, accurate—account of their association.

19. Mott, *The Seven Mountains of Thomas Merton*, p. 455.
20. Merton in Mott, *The Seven Mountains of Thomas Merton*, p. 450.
21. Mott, *The Seven Mountains of Thomas Merton*, p. 533.
22. Merton, *The Springs of Contemplation*, p. 240.
23. Merton, *A Thomas Merton Reader*, pp. 434-35.
24. Mott, *The Seven Mountains of Thomas Merton*, p. 438.
25. Thomas Merton, "Certain Proverbs Arise Out of Dreams," in *Eighteen Poems* (New York: New Directions, 1968).

19

The True Self

1. Shannon, *Thomas Merton's Dark Path*, pp. 80-81.
2. Ibid., p. 81.
3. Merton in Shannon, *Thomas Merton's Dark Path*, pp. 116-17.
4. Shannon, *Thomas Merton's Dark Path*, p. 179.
5. Merton in Shannon, *Thomas Merton's Dark Path*, p. 179
6. Merton, *Contemplative Prayer*, p. 24.
7. Shannon, *Thomas Merton's Dark Path*, p. 121.
8. Ibid., p. 195.
9. Merton, "The Inner Experience: Kinds of Contemplation (IV)," p. 296.
10. Merton, *Zen and the Birds of Appetite*, pp. 23-24.
11. Ibid., p. 31.
12. Merton, "The Inner Experience: Some Dangers in Contemplation (VI)," p. 143.
13. Shannon, *Thomas Merton's Dark Path*, p. 201.
14. Merton in Shannon, *Thomas Merton's Dark Path*, p. 134.
15. Carr, *A Search for Wisdom and Spirit*, p. 44.
16. Merton, "The Inner Experience: Kinds of Contemplation (IV)," p. 289.
17. Merton, *Thoughts in Solitude*, p. 96.

20

The Contemplative Life

1. Merton in Shannon, *Thomas Merton's Dark Path*, p. 73.
2. *The Rule of St. Benedict*, chapter 7, p. 232.

3. Merton in Shannon, *Thomas Merton's Dark Path*, p. 125.

4. Thomas Merton, "The Inner Experience: Society and the Inner Self (II)," p. 134.

5. Shannon, *Silent Lamp*, p. 137.

6. Shannon, *Thomas Merton's Dark Path*, p. 27.

7. Thomas Merton, "The Inner Experience: Some Dangers in Contemplation (VI)," p. 145.

8. Merton, *Zen and the Birds of Appetite*, p. 118.

9. Ibid., p. 137.

10. Shannon, *Thomas Merton's Dark Path*, p. 25.

11. Merton, "The Inner Experience: Some Dangers in Contemplation (VI)," p. 150.

12. Carr, *A Search for Wisdom and Spirit*, p. 146.

13. Merton, *New Seeds of Contemplation*, p. 153.

14. Merton, *The Springs of Contemplation*, p. 190.

15. Patrick Hart, O.C.S.O., "On the Photography of Thomas Merton," in *The Photography of Thomas Merton* (Louisville, KY: Louisville School of Art, 1978), unpaged.

16. Merton, *The Springs of Contemplation*, pp. 64-65.

17. Merton, *The Asian Journal*, pp. 333-34.

18. Thomas Merton, *Woods, Shore, Desert: A Notebook, May 1968* (Albuquerque: University of New Mexico Press, 1983), p. 48.

21

Prayer

1. This is a summary of Merton's comments from *The Climate of Monastic Prayer* articulated by William H. Shannon, *Thomas Merton's Dark Path*, p. 174.

2. Carr, *A Search for Wisdom and Spirit*, p. 134.

3. David Steindl-Rast, quoted in Hart, *Thomas Merton, Monk*, p. 87.

4. Merton quoted in Hart, *Thomas Merton, Monk*, p. 86.

5. Ibid., p. 82.

6. Merton, *The Hidden Ground of Love*, p. 503.

7. Merton, *The Springs of Contemplation*, p. 15.

8. Merton, "The Inner Experience: Kinds of Contemplation (IV)," p. 292.

9. Merton, *The Climate of Monastic Prayer*, pp. 35-36.

10. Merton, *The Springs of Contemplation*, p. 48.

11. Ibid., pp. 188-89.

12. Ibid., p. 189.

13. Merton, "The Inner Experience: Society and the Inner Self (II)," pp. 128-29.

14. Ibid., p. 129.

15. Shannon, *Thomas Merton's Dark Path*, p. 185.

16. Merton, *The Climate of Monastic Prayer*, p. 91.

17. Merton, *Silence in Heaven*, p. 26.

18. Thomas Merton, *Contemplative Prayer*, p. 106.

19. Merton, "The Inner Experience: Kinds of Contemplation (IV)," p. 294.

20. RB 1980:*The Rule of St. Benedict: 1980*, p. 171.

Conclusion

1. Thomas Merton, *The Secular Journal* (New York: Farrar, Straus and Cudahy, 1957), p. 184.

Acknowledgments *(continued from page 4.)*

Excerpts from *The Springs of Contemplation: A Retreat at the Abbey of Gethsemani* by Thomas Merton, copyright © 1992 by the Merton Legacy Trust, reprinted by permission of Farrar, Strauss & Giroux, Inc.

Excerpts from "The Inner Experience: Notes on Contemplation" by Thomas Merton, offprint from *Cistercian Studies,* vol. 18 and 19, reprinted by permission of the Merton Legacy Trust.

Excerpts from *The Seven Storey Mountain* by Thomas Merton, copyright © 1948 by Harcourt Brace & Company and renewed 1976 by the Trustees of the Merton Legacy Trust, reprinted by permission of the publisher.

Excerpts from *The Sign of Jonas* by Thomas Merton, copyright © 1953 by The Abbey of Our Lady of Gethsemani and renewed 1981 by the Trustees of the Merton Legacy Trust, reprinted by permission of Harcourt Brace & Company.

Excerpts from *No Man Is an Island* by Thomas Merton, copyright © 1955 by The Abbey of Our Lady of Gethsemani and renewed 1983 by the Trustees of the Merton Legacy Trust, reprinted by permission of Harcourt Brace & Company.

Excerpts from *The Seven Mountains of Thomas Merton* copyright © 1984 by Michael Mott. Reprinted by permission of Houghton Mifflin Company. All rights reserved.

Excerpts from *The Asian Journals of Thomas Merton* copyright © 1975 by The Trustees of the Merton Legacy Trust. Reprinted by permission of New Directions Publishing Corp.

Excerpts from *Zen and the Birds of Appetite* by Thomas Merton, copyright © 1968 by The Abbey of Gethsemani, Inc.. Reprinted by permission of New Directions Publishing Corp.

Excerpts from *New Seeds of Contemplation* by Thomas Merton copyright © 1961 by The Abbey of Gethsemani, Inc.. Reprinted by permission of New Directions Publishing Corp.